THE
JAGGED
HALO

PATRICK BENTLEY

ORIGINAL WRITING

978-1-907179-85-3

A CIP catalogue for this book is available from the National Library.

Published by Original Writing Ltd., Dublin, 2010.

Printed by Cahill Printers Limited, Dublin.

DEDICATIONS

I would like to thanks the following people for their endless love, support and advice as I was putting Jagged Halo together. To Sharon, for all her help in getting behind me all the way from start to finish.

To my Son Jamie, my biggest fan.

To Paul Carson, whose friendship down through the years was a big part of writing this book.

To Terry Carroll who got me into motor bike racing.

Thanks to all my family – Caroline, Raymo, Stuart, Simon and my little sister Fran.

But especially to my sister Breda and Alex who let me write about their childhood into this book.

Special thanks to Trish Halligan and Donagh from Cyber Zone in Balbriggan.

To my friends Dean Monahan, Nora Leahy , Jenny Weir , Suzanne Guildea , Bobo Colman , Kevin O'Malley , John Kennedy , Myles Lally , Jack Corry , Donna & Mr Keith Costello , Tonia McNally Anne , Sharon & Tyrone O'Flaherty Mottam. Marie Kane, Moya Brennan, Aslan, and the one and only Gary Numan.

Dermo, Paul and Vino Carroll who are all my close friends. Mick Power who's worked close with me in writing this book. To Jackie & Demy Traynor, for all their feedback on earlier chapters.

To Gavin & Brian two motorbike fans. To my good friends Tadgh Killcummins Michele Griffin + Adrian Foley also Gary Numan fans, thanks for never giving up on me.

To both Skerries & Balbriggan taxi cab drivers whose ears I burned talking about this book.

To my two barbers Bert of Skerries and Tee Reed , keep up the competition lad's.

To all you people in the Fingal area who never stopped encouraging me, thanks so mush for all words and best wishes.

To the Fingal community church based in Swords & Corner stone church based in Skerries thanks for all your love and encouragement.

I hope and pray this book in some small way touches someone's life in a lasting way.

What writing this book proves beyond doubt is if you have a dream and you allow it to become your passion then one day your dream will become real.

This book is dedicated to Jesus the Lord of glory,

My Ma and Dad. To all survivors of abuse.

And to all those who never got to see justice. To Micky Flanagan the Boy with the broken arm R.I.P

With love ...Patrick Bentley

CONTENTS

THE
JAGGED
HALO

Chapter One

ADOPT ME BEFORE I'M BORN

Here it comes again
I'm tortured and deceived.
Here it comes again
If only I'd believed.

Before You Hate It
Gary Numan, 2006

For most people, if they were asked to think about something tragic surrounding the month of September, they would say 9/11, the day the world stood still in shock as both the World Trade Center Twin Towers in New York fell. It's a day we will never forget. But for me, it's not September 11th, 2001 that comes to mind. It's September 1st, 2007.

12.30 am. I get up off my sofa and make my way across the room. I'm flying from a night of coke. I roll up a €50 note and place it up to my nose. I've already taken twenty or twenty-five lines. I bend over and snort two more. I step back and turn to Sylvia. I can hear Gary Numan's music playing in the background as I head down the hall towards the loo.

It was at that moment that the most awful, fearful feeling I'd ever imagined swept up my body and into my heart, mind and soul. I stopped in my tracks. Then this soft voice whispered to me,

'You have just overdosed on coke. You have stepped over the line. You are now in the first stages of dying.'

1

Panic swept over me. My body felt like my mind was leaving it. Sylvia came down and grabbed me.

'It's all over, Sylvia,' I said.

'It's OK, Patrick,' she said. 'You're OK.'

But I felt myself slipping further away. The voice spoke again.

'You're dying, Patrick – it's all over.'

The next thing I knew, I was standing outside time. I had left this world and slipped into eternity. The awful fear left my heart and soul. I was now in heaven standing face to face with God. I couldn't see his face, but I knew it was him. This wasn't a drug experience of any kind – this was really happening. Sylvia could see that I was sitting on the sofa, but she knew something had happened to me. Even though I was in the room, she knew a part of me was gone. She was crying, and asking me to come back. But I was now in front of God, and he was about to speak to me.

Why, why, why now after taking coke? Why did he take a hold of me in this state?

All the truths were about to unfold before me.

I trust as I take you back to the beginning, you will take your time and let me walk you through the story of how my life ended up where it did. I hope to take you behind who the real Patrick Bentley is. I hope that it will give everyone who reads this book not just an understanding of my life, but something more than that. I hope it gives readers a perception of what life is about beyond that which is just seen with the naked eye.

So now, as I sit in my warm, safe house, with a peaceful heart and soul, a warm bed to sleep in and all the love in the world to enjoy, let me take you back to where my story began. I step aboard a time machine, take a seat and close the door behind me. My heart races at the thought of going back, but I smile, knowing that it was destined to happen in the way that it did. I press the time button and turn the clock back as far as I can, until I'm back to where my life begins. My first memories are now about to unfold.

I've just turned two years old, and my eyes are filled with tears and fear. The sound of screaming and the clatter of pots and pans falling surround me. I'm standing in a frozen state watching as my dad's blood-red face flashes before me. There's a row going on between him and my uncle from my ma's side. My ma is screaming and trying to stop them. Inside, I feel so scared and lost. I just want the noise to stop and for my ma to hold me close, and for everything to be normal again. No such hugs come, but the noise stops, and life goes on.

My ma and dad never seem to talk, or laugh or hold each other. Everything is just cold and lifeless. No-one loves or shows love. You just feel alone all the time, as if you were not alive at all. My sisters Laura and Breda and my brother Alex are living in this cold house with myself and my parents. We live in a very small two-bedroom house down at the bottom of an old lane a mile outside Lusk, Co. Dublin. There's no running water or anything clean about the place. The year is 1966, and as a two-year-old, the feeling inside of me is just of pain and loneliness.

My next memory is even more terrifying than the first. My ma takes me up for what I think are hugs, but then she puts me in a cot in the room with Laura. I know she's leaving us. She has her coat on and a bag in her hand. She's going away, and Alex and Breda are going with her, and I'm being left alone in my cot. The tears and fear rise within me. She says, 'I'll be back,' but as she speaks, I'm choking with screams. My tiny hands reach through the bars of the cot for her to take me with her. She turns and walks out, leaving me screaming. My tears and screams deepen as the fear of being abandoned overpowers me. My crying and screaming seem to be going on forever, and then as I tire they turn into a slow, fretting, trembling cry, my mouth wobbling from the uncontrollable tears that flowed for so long.

Later, the door opens and my ma walks in. She had to go to the shops, but I didn't know that. I thought she'd left me forever. She gives us a bar of chocolate and it's forgotten – by her, at least. For me, the damage is already done. Where was all the love that a kid should be enjoying at such an early age?

My dad seemed to live with the world closed up around him. He never spoke, and most of the time, he never looked my way. He worked hard, dropped in for a pint on the way home and went straight to bed after dinner.

My mother seemed to be lost trying to keep a house going and taking care of four young kids. She hadn't time to pay real attention to me or any of the others. As time went by, I could feel my heart slipping into some unknown place where everything was cold and lifeless, and no one could touch or help me. I was just a child, yet already I felt like I was dying some kind of slow death. Even with my brother and sisters around me, I still felt like I was alone in this strange world. I had no one to reach out to, no one to find me and love me.

*

In 1968 we moved into a three-bedroom council house in 61 Sherlock Park, Skerries, Co. Dublin, an area nicknamed the Cabra. It was to be my home for the next thirteen years, and if homes and walls could tell stories, this was one sad hallway that painted its own grim tale.

My first memories of this house were that of being led from it to my first day at school. I gripped my mother's hand tightly, not wanting to let it go for a second. A couple of jam sandwiches packed in a paper bag was all I was left holding as she said goodbye, mouthed a brief word to the teacher and then headed out the classroom door. Again, I was left in this awful state of fear. I was left alone, this time among a classroom of strange kids and a teacher.

Miss Tierney. I'll never forget her. She was a kind old lady who, to this day, I could never say a bad word about. School back then was ruled, as you know, with an iron rod. But Miss Tierney was fair, and you always felt she cared about everyone without showing anyone special attention. She would, on certain days, put a penny on the bottom of the blackboard and tell the class that whoever was the best in the class that day would get the penny. I'll never forget the day when she announced,

'Today, the penny goes to . . . Patrick Bentley.'

To me it wasn't the penny that was important – it was something far greater than a million pennies. It was the warm smile coming from this woman's face as she walked towards me. It was the warm hand taking mine and placing the penny in it. For a kid today this would be nothing, but for me, back in that classroom, it was the very first scrap of love I had ever felt. My small body with a cold lifeless face had taken its first ray of sunshine. I was four years old, and I remember wanting to keep smiling, to hold that moment in my tiny heart forever.

But warm moments don't last forever. Soon I'd be walking back through the door of my dark, cold, empty house. The absence of love engulfed every corner of every room, and nothing seemed clean or hygienic. At times I was met with the loud noises of a washing machine, and beside it was what seemed like an endless mountain of clothes to be washed. Splashes of dirty water covered the kitchen floor.

I looked up from the clothes on the floor to my mother's tired face as she strained to twist the handle of the mangle to rinse the clothes. You could see in her face that she hadn't known a taste of love in a long time. She bore the marks of a woman just trying to hold the world around her together as best she could. I'd often reach out, maybe just for one hug, but as time went by nothing ever came back, so that part of the mother and son relationship closed down. My sense of being lost and alone grew ever deeper. In my mind, I felt like I had to find something to hold. Something that was mine, something that was warm to take the pain away. But there was nothing but cold empty hands around me at all times.

My brother and sisters lay in the same trap, and they had their own ways of dealing with a loveless home life. But for me, things were just slowly getting worse. I started to feel weak and tired all the time. Our home was going to rack and ruin. It was never tidy, and we never seemed to have clean clothes to wear. We just wore the same clothes all week long, and they must have smelled bad by mid-week. The weakness and tiredness was down to not eating properly. Most of the time, we had no breakfast, and just a couple of sandwiches to eat for lunch at school. Most of the families around Sherlock Park were well looked after – they all had warm houses, warm beds to sleep in and warm food to eat. They all came to school well-dressed and with school books and decent lunches. All the kids seemed to be in school on time, and most seemed to have families that would leave them off to school and give them a big smile as they headed in the gates. Everything they had I hadn't got, which, in time, singled me out as 'different'.

I wasn't just seen as different, I was beginning to *know* I was different. That feeling soon turned into a new feeling that I'd never known before. Self-hatred. I hated who I was. I hated the fact that I was looked at as different and that people looked down at me, even though we were all still just kids. I was grateful for one of the kids around Sherlock Park I often hung out with – Ian Watson. He always shared his lunch with me on days

I'd pretend to go home for my lunch. He was the only kid that showed me kindness, and you could tell he felt sorry for me.

Even at that young age, getting to school late resulted in six of the best from the head teacher, Mr Jones. My first visit to him spelt the start of a relationship that was to be one of constant visits to his office for punishment. That first visit was when I was late for school and was sent to him, my small hands still numb from the bitter frost of the morning. I was met by this cold-faced man.

'Bentley,' he grunted, 'you're late again. Stretch out your hand, boy!'

I stretched it out as far as I could. Then he produced a long cane, drew back his whole arm and brought it down with cruel speed. The pain shot through my fingers and up my arm.

I broke down crying long before he had got through the six slaps. I went back to the classroom with tears in my eyes, knowing everyone knew it was because I was late for school.

As time went by, my relationship with the headmaster grew worse as being late turned into a habit. It wasn't my fault, as my ma would sleep it out and still send us in, knowing it was late. There was nothing worse than walking cold and hungry to school, knowing you had to face six of the best for doing nothing wrong at all. Feelings of anger were now turning to hate, because I knew none of this was my fault, yet I had to face hard days at school and then come home to the oppressive atmosphere that seemed to live in the very walls of our empty-hearted house.

Most afternoons my dad would be in bed or at work, so we'd just head out to play or be asked to go to the shops, which I hated to do. As I headed to the shop, still feeling the pains of hunger and a sense of weakness in my legs, I'd go through the nun's convent, and I'd pick apples from the trees and scoff them. There were times when the nuns would come out shouting at you to stop, and run after you. You'd run for your life in total fear. I was never aware that it was hunger that was causing me to feel weak; I just knew I didn't feel well most of the time.

Within a year, my life started to change in many ways. My school life was getting worse. I was learning nothing, and spent all my time looking out the window or just drawing pictures of war and people getting killed. As I still had no school books, my mind drifted more and more into a place that was very much closed-up to the outside world. I felt so alone, as if I were an alien of some kind, sent here to endure nothing else but pure pain forever. I always sat down in the corner away from all that was being taught by the teacher. At times it was unbearable watching how clean and well everybody else looked compared to me, with their tidy school bags full of carefully-covered books. It was hard to imagine what it was like to be one of them. I would often wish to swap places with them and have all they had, but all that was an unreachable dream, another world far, far away from the nightmare world I found myself in.

*

It was around this time on my way home from school that my life took yet another turn for the worse. I went into a local shop, and as the shopkeeper had his back turned, I made off with a full packet of biscuits. I hid down the beach, and in no time I had scoffed the lot. I had taken my first step on the road to a life of crime. I knew I needed to eat, but food at home was now down to one meal a day, so hunger pushed me into the first steps towards stealing.

Before long it was a daily ritual. My brother Alex and I set out, thinking we were just like the James Gang in the cowboy pictures. (Alex, I remember, wore a long coat down to his knees and just looked like Jesse James). Any kind of robbing back then was seen as very serious, and the cops were hard on anyone that was caught doing it. But we didn't give a toss – what hungry kid would?

Skerries was such a small town back in the early 70s. Everybody knew everybody, and it wasn't long before people were talking about Alex and me running wild around the town like a pair of cowboys.

My first visit to the cops was after two older boys asked me to help them steal a whole coal sack of sweets from O'Neill's shop in the town. Mr. O'Neill always went away on a Thursday to pick up stock, and closed his shop for half a day. That's when we struck. We went 'on the hop' from school and carried the sweets up to the graveyard. We stayed there enjoying what must have seemed like a mini Willie Wonka factory, judging by the amount of sweet papers we left behind. We buried the sweets in the graves, and headed home just as everyone got home from school.

A couple of days later, cops came knocking at the door asking to talk to me. My ma asked why. They said,

'We believe he was seen near O'Neill's shop on Thursday after-noon, and we just want to ask him a few questions.'

My ma was gobsmacked.

'But Guard, he was in school on Thursday.'

We've checked the school, Missus,' they said. 'I'm afraid he wasn't in that day.'

There was no getting out of this.

'Yeah, Ma,' I said. 'It's true. I . . . I broke into O'Neill's shop.'

Dad came home and told me to go up to bed. He followed me up, took his belt off and lashed it across my half-naked body until I was screaming for him to stop. The pain shot up my body time and time again until he finally stopped. I lay there curled up on my damp bed in the dark.

The next day I was told I had to go to court. On the day of the court, we got a warning and were told we'd be sent away next time. The Fingal Independent stated that the judge said I was young enough to be still at home in a pram. This in no way stopped the crime wave. It slowly got worse as Alex and I found what was to become our money den for the next few years – the Catholic church in Skerries.

We were very careful as to how we went about robbing the church. We'd wait until mass was over at one o'clock on Sunday and watch the priest leave. We had our place to watch from until everyone left; there was a small lane that ran from the right-hand side of the church out onto the main street, which was a perfect hiding place and get-away route. There was a big money box at the main entrance to the church, and one on each side of the two side entrances. There were also four candle boxes inside, and on Sundays you'd always find money under the seats after a full day of masses. We nicknamed the two side entrances the bright side and the dark side, not for reasons found in the Bible's Darkness and Light. We chose those names because when you opened the box at the left entrance, you could see into it perfectly clearly as the sun always shone on that side of the church, but on the other side, you couldn't see a thing when you opened the box and had to put your arm in and feel around to see if there was any money left behind.

On Sundays we'd check all the boxes first, then look under the seats. We'd then head for the door into the sacristy. If it was open, we'd scout around for money. The biggest money earner was envelopes sent by people to pray for the dead. The envelopes would be sent in during Lent and the run-up to Easter. People would drop them into the boxes throughout the weekdays when the boxes at all three entrances were not locked. Alex would get down early after 10 o'clock mass to check all the boxes, and race home to tell me how many envelopes we got. Sometimes we got four or five, with the largest sums at £3 in some and £1 in others. That was a lot of money to be dropped into a kid's hand in the early 70s. We'd head downtown in the afternoon to buy sweets, drinks and have a day at Bob's Casino, the local seedy amusements arcade, living like a pair of kings. We were that hungry one day we bought a full-sized cooked chicken and ate it down the beach with our bare hands like a pair of starved seagulls.

It wasn't long before word got out that we were stealing from the church. In the early 70s, to be robbing was bad enough, but to be stealing from God and priests was seen as the lowest and most sinful thing a person could ever do. It didn't bother us – we saw it as God feeding us with what was, after all, his money to give. It was giving to the poor, and we were poor and hungry, so as God said in the Bible, 'Whoever comes to me will never go hungry.' You could say we took God at his word, and in our small minds we believed God was passing this money on to us as our means to live.

But everyone else didn't see it that way, and soon, things got out of control. Alex and I went to the church when everyone left one day and searched the place upside down, but found nothing. Drastic action had to be taken to get money, so we turned over a couple of candle boxes and jumped up and down on the door to the money box to bang it open. Money came out everywhere. Well, as the saying goes, 'Keep knocking and the door shall be opened to you,' and this door opened up buckets of money. (If you go into the Church today, the broken door of the candle box can still be seen).

But now we had stepped over the line – breaking a box in the church was a serious matter. Up to now, no one had missed the envelopes. But a candle box being smashed open had the whole town talking, and the cops were soon knocking at our door again. They questioned us about it, and in the end, we told them it was us who broke it open. We both made statements about how we took the money and spent it on sweets and drinks. When dad came home to the news it was another beating with the belt across our half-naked bodies. I was also grounded for a week after school.

But it wasn't long until we were out and running wild on the streets of Skerries again. We turned our attention to other crimes. Breaking into houses and caravans had become an everyday habit. We often ransacked caravans and broke all the windows in some and robbed stuff that had little use, like flashlights and toys, which we broke up just for fun.

Our next target was the school. We knew it had a poor box, and a payphone with money in it. We got in through a small window, and started ransacking the classrooms in search of money or anything else we could find. We got the payphone open in the head office by breaking the lock with a small bar we found in the school. We slid the bottom of the phone across and down came all the money that was inside, hitting the floor and spilling all over the place with a crashing sound. We hit the jackpot that day, as the phone was half-full with a mixture of silver and brown coins. We filled our pockets and fled the scene as fast as possible. We hid the cash and headed home as it was getting late.

Next morning we got to the gates of the school to find the cop car outside, and a lot of tension in the air. I went into my class, but it wasn't long before I was called into the head office to find two cops waiting to ask me a few questions about where I was the night before. I said I was out playing up near my house all night. My voice didn't sound convincing enough, so they pushed me further.

'You're lying, Bentley. You were seen at the school last night by someone, so tell us the truth.'

Mr. Jones, the head teacher, pushed me further, saying my fingerprints were left behind.

'I didn't do it.' I said. 'I wasn't anywhere near the school.'

I felt a crash across the back of my head as Garda Boyle hit me a slap for talking back to Mr. Jones. But I didn't give in, and was sent back to my class.

After school it was time to spend the takings with Alex, who was waiting at the spot where we had hidden the money. We counted all the silver first, then all the brown money, and split it fifty/fifty. We headed to the shops and started to spend it, mainly on sweets and food. But word soon got round that we were spending money and changing coins into notes in some of the shops, and some days later the cops were at the door again, asking more questions. They had no proof, but knew it was us that were robbing not only the school, but half the town.

We paid a couple more visits to the school, plus the church on Sundays after mass to find what God had left behind for us to spend. Another den for money was the hockey match, which was held every second Saturday in the nun's field at the back of the convent. We could get into the changing rooms through the caravan site and be in and out with cash in minutes.

As our crime wave spread to all places in Skerries town, so did the risks, and it wasn't long before we were caught for a number of jobs. Twice we got caught, through fingerprints, robbing the school, and we got caught in the caravan site for smashing up a whole caravan to bits with two sweeping brushes.

We found ourselves in the church one Saturday trying to open a box up. But we were unable to break the lock, so we decided to lift the whole box up and take it out of the church and down the nearby right-hand lane. It was a sight to behold, two kids running down the side church lane holding one of the church collection boxes. One of us was holding the box part and the other the legs of the box. We took it to the back garden of an old run-down house and smashed it open, only to find there was just 50p in it. We were seen on this occasion and dragged into the cop station for this and for other jobs that they could now prove.

Besides the beatings we got from our dad for bringing the cops to the house again, we were now branded the worst criminals in Skerries. Back in the 70s it was much worse to be known as a robber than it is today. The shame you were made to feel for theft back then was worse. People were appalled at the fact that two kids were robbing the church and half the town, and most kids were told to stay away from us completely. When you walked down the street, mothers would call their kids and you'd hear them telling them not to be seen with kids like us.

Looking back now, years later, I find it hard to believe the extent of our crime spree, and feel totally ashamed and to some extent mystified.

Behind the mask that I had perfectly fitted to my face to show the world that this six-year-old boy didn't care, lay the real story of the boy crying out to be loved, to be cared for like all other kids. A boy who wanted his dad to take him in his arms, look him in the face and smile and tell him he loved him. A boy who wanted his dad to help with sports, who would be there for him when he returned home from school, who would be waiting for him with a hug and a smile and to ask how school went. A young child looking out from behind this cold, constructed camouflage, wishing with everything that lay in his empty heart for a life of warm love, warm food and a warm bed. Just to wake up in the morning to a smile and a hot breakfast, to put on a clean coat, pick up a school bag and head off, skipping with a smile. A child that would sit in class and learn from his teacher and enjoy being at a place called school.

Beyond all that, what I craved for most was my mother's love. I craved to reach out from my childlike world with my cold hands and feel the heat from those motherly hands I saw making the dinner and washing clothes. I wished to see her eyes smile from her world into mine and to hold me in times of dreaded fear. But my ma was as lost as I was, and her world lay as empty as mine. I felt sorry for her, and wished I could help her and make things better. But I was already slipping, with my self-made wall around my pain, into a deeper, hopeless place that bore all the hallmarks of hell on earth. Inside, the boy had found his hiding place from the world that lay around him, a world that was frozen to numb out the pain that would otherwise tear his existence apart and leave him nowhere to hide.

As he hid away from the cold world outside, he projected an image of a young boy who didn't care what the universe did to him or what might happen to him. he gave everyone the wrong idea that he didn't care about anything or anyone, that he was on a road to destroy himself, while all along behind this stone wall lay a little boy so lost and confused in a world that he never made or wished for. In his eyes, if you looked clearly, if anyone had taken the time to look, they would have seen the message there:

Please help me, I'm just a kid.

But no one had the time to look, and so out of the cold years of the early 70s came this thin, innocent-looking boy who was to hold the town in the grip of crime.

Now, with the cops on my tail and the beatings at home and at school on the increase, my world roared further out of control and into more turmoil for everyone around me. Alex and I upped our crime, and found ourselves shoplifting and going over to the holiday resort at Red Island in Skerries to rob holi-daymakers. Walking past the rented apartments we'd look in-side and see money left unattended, easy pickings, as on hot summer days people often left windows open with money vis-ible. One grab and it would be our holiday at the carnival and Bob's Casino for the day. An all-expenses trip for two. More trips to the church would pave the way for even richer days of sweets and food ahead.

We went down in history as possibly the only robbers who nicked all the cash from a big church box without opening it. The box was locked away in the sacristy and was three-quarters full, but we couldn't get the lock off – so we came up with the idea of wedging a small thin bar into the side of the box between the lid and the box itself, then pushing it up to make a small gap. We then simply turned the box upside down, got it by the legs and shook it. The money came crashing out all over the floor of the sacristy. 50p and 10p coins and pound notes all flew across the room. When our pockets were full and we could carry no more, we took the bar out and put the box back as if nothing had hap-pened, and went to Dublin to spend to our hearts' content. We revisited the box until every penny was emptied out. We always laughed at how the priest would get his head around that one. A box empty, with the lock still on – pure magic in a kid's mind, a master trick that Houdini would have been proud of.

But the innocent side of kids at that age was never far away. We robbed the jewellery shop in Red Island and got loads of old ladies' brooches with all kinds of strange colours shining from them. We pinned them to our jeans and jumpers and walked up the main Street of Skerries and into the cop station. I knocked on the door, and Garda Mason opened it with a look of disbelief.

'Hi,' I said, 'we robbed these brooches, and we want to hand ourselves in.'

It took the cops quite a while to get the brooches off. We sat in the cop station confessing to any jobs we might have done that we were not yet caught for. The cops gave us a lift home. This of course meant another beating for bringing them to the house again.

As time went by, we were the main ringleaders for any other boy in the town who wanted to earn money by robbing the town blind. We had all the experience, even at such a young age, plus we had no fear of getting into places. The only downside to bringing other kids with us was when we did get caught, we were singled out as the ringleaders who were dragging the other kids down the road of crime. Their mams and dads banned them from hanging out with us. It furthered my sense of alienation when kid after kid told us,

'We can't hang out with you anymore.'

The feeling of being different from other kids had been so enforced upon me that I was now beginning to adapt and even like how I felt. I knew my life was different to anyone else's in the town, and even at such a young age, I felt I wasn't human at all. To be human seemed like a faraway dream. I couldn't scream out how painful it felt to walk down the streets of Skerries and see grown-ups giving you hard looks, to walk into school and see the same looks from the teachers, to walk into your home to stone-cold feelings and that awful expression of hurt and pain in my mother's face. How safe would it be for a seven-year-old child to let out a never-ending scream of pain to be normal, to be loved, to have a normal life like the rest of the kids around the town? Could things get any worse than the place I found myself in as a young kid?

Chapter Two

DAD, ARE YOU SMILING AT ME?

By the summer of 1972, there had been two more additions to the family – Ray, who was born in 1970, and Stuart, who was born two years later. With the added pressure of the new kids to look after and feed, my ma must have been worn out.

As the summer came and we got our holidays from school, a nun from Temple Street Hospital got in touch with my ma and offered her some help. The nun, named Sister Frances, came up with an idea to give Ma a break from all the stress by offering to take me and my sister Laura and put us in a school in Baldoyle for speech therapy. It was really to give our ma a break more than anything. My ma agreed, and off we went by car with Sister Frances to Baldoyle.

I found Sister Frances to be a lovely woman who went out of her way for years to help and support the family. But as we got dropped off, to start what we thought was a nice holiday for two weeks, we soon realised that the moment we went through the doors of this place it was the beginning of two weeks of fear and abuse.

The school was mainly a place for handicapped kids and kids who had speech problems. The nurses who ran the place beat the kids on a day-to-day basis. We saw kids being beaten and kicked for doing no more than wetting themselves. Their screams for help echoing in the bathrooms filled me with a dreaded fear that I could be next. The horror of seeing innocent, helpless kids being beaten by cold-hearted nurses subjected me to a deeper fear of people in authority, a fear that took control of me from this point forward in my life.

I walked in deep terror for the whole two weeks. I did everything I was asked to do as fast as I could to avoid the same fate as the other kids. At bedtime I was always first into bed, not because I was being a good boy, just out of total fear. After lights out, I peered from my bed through the window that was next to me, and I longed to see my ma's face again. I felt so far away from home, and the time seemed to drag by in years rather than weeks.

My sister cried every night as she was taken to the girls' ward to sleep. Her only security lay with us both being around each other throughout the day, when we spent our time in playgrounds and inside playrooms, mixing with kids who couldn't do much to help themselves most of the time. Frantic screams from frightened kids unable to protect themselves from the daily beatings could be heard for the whole two weeks we were there. It left a trauma within me that I felt would only be cured with a long hug from my ma.

When we were told that Sister Frances was here to bring us home, my heart jumped inside with relief that I was getting out of this nightmare place. All I wanted now was to hold my mother. I couldn't wait to get home. The drive home seemed to take forever. Eventually, we came to Sherlock Park and stopped outside my house. My heart was racing as I jumped out of the car and ran towards the front door. It was already open, and I found myself rushing into the hall and then into the sitting room. There was only my brother Alex sitting there watching TV, so I turned and headed towards the kitchen. My ma was at the sink washing up after the dinner. I ran frantically towards her, stretching out both my arms to hold her. As I grabbed her with both hands to find a place of security, safety and warmth, she turned towards me and pushed me away. I landed halfway back across the kitchen floor, and everything inside me froze. My heart dropped, and any attempt to say anything was lost in that moment.

For two whole weeks, everything in me had cried out to hold my ma and to feel safe again. After all the nights I looked out my window yearning to get home to see her again, she was now pushing me away when I needed her most of all. The damage that was done in that one act froze everything inside of me. At that age, I couldn't say how I was feeling as I didn't know what I felt. All I knew was something died inside of me.

From that day forward, I felt a deeper sense of being alone in the world. People, even my own siblings, seemed alien to me. It was as if this young boy gave up on ever being wanted or loved, and fell back into some unknown dark place deep in his own heart as he closed over the door to the painful world that lay all around him. All my trust in people slipped away in what I saw in those two weeks in that hospital in Baldoyle.

*

Within days, I was back robbing the town blind. Money wasn't safe anywhere. Dowling's Shop became a new place where money was easily stolen. We used to go in and stand at the counter, and in front of us were the shelves of sweets. There was a mirror running along the back of all the shelves from one end of the shop to the next. You could see through the mirror if there were any 10ps or 50ps left sitting on top of the steel drawer of the cash register. If there were, and most of the time there were, you just had to sneak your arm around the side of the cash register and slide the money slowly around and into your pocket. We always made sure we got whoever was serving to go down to the back of the shop while we made our move. Another place we found to steal money was from anyone who left a pram outside a shop or house and left a purse in under the covers. In truth, nothing was safe anymore. If we couldn't find money to steal, we got empty Coca-Cola bottles and took them back to shops. In those days you got a couple of pence a bottle. But even these were stolen from the back of pubs, shops or houses. Our name around the town just got worse as time went by. Week after week, the cops would be up knocking at the door over some robbery that had taken place, and after they'd gone it would be another beating by our dad.

Home life got worse and with two more mouths to feed, food got scarcer and scarcer. At night we'd hear the rows going on as my dad came home drunk. I'd lie in my bed wishing the shouting would stop, hoping that somehow, some way we would all find happiness like other families around Skerries. That dad would change and become warm-hearted and give our mother the right money to feed us, clothe us and buy us our school books so we could all learn like other kids in school. With dad working in the airport we knew he had lots of money, so why didn't he look after us all?

I hated seeing my ma worrying over food. There were days when she'd ask us to go up and wake dad and ask him for money for food for the day. Some days he'd say no. I can still remember eating custard for breakfast, lunch and dinner one day. My ma ate nothing as the worry of having no food or money seemed to have taken its toll on her, now that she had Ray and Stuart to feed as well.

Things in school only got worse. Run-ins with teachers for being late or having no homework done only led to further beatings with the cane. One teacher who took a bitter dislike to me was Miss Redman, who made it her job when I was in her class to torment me in front of the whole class. She would ask me to come and stand up at the front of the class and face everyone, then ask me why I had no lunch or school books. I never answered her. She would continue by asking me why I stole money from the Catholic Church and why I broke into the school and steal money. She would push it until she had the whole class laughing into my face. Still, I never opened my mouth or gave any reply. She made a laugh of the fact that everything about me was somehow wrong in some shape or form.

In the silence of my heart, I knew where to hide and to protect myself from such pain. Again, in those frightening moments I could switch off and withdraw to a place deep inside, and look out through stone-cold eyes as if nothing could reach me or hurt me. Within the walls of this world I had made, behind that stone-cold face lay a frightened young kid crying for all this pain to stop. Hoping that somehow someone would come into his life and impart feelings of love and support, and give him all the nice things other kids had and enjoyed.

Maybe the worst part of what was happening inside me was that I was beginning to like this world I could step into at any time. If everyone thought I was the worst person in Skerries, well, maybe I should just start being who they all said I was. If I was to hold this name in the town, then I should become everything that was being said about me.

With the abuse by Miss Redman in school, my anger grew more out of control. To watch such an evil person rip me apart in front of the class and then turn and pray 'In the name of the Father, and of the Son and of the Holy Spirit' just made me hate grown-ups intensely. It pushed me further into a life of self-destruction and crime. I just didn't care anymore. Life was the worst thing anyone could imagine it to be. My crime had marked me as the worst person around the town, and I now accepted the name.

With my crime came another very bad habit – lighting fires. Fields of hay were my main target, or just ditches. I loved standing back and just watching places burn. The higher the flames, the bigger the buzz. With all this crime and lighting fires came another identity – I was a hard kid, someone not to get into a row with. Nothing could have been further from the truth.

I don't think I ever won a fight as a kid, because I was too weak from lack of food and too frightened of every human being around me to fight. Any row I ever remember being in only deepened my fear of the world outside of my own self-made one. There was nothing outside my world that ever seemed to match how I felt or who I was.

I could sit and watch as grown-ups were hailed with great respect, but from where I sat I knew the truth about them all. Any one of the teachers, cops, nurses, and parents of other kids was a potential abuser of one innocent child, though they might even sometimes be unaware of the harm they were causing down the years. Any hope of me living a normal life like any other kid was gone forever.

From within the frozen world that I inhabited, I would now just sit with a dead, unemotional look on my face. I grew to love my new world, and as I did, the world outside grew more hostile towards me. I knew how to hide away with all my pain from everyone that I knew could hurt me and make me shed tears to justify their needs. In truth, all my nightmares up to this point were just the beginning of the nightmare still to come.

My young life of crime had gone too far. With Alex and me upping our crime wave across Skerries town, the cops were sick to death of us both. After a day smashing another brand new caravan to bits, it was time for the cops to put a stop to what seemed like an endless day-after-day job for them.

I had reached the age of nine when we were brought into the cop station and told we were going to court in four weeks' time. I had over twenty charges of house break-ins and other crimes. Alex had twenty-five. Our ma was called to come down to the station as the charges were read out, one after the other. Alex and I didn't give a toss and just smiled away, unaware that we were in a lot of trouble this time.

The day of the court came. Dad came with us, and we sat down the back. Myself and Alex just smiled at each other through our fear all morning. In the afternoon, our case came up. The judge called us forward. Our solicitor, Mr. O'Toole, gave his say on our behalf and the cops gave their say as to the charges that were set out against us. We couldn't take in or even hear what was being said throughout the case.

My dad stood on my right side, and every now and then I looked up at him. He was my dad, but somehow I didn't know him from Adam. He never spoke to me or looked my way with any kind words of love or support in all of my nine years. All I knew was he shouted at us and beat us anytime we brought the cops to the house. I knew him and Ma never got along and that he drank a lot. That's all I knew about him. Now standing facing a judge in Balbriggan Courthouse, this cold man who seemingly cared very little about his kids faced the judge's statement that both me and Alex were sentenced to two weeks in St Laurence's School, with the prospect of one year to follow in the bigger section of the school.

The cops came to take us out of the court. My head turned around and in one of those moments that to this day I'll never forget, there was my dad looking down into my face and into my eyes for the first time in his life with a lovely smile across his face. For a moment, I thought, *Dad, are you smiling at me?* Then I noticed sweat running down his face and his eyes looking different. Even though I was just a nine-year-old boy, something told me something was wrong with my dad. I wish I could have reached out at that moment to hold him close and say, *Dad, everything is going to be OK.* But within minutes, we were taken out of the court and away to Dublin to St Laurence's School for Young Offenders.

We got there around five in the evening. It was May 1974. We were greeted by a Christian Brother named Brother Carl. He couldn't have been nicer to us. The school was a small place, but just across from it was the bigger section where up to sixty kids stayed. But this place was to let you settle in for the next two weeks with the prospect of a year in the bigger place. Brother Carl took us around and showed us the whole place. It was so nice. The bedrooms were so clean and warm. The smell of fish fingers and chips seemed to fill the whole school from the kitchens.

Brother Carl told us the simple rules of the school. He also told us that they showed films, and that there was a swimming pool and a shop. To me it seemed like a holiday camp, and seemed far better than my home life of no food or warm, clean clothes. Alex felt the same, and after Brother Carl had got us clean clothes to put on, it was time for tea. The food was so nice and there was a load to go round. The whole place seemed like paradise compared to what we were used to back home. To sleep in such warm beds for the first time in our lives seemed to make life in St Laurence's seem like a place you'd be happy to spend your childhood.

We settled in fast, and come Sunday Brother Carl called us and said our mother and father were here to see us. We ran out to see them. We were met first by Dad who, for the first time in his life, hugged me. As he was pulling away I looked into his face and saw that same look I saw in the courtroom. The sweat was running down his face and he seemed so different to the man I knew for the past nine years. My ma seemed happy that dad had changed so much. She bent over and said,

'Your dad is a changed man. He's handing up money and he's going to do up the house.'

As they were leaving, Dad hugged me again. I wondered if this was the turning point in our family life. Was Dad now seeing that he had a responsibility to take care of his kids? Would this be the start of a new beginning, of a new home life like all other kids around the town enjoyed? I saw the hope in my ma's face that Sunday, and with all my heart I hoped when we got out of this school, life would be different for all of us.

A week later Ma and Dad came in again to visit us. The news was that Dad was doing everything to sort out the family home. But there was a look of concern on my ma's face that, as a nine-year-old boy, I couldn't make out. All I knew was our dad was hugging us, and even though I couldn't understand it all, I was so glad to have a dad for the first time in my life. I had this new hope that everything was going to be OK now, and it helped me cope well with my new surroundings.

We went back to court after the two weeks were up and were given the full year sentence in the bigger part of St Laurence's School for Young Offenders by the judge. I noticed my dad wasn't in the court but my ma turned up looking like she had the world on her shoulders. We were taken away by the cops to the school. I can still smell the brass polish as we walked through the main doors and into a long hallway leading towards two main yards with walls around them both. The sound of kids' voices ringing out left me feeling that this place was very different to the smaller part of St Laurence's that we had spent the past two weeks in. The smaller part was just a stepping stone to get us ready for the main school.

We were met by the main Christian Brother, Brother Doyle, who gave us a lovely welcome and took us into the main office to explain the rules. He explained the difference here was that you got home at weekends, but that the number of kids was sixty rather than the ten over in the smaller part of the school. As he spoke, all my fears came rushing through my body. I just didn't like this place at all. It began to sink in that I missed my ma and dad and home life, even though my home life wasn't a great one. The reality sank in that I was being locked up; that my freedom was being taken away from me. All my old fears of people in authority took hold of my heart, leaving me unable to speak a word.

Brother Doyle led us into the main yard, where he opened the door and told us to go and mix with the other kids. Before I could catch my breath, I was standing with Alex and sixty wild kids from all over the rough parts of Dublin. The fear was so bad my small frame kept shaking as kids with rough and ready faces came our way, with hardcore Dublin accents asking,

'What's yer name?'

'Where ya from?'

'Whatcha in for?'

Four kids with fags in their mouths, talking at the same time, just made me more tense and fearful than I already was.

For all that was said about me across Skerries being a hard man, it was certainly shown to be so untrue in those moments. I suffered greatly with all kinds of fears that maybe back home weren't noticed that much, and yet they hung there, all around every room of my heart. In a nutshell, people frightened me in every sense, and now the full-blown reality of those fears came up my throat at a time you didn't want them to. The last place you want to show a weakness is in prison. But it was hard in this situation to hide away from what you felt.

We were later shown where we would sleep – in a large dormitory that had four beds to each section. Each dormitory held twenty-four beds, and there were three dormitories in all. Our first night was OK, and we both slept. We awoke to the loud voice of a headmaster telling us all to wake up. After we got washed and dressed, we were led to the main dining room to have breakfast. Then, it was off to classrooms until dinner time. After school, at three o'clock, we had to tog out for sports even if it was raining or snowing. After our six o'clock tea, the evening was spent playing in the yards or watching TV until our supper of milk and biscuits.

That was very much the daily routine until Friday afternoon when at four o'clock you were let home until Sunday night. Come Friday, I was dying to get home to my ma and dad. This place was nothing short of a nightmare for any nine-year-old boy. We were let travel home alone by train, and all I wanted to see was my house, which you could see as the train pulled into Skerries train station.

I ran from the train station all the way home. As I went in through the front door, the whole house seemed different as I turned to my ma and asked where was Dad, hoping he'd be here to get a hug from. But Ma sat me down with Alex and told us dad was in hospital. She didn't go too far into what had happened, just that he took sick and would be OK. Next day, the full horror of what had happened was told to me by Breda.

The day we were both were sent away, Dad came home but couldn't eat his dinner. He went upstairs and Ma went up after him, and Breda could hear him crying and saying,

'I want my two boys back, Clare. They took my boys away.'

The truth was that the day I saw my dad smiling at me in that courtroom was the moment his mind snapped. From the moment the judge passed sentence on Alex and me, something gave way inside my dad. He was smiling down at his nine-year-old boy who was being taken from him, and it broke his heart in two. He knew he should have done more to keep us on the right road, and now it was too late.

He was on his way to a major breakdown, but this was back in 1974, so no-one noticed it. My ma thought he had changed into a new man who was going to put the house back together and that we were all going to live happily ever after. To make this whole sad story worse, it was in the eyes of the people of Skerries, in the middle of the town in broad daylight, that his final breakdown happened.

My ma took Ray and Stuart in the pram for a walk down to the shops with Dad. Without warning, he stopped some guy and started shouting at him to give his boys back to him. Within minutes, he stripped naked in the street. The cops were called, and they knocked him out. They put him into a car and drove him to a doctor, and from there he was sent into Portrane, a hospital for people suffering from mental illnesses. In there, he was given shock treatment to try help him get back to normal health.

Sitting at home that weekend, I felt so disappointed that all my own hopes of our family being fixed and being happy had taken another terrible blow. As Sunday evening came and it was time to head back to St Laurence's, my feelings turned into a new kind of fear that I'd never experienced before. I can still feel the sick feeling deep inside as Alex and I said bye to Ma and headed off to face the unknown events of staying in a cold-hearted place like Laurence's.

*

By the time we got back there it was seven o'clock in the evening and all the kids were in the same mood. You could feel sixty young kids' hearts crying out in the silence of the chilly air in the main yards, and see on their faces the hurt of being away from home and family. But everyone hid their feelings behind bursts of anger, resulting in big one-to-one rows and even bloodshed. Back home I was seen as a crazy guy, but in here I was out of my league by a long way. Some of the kids would eat you for break-fast. I was just a shy, frightened young country boy to these lads from the inner city.

It wasn't long before I was getting into rows myself and losing every one. I just froze when a row broke out; it just wasn't in me to fight at nine years of age. The moment someone picked on me, my body just filled with a paralysing fear that I had no control over. This left me as easy prey for the bigger guys to pick on when they were in bad form. But one guy came to my aid more than once to tell anyone who picked on me to back off and leave me alone. And that young kid, whom I've always been so thankful to up to this day, was none other than Gerry Hutchinson, otherwise known as The Monk. So, as you can imagine, every time I see Gerry's face in a paper it brings a big smile to my face. To me he was a hero.

But Gerry couldn't be where I was all the time, and the abuse did get worse. With time it wasn't just the other kids but some of the housemasters who gave out beatings to me and other kids on a daily basis. Plus the Christian Brothers who co-ran the school would use leather straps to beat us if anyone stepped out of line. All this just led me into a more damaging fear that deepened and took a greater hold of my whole life.

My already deep-seated fear of people in authority had now fully taken over my heart and mind. Anyone with any kind of authority or strong personality would now leave me in a state of powerlessness. The violence in St Laurence's had pushed a young nine-year-old boy beyond the point of attaining the normal life that every young boy deserves. I had become a cold, lifeless child, with a confusing, painful anger against anything that bore any hallmark of authority.

*

As Alex and I tried to settle down into our new life in St Laurence's, we were all too frequently picked on by some of the bigger boys, who enjoyed beating us up. On one occasion, I was running from a gang of them and I hid behind the Brother who was in the yard at the time. He chased the gang away, and turned to me and smiled.

'Don't mind them, Patrick,' he said, in a warm, friendly voice.
He knows my name, I thought, *but I don't know his.*
Despite his tall, thin frame, the protective hug he gave me was like a wall around me. I felt reassured and secure.

'If any of them give you any trouble, just come to Brother Mark. Do you hear?'

From that day on, I loved seeing him in the yard. I knew I was safe when he was around. I'd even run over and sit on the bench in the shelter, just to be near him. He was a man of few words, but everything he did, from always smiling at me to holding my hand, made me feel that I was special and that he cared about me. In a playful way he would tap me lightly on the head, then tickle me by running his fingers around my neck and down my back till I giggled. Maybe I felt that, like the father I wish I had, he was someone I could look up to and respect.

One particular afternoon, I was playing alone in the yard, buried in sad thoughts.

'There you are, Patrick!'

I looked up. Brother Mark was walking towards me, beaming as usual.

'Listen – how would you like to get away from the yard here and come up and see the library! Would you like that?'

'Yeah, sure, Brother!' I gasped in excitement.

He took me by the hand and led me in through the main doors, up the long stairway and into the library.

I stood there for the first time in my life, looking at the rows and rows of books in their bookcases. I heard the click as he locked the door.

'Now, Patrick, I'm going to get you to do some exercises, how about that?'

'Yeah, sure, Brother.'

'OK. First you just lie down there now and start by doing some press-ups.'

Then he knelt over me and turned me over on my back.

'Great, Patrick. Now you can do some sit-ups.'

He held me down by the ankles, and gradually started moving his grip further and further up my legs.

'Great. That's it. Keep your hands behind your head now.'

He then pushed my jumper up so that my stomach was now bare. His voice changed and he started breathing heavily.

'Your belt is too tight, Patrick,' he said. 'Here. Let me open it for you.'

My body grew tense and nervous as he held my waist with one hand and with the other opened my belt and trouser buttons. This Christian Brother whom I trusted as my protector and friend was about to sexually abuse me, and a new sense of fear and shame was born into my 9-year-old life.

Other attacks followed the one in the library.

On one occasion I was at my lowest ebb and most vulnerable as I lay, suffering from the flu, isolated in the sick bay. I was a weak and easy target for Brother Mark, who came in, on the pretence of asking how I was, and took advantage of me in the cruellest way.

The last time he ever molested me was that summer when we were taken on a two-week holiday to Wexford, an annual sea-side treat for all the boys in St Laurence's. We were taken out fishing on a small boat. A while into the trip I became sea-sick. While I was leaning over the edge of the boat, puking into the water, Brother Mark came up behind me to comfort me, his hands touching my back and sliding down my body. The other boys could see what he was doing, but could do nothing to help.

You couldn't scream. You couldn't tell anyone. Who would have believed you? The fear in those moments no-one can explain. He was supposed to be a man of God, someone who, above anyone else, you could trust and come to. But all I was given by Brother Mark were life-long scars that were to haunt me for many years to come.

Apart from me, he took it upon himself to sexually abuse many of the younger kids too. The abuse was aimed at the weaker and innocent boys who couldn't fight back. He even tried it with my brother Alex. It was a well known fact that some kids were actually raped by him but it was covered up, like everything else in St Laurence's.

On the days when we played sports and had to strip naked to change, Brother Mark would stand there, watching our every move. You were given no towels to cover yourself up with until after the sports were over, so as we togged out, you always knew that he'd be enjoying watching us. Then after sports we had to shower and he'd be there watching us all intently. Some of the older kids would slag him off, calling him 'bent' or 'queer'. But that just resulted in a beating, as no housemaster or the other Brother would have believed Brother Mark was doing what he was doing.

*

Back in Portrane Hospital, Dad was starting to get better and was let home, but was being treated with medication and still had a long way to go to get back to full health. Seeing him for the first time was sad. He'd lost weight and looked out of it from tablets and the stay in hospital. But at least he was OK and back home, and for that I was thankful.

By the time the year was nearly up in St Laurence's, there wasn't one of the younger boys who'd come in to this school with problems that wasn't now leaving in a worse mess than before he arrived. In the last two months, I got my head split open and needed stitches. I suffered very badly and was unable to breathe properly at night. I was having nightmares, and throughout the day I wasn't able to watch anything on TV as it seemed to trigger off panic attacks. It took a long time to clear up. I never told anyone but Alex about it – I was just too afraid to say anything because I didn't know what was wrong with me. It wasn't until later years that I found out it was diagnosed as a case of severe concussion.

When it was finally time to go home for good from St Laurence's, many thought that the year away would have sorted out our wild ways back home and that we'd go straight and live normal, crime-free lives. But St Laurence's did very little to solve anything inside me. What it had done was leave me traumatised, hurt, sexually abused and in an even more lost state than before I went in. As for Alex, he came out pretty much the same, but we were different to each other in many ways.

Alex left his life of crime behind, but I picked up where I left off. Only this time I moved to bigger crimes, as the cold-faced child with no identity was driven along life's paths by anger, fear and a desire to get revenge on people in any place of authority that had hurt him and left him in this cold state of being.

> *So I turned on the crowd and I screamed, you and you,*
> *It could have been you.*

> *Replicas*
> *Gary Numan, 1979*

Chapter Three

IN A GLASS CAGE

I put my fear back in its box
And I put the box where love
is blind.

Blind
Gary Numan, 2006

Just before my departure from St Laurence's in 1975, I broke my arm and spent a long stay in Cappagh Hospital getting it pinned back together. By the time I got out, the best part of 1975 was gone and with still no encouragement at home, I soon returned to the life of crime.

My dad had now made a full recovery from his breakdown, but the dark old days continued, with home life as bad as ever, with no money for decent food and schoolbooks, and school life as grim as before – no support or encouragement from the teachers that all ten-year-olds need to make it through the week. From my experience in St Laurence's I had little or no respect for any form of authority. I didn't give a damn if I never learned a thing again in life. And teachers like Mr. Webb in 5th class just handed out beatings to whoever stepped out of line. Younger readers may find it hard to believe that that was just the norm back in those days.

By now I didn't care what happened to me. My revenge would come at the right time against all who misused their powers to hurt me. Any person who had a state-given place of authority and misused it against me were all marked down in an imaginary small black book stored in the back of my mind until I found the best way to strike back at them all.

Around the town I was now branded as an ex-con. What a joke to hang such a harsh sentence around the neck of a ten-year-old child, without asking *why*. I always felt so different to the whole world around me because in all truth I *was* different. I was cold inside and out, with crime as my only outlet. I had no interest in any sports or games like most kids, bar one funny story that gives me a laugh looking back.

Just out of the blue I came up with this great idea to sort my life out. I'd give up my life of crime and join the rugby club in Skerries. Of course, I had to ask dad for money for boots and shorts. Alex and I went up to him when he was in bed and asked him for the money, explaining that we wanted to join the rugby club. He gave us enough money for two pairs of shorts, but no money for boots. So down we went to Ireland's No. 1 clothes shop, Sharkey's in Skerries, and we got the shorts. Come Friday, we showed up for training with all the kids from my class. Out we came in our red shorts, but in the shoes and jumpers we'd wear day to day. All the other kids were fully kitted out, with proper jerseys and boots.

At the training session I think I touched the ball once, and stood there trying to fit in and look like I knew what I was doing. As for Alex, he got the ball and took off like a greyhound, but it all went unnoticed. At the end of training we were told that the game for the next day was in Navan.

Next morning Alex said he wasn't going without boots, but Braveheart me got up to go. A disaster waiting to happen! First thing I noticed was the jeans I had worn the night before had gone into the wash, and the only other pair I had were still damp. So my sister, Breda, came up with the only other possibility – if I really wanted to go to this game, the only pair of trousers that I could wear that would fit me were her blue pair of Bay City Rollers tartan trousers. They were so wide in the leg you couldn't see your feet even if you had size twelve boots on, plus they were girls' trousers. But on they went, and with my shorts under my arm, off I went, looking like a right plonker. I didn't know whether to laugh or cry.

I got to the meeting spot and noticed the other lads looking me up and down in disbelief. I stood there not daring to open my mouth to say a word. In my all too familiar withdrawn state, I stood waiting for the cars to come to pick us up to drive to Navan. When the cars did come, everyone got in bar me. With everyone looking at me, the last man standing, one of the drivers broke the silence by saying,

'Well, there's room, get in.'

So in I got and went away to my first big rugby game.

On arrival at the Navan club, things just went from bad to worse. I was left standing in the middle of the dressing room on my own as everyone togged out for the match. Some of the dads who went along to support their sons interacted with them, but I might as well have been invisible. No one spoke one word to me, and as we headed out to play the game, I was left to walk behind the team to the sideline of the pitch, and stood alone for the entire game. To make matters worse, it started raining.

Alone on the sideline, with my sister's Bay City Rollers trousers on, my rugby career melted down with the raindrops into the pitch under my feet and was lost forever. It was a lonely return to the dressing room after we won the match by the one and only try of the game. A sinking feeling had already gripped my heart, and I knew I would never return to this experience ever again.

It was a lonely trip back to Skerries. When I got home, I made up my mind that even though my rugby days had ended before they started, I really wanted my life to change and I wasn't going to give up that easily. I'd come to a place that I was tired of. I'd had enough of being this strange kid with no hope. I was fed up of being in trouble with cops and teachers and other kids from around the town. So I stopped nicking stuff, and made sure I got to school on time.

*

After a while I started to feel good about myself, and felt I was starting to slowly turn my life around. My anger towards people in authority was far from gone, but I didn't think about it as much. I felt like I was at last gaining ground out of my dark existence. When I got to school in the morning, I started to make a habit of saying hello to any teachers I met in passing. As an eleven-year-old child, it just made me feel that if I was nice to people, they would forget my past and accept me like any other kid in the school.

With my new-found hope came what was maybe the first smile on my face. I knew I was on the right road, and it felt great getting up in the mornings and heading across by the Old Mill Bakery to school. Smelling the freshly-baked bread in the morning air just added an extra touch to my growing smile. I hadn't got school books yet, but felt it didn't matter as long as I was keeping out of trouble and being nice to grown-ups. That's all that mattered to me in the whole world. I started to find a trust inside myself that I don't think I ever had before, and it seemed to give me great hope for the future.

Then as this eleven-year-old child walked down the school hallway one morning with high hopes and my new-found smile, I met Mr. Jones. I had been saying hello to him for the past while, so it was just another opportunity to show that my whole manner had changed and that I was at least improving from what I once was. As he passed by I smiled and said,

'Good morning, Mr. Jones.'

I had just passed him when he called me back. I slowly went towards him. He looked down at me and said in a cold voice,

'Don't you ever say hello to me again, Bentley. I don't want anything to do with the likes of you.'

He turned and walked away.

In that one moment every hope, every smile, everything I had built up over the past few weeks were all lost forever. Those few words from his mouth took away all my hope and left me in a worse mess than when I started trying to change my life around. I slowly walked to my classroom leaving all hope of ever wanting to be nice to anyone ever again behind me in the hallway. I would strike revenge against anyone who caused me unjust harm like Mr. Jones did to me that day.

I turned back to stealing again, and was soon in trouble with the cops. This time I was doing jobs myself, breaking into houses and visiting the church to help myself to what God might have left for me after Sunday masses.

My school days went from bad to worse, and I ended up in more fights with teachers as my anger and hurt began to totally spill out of control and push me further and further towards another disaster in my life. Things got so bad that the cops assigned a plainclothes cop to me whose job it was to help and work alongside kids like myself. His name was John Hyde.

John came to our home to talk to my ma and myself about my crime wave, but all my trust in people was well and truly gone. He opened a youth club in town that opened its doors to just about everybody who wanted to come along. But in 1976 a Christian Brother who was working there assaulted my close friend, Paul Webb, when we came up to the door to get in one evening and he told us we weren't getting in. We had never seen him before, so we pushed at the door to get in. He opened the door and gave Paul a full-force kick between the legs, leaving him on the ground screaming in agony and bleeding badly from a deep cut to his testicles. Paul had to be rushed to hospital to be stitched.

The Christian Brother was removed from the town that very night, the youth club was closed down for good, and the whole issue was hushed up to this day. The experience reinforced my fear and hate of people who claimed a place of authority but who abused kids they were meant to care for, encourage and do no harm to.

I slowly found myself experiencing an even deeper withdrawal from all around me, and my wave of crime went on the up as I started to steal whatever came my way. A lot of the time I got away with it, but sometimes I did a few jobs with guys who couldn't keep their mouths closed. So I got caught a few times, enough to put myself in striking distance of going to court again. But at this stage I didn't care what happened to my life, so I continued to push ahead with my crime spree.

By late 1977, I pushed the cops too far and found myself standing before the judge in Balbriggan Courtroom again. This time I was alone, without Alex. As I stood up in front of the judge and the charges were read out, I found a picture flashing across my mind of a young teen sitting in a glass cage looking out across a sea of people who were looking in at this cold-faced boy who had grown from a child into an untouchable teenager, and who seemed to care little about what was happening in the courtroom that day. But deep down, under all the coldness and the lifeless eyes of this thirteen-year-old, lay just another kid wishing his life was so different than what he was experiencing at that time.

The judge passed sentence: another year in St Laurence's. Inside, all my fears of this place returned, but I tried so hard to remain in a frozen state and not let anyone see what I felt inside. I was taken away out of the court to start another year in the dreaded place in which I had suffered all kinds of abuse as a nine-year-old child. I got out of a cop car wearing a black blazer and trousers and saw a housemaster waiting for me at the main doors of St Laurence's. He came up and shook my hand to welcome me back. It was Mr. Grimes, whom I knew from the past year I spent there. He never liked me because I once got sick in his car, and he was to become one of the main figures of abuse in my life for the next year in St Laurence's.

Walking into the main yard for the first time in three years sent a chill down my spine. I felt alone and not ready to face sixty other kids whom I didn't know from Adam. I walked out into the yard as the door closed behind me with a loud bang. I was soon surrounded by a big crowd of kids firing all kinds of questions at me, who I was, what was I in for. I was back in the hell hole, St Laurence's, and it felt worse this time around than when I was nine years old. I was on my own this time, and I knew just what to expect.

With Brother Mark still roaming around abusing new victims, it was only a matter of time before I would experience more of the same abuse that I had suffered three years ago. The only positive was that Brother Mark went for younger kids, as the older kids would fight back. But you still had to change in front of him, and there was nothing you could do about it. Plus you knew kids were being abused behind the scenes, though none of the other staff picked up on it. At the end of the day, no one would have believed you if you did speak up.

On top of Brother Mark's abuse, I had Mr. Grimes who, as I said, caused me great harm throughout the year. He was over my class, and each week he held what they called a 'Marks Day'. Different classrooms had different housemasters doing marks to see how each kid behaved over the week. They would ask different teachers how we behaved and did we do the work they had set out before us. I found most of the school teachers at St Laurence's great people and very easy to work with. They never, in any way, abused the kids and did everything they could to further our education. So I started to learn how to read and write for the first time and opened up a little.

But each week, Mr. Grimes tried to find fault with me and my work. When he had the whole class together, he'd let some lads who did nothing in school but cause fights with other lads and teachers off the hook. But when it came to me, he just twisted things around to make me look bad in front of the class. Then sometimes he'd have me in tears telling me I was losing my weekend home, even though he was actually planning on letting me go home. I tried harder in school each week, but the harder I tried the worse he'd make me feel.

This experience went on for the whole year, and I grew colder and stopped crying as my heart closed over more than ever before. It felt like my whole life made no sense to me anymore, and what I longed for more than anything else was something that I could identify with that matched the world I was living inside, deep in my innermost thoughts.

I yearned for something or someone to understand me and accept me for who I really was. But even that was something I wasn't sure of, who I was, what I was. All I was sure of was that I was slipping slowly away from the world outside me. I felt more of an alien than a human around people. I saw nothing but cruelty and pain outside me from all around, and my only wish now was that someone would find me and help me come back to life. Could someone care enough to show me the way without hurting me? Could someone come through my almost closed door and sit down in silence, put their warm arms around my icy heart and melt away all the coldness and hurt and pain, and bring me back to some normal existence where love is not something that you dreamt about and lost when you opened your eyes on a cold wet morning in St Laurence's?

But the harsh reality was that I was on my own in a state of loneliness, and had always been from as far back as my mind could reach. I could see nothing in the near distance that would help me out of this cold world that surrounded me inside and out.

*

Outside my little confused world, a new front page story was causing great talk in the music realms. Punk rock music had come to life in the form of one of the main punk bands, The Sex Pistols. The punk trend was shocking all sides of society as fans of the new music dressed in torn-up clothes and pins, dyed their hair different colours and gave two fingers to all authority figures. The Sex Pistols themselves were headed by Johnny Rotten on lead vocals, Sid Vicious on lead guitar with Paul Cook and Steve Jones making up the band that were causing the main stir-up in England with their new rock music and their two banned number one songs, *God Save the Queen* and *Pretty Vacant*. Their first and most famous album, *Never Mind the Bollocks*, saw the Sex Pistols hit number one with the album's famous and distinctive yellow cover, and before you could say stop, punk rock music exploded onto the scene and nothing could put a halt to it.

Like everything else in Ireland, it took a little longer to hit here. I'd had little interest in any type of music before this, but I was just at that age where my music taste was starting to kick into gear and my ears were waiting to hear the right kind of music to suit my own musical taste. Up to this date, the only song that I'd heard that did anything for me was a love song called *Nights in White Satin* by the Moody Blues. For me it was, and still is, one of the greatest and most moving songs ever recorded. But as punk rock music came across the Irish Sea to hit our small island with a wave the size of Ireland itself, its music and image struck me as something I wanted to get into right away. So I became one of the first original punk rockers with my hair dyed four colours and my clothes full of safety pins and covered in punk rock badges. Alex jumped on the bandwagon too, as well as Breda.

Soon we had our hands on the famous Sex Pistols tape and it was played every weekend when I got home from St Laurence's, much to the dislike of my dad, who was upset at the way we were dressing up at the weekends. But the show went on. For me, nothing was better than causing great shock walking around the streets of Dublin at the weekend to the disbelief of people who nearly fell over themselves and others to get a look at one of these rare punk rockers who didn't give a toss about the world around them, and openly portrayed a message of two fingers to all those who held any post of authority. Deep down, it was my own release of anger to all those people – cops, teachers, Christian Brothers – whom I hated with all my heart for the hurt they had imposed on me down the years.

To get into a disco was hard, going dressed in this fashion. The trend was not catching on as much over here, and the guys on the door of the local discos told us we were not dressed the right way to be let in. But in time we started getting in, and then the next mountain to climb was to get a DJ to play a Sex Pistols song so we could go mad for five minutes. It was a normal rule for punk rockers never to dance to any other type of music but punk rock. So it was five minutes in the whole night. The rest of the time was spent just looking around at who else was at the disco. You had your skinheads, your Thin Lizzy fans, your Horslips fans all together under one happy roof. For me, so much more was going on inside that no-one saw.

I watched as the music died down and the slow sets came on, and people started dancing wrapped around each other and kissing. The first wave of feelings for girls overwhelmed me. But I was not like any normal fifteen-year-old teenager who had no problem asking a girl for a dance and showing her warm feelings and kissing her. The very thought of getting close to a girl sent a wave of intense fear through me, and seemed so frightening that I felt myself trying to back away as far as I could. A part of me wanted to be that close to a girl, but I was far too frozen up inside to be able to have any kind of normal chat or dance with anyone, plus I had zero confidence. So, for me, it was just another distant dream that seemed very much out of my reach.

Still very much underage, we started our beer-drinking days. There was always some bigger guy who could get us drink and pass it on to us down a lane. The drinking gave me false confidence, but that was better than no confidence. So it was a couple of bottles of cider and then falling into my local disco. With the drink, I blocked out all my problems, like alcohol does to anyone who drinks. Most of the time I just got sick or fell asleep, but the times I didn't, I enjoyed the buzz from it.

In the midst of my punk rock disco days, my eyes fell on what I would call the first girl I truly fell for. Her name was Nora, a local from the town of Skerries. The first thing I noticed about her was her eyes. Truly amazing and by far the most beautiful girl I had ever seen in my life. At discos, I'd be watching to see if she was there each week. I was now smitten. But how was I to get myself out of the cold, closed-down world I lived in and get to a place where I'd ask this girl up for a dance? It all seemed so impossible, and too far out of my reach.

The fear of her saying no, and what that would feel like kept me firmly in a corner of the disco, and each slow dance came and went as I tried to find the courage to make that lonely walk across what seemed like a ten-mile walk to where she was sitting with her friends. In the end I found the courage from somewhere to make the long trip across the floor to where she sat. I muttered the words,

'Do you want to dance?'

In the back of my mind I was saying,

If she says no, run and throw yourself into the harbour.

But she said yes, thank God, and I walked nervously out to the dance floor and moved close to her, putting my arms around her, drawing her close. My heart was racing, but I just forgot everything and took in the fact that I was dancing for the first time with the nicest girl in Skerries.

45

Away from the all-seeing eyes of the world around, no-one would have realised the staggering truth – that this was the first time I ever felt something warm from another human being in the fourteen years of my life. Everything up until this moment was hurt, pain, abuse and rejection. I'd spent all those years locked safely away in a cold and lifeless world, and nobody was let past a well-closed door to my heart and soul. But this moment was pure heaven.

This was a girl people only dreamed about. Nora, with her cute shy smile and amazing eyes, was dancing with the most messed-up teenager that ever lived in Skerries, yet she danced with me as if I was just another one of the guys. I never spoke a word to her; I was too lost in the moment. The smell of her skin, her hair, her neck was better than any perfume on the planet. But just as I wandered along in a fantasy about this amazing girl, fear struck its hold over my heart and mind as recollections of my abused life flashed before my very eyes. As the dance ended, I thanked her and walked away back into my cold lifeless world where I felt safe and secure. Without doubt, I had met my first love, but I was too messed up to get close to anyone long-term. But for a moment, this cold messed-up boy tasted his first moment of warmth, his one moment of a taste of love. However, that moment then caused more doubts about my self-worth to creep in because I couldn't go beyond the moment and interact with a girl beyond a dance. So, I just went back to the world I was used to.

By the time I got out of St Laurence's my life was in a worse state again. Throughout the year there I saw kids being beaten, along with myself, by housemasters and Christian Brothers. The knowledge of kids being sexually abused left more harm done to my life, but that would remain a closed secret for many years to come. On my release, I entered secondary school but within weeks lost my head in a religious class and left school for good. With no education, I went to work on the land for a farmer, Christy Grimes, who was the best farmer around Skerries at the time.

As for my punk rock scene, I carried on with the dressing-up part, but in my heart it all meant nothing to me. The music was great, but it had nothing personal to say to me about how I felt. It was just a load of anti-government words about hitting back and not caring about anything or anybody. For me, the whole thing didn't fit into my world and never did. Jumping around a dance floor spitting at each other was not what I wanted to take into my world. In truth, I now hated the punk rock thing. I was hurting badly and punk rock wasn't helping me with any of what I felt inside. I hit a very low time in myself and couldn't see any way forward. I couldn't be with girls like all my mates were. I couldn't shake off the name I had inherited. I couldn't get all the abuse out of my head from St Laurence's. I could see I was truly sinking down into myself without a way up again.

There was nothing around that I could bounce what I felt inside off or something that I could identify with from what I had become inside. Nothing that I could say was mine and that I knew would be safe to take into the world that I seemed to be locked away in. Something needed to happen fast or I felt I was going to break and be lost forever in some kind of emotional breakdown.

On top of this growing concern, Ma and Dad called it a day in their marriage and Dad moved out and back home to his mother's house. He took the three younger brothers with him, Ray, Stuart and Simon. So with a broken family to top off the rest of my grow-ing concerns, it seemed that my whole life was coming to an end at the tender age of fifteen. But there was yet another twist just around the corner waiting to change something in my life forever.

That something that I'd been searching for all my life to identify with how I felt inside my isolated world awaited me. As my life dangled on what seemed like a thread, looking down into an endless pit of despair and pain, a cold voice never heard before was about to enter into my life and world. A voice that would take centre stage in my life, and help me feel for the first time that at last I was no longer alone.

Chapter Four

THE EXODUS TO REPLICAS

I'd give it all up for you
I'd even be a number just for you
The strangest living boy
You could ever wish to see
. . . That's me.

The Machman
Gary Numan, 1979

It was a Thursday evening in May of 1979. Myself, Breda, and the rest of the family scrambled for a place to sit to watch our weekly *Top of the Pops*. Even my youngest sibling, Fran, would be watching it in her own way from her highchair even though she was only a baby at the time. For Breda, she watched the show to see what punk bands would be in the Top 30. For me, it was just going through the motions, as I'd long given up on punk rock. Strangely enough, I still wore the punk rock gear, but the buzz was well gone from my life. Punk rock wasn't the easiest thing to give up. It was like a cult in many ways, and if you got out of it, you'd be given an awful time by other punks around the town for doing so. So maybe I was a little scared of the backlash of walking away from it all. But inside, it was well gone from my heart and my mind.

I had other things on my mind than *Top of the Pops* that Thursday night. As I stated in the last chapter, I was going through what seemed like a dead-end experience. Everything seemed dark and I couldn't see anything good down the road in my life. Fifteen years of abuse, hurt and pain seemed to have caught up with me in some very strange and painful way. Nothing I saw, thought or felt seemed to help pull me up from the dreaded place I found myself so lost in. If there was any ray of light out there, somewhere in the world, it was something I couldn't find. I'd hit a real life low point and couldn't see any way out.

I sat with my arms folded, my eyes staring in a trance at the TV as *Top of the Pops* ran down the Top 30 songs in the UK. Deep in my own thoughts, I wasn't taking much notice of the bands that came and went that night. Then the presenter said there was a new entry into the charts, and said the name Tubeway Army with a song called *Are Friends Electric*. Next thing I recall was seeing this pale-faced guy with a cold look in his eyes and the strangest music I'd ever heard in my life. Then he started to sing with the most incredible voice that almost didn't sound human. His eyes looked sharply to one side, glaring out as if he was saying *I'm untouchable*. The fact that he was wearing all black just added to the mystery of the man.

I sat in a state of shock, mainly because the whole song and image was something that touched me like nothing ever had before in my life. Before the song ended, I'd fallen deeply in love with this band and its music. I felt like a beam of light had come through the TV that night, and somehow this lifeline was thrown to me in my depressed state and a light came on in my heart that was never there before. The singer was, of course, Gary Numan, a young singer making his debut on *Top of the Pops*.

Something happened in my life that night. I had found a life support machine in Gary's music, and it was like it was all planned to happen the way it did. Everything I'd ever felt all my life, the hurt, the pain, the coldness inside was now OK to feel, because in Gary Numan I'd found my mirror man and for the first time in my life I didn't feel alone. They say things happen for a reason and I'm sure that's true in everyone's life. For me, I was rescued in the nick of time. I'd found a music that mirrored how I felt inside, and that was the one thing that was missing from my life. No longer was I sitting alone in my self-made world where it all seemed so cold and lifeless. Now I had someone whose music seemed to make me feel understood for the first time.

With the music came a lifelong bond. Gary Numan seemed to me to be the perfect deal; everything about him and his songs stood out from the rest, and gave me my first and only true love of music. But on a deeper, personal note, I discovered Gary Numan's voice had a way of reaching me in a split second and making me feel that I wasn't alone with my struggles and hurt. So, in those five minutes that Gary sang on that Thursday night in May 1979 on Top of the Pops, my life was turned upside down.

As I closed my eyes that night to drop off to sleep, a slow echo of Numan's voice reverberated in my mind. I'd found something in my life that was mine, that I loved and that no one could take away from me. I couldn't wait to see him again the following week on Top of the Pops. But for now I had gone from being down at my lowest point in my life to being raised up to what seemed like the best place I'd ever been to.

Tubeway Army were no flash in the pan. Within a couple of weeks *Are Friends Electric* topped the charts and stayed there for three weeks. Gary Numan with his new sounding synthe-sised music and distinctive voice was here to stay. If punk rock wasn't gone out the window already, it was now, and my next step was to get the single *Are Friends Electric*. But I had no money, plus I had no record player as I had broken the old one. So it was time for a night trip to nick something I could play records on fast. I ended up nicking a twin tape recorder from the school, something that was valuable then. The word got out around that Tubeway Army had an album out to go with the single. A close friend of mine, Joe Burns, told me he heard the whole album and it was out of this world.

'Every song on it is brilliant,' he said. 'Wait till you hear it.'

With a night out nicking around the town complete, I got on a train on my own personal mission to buy Tubeway Army's new album entitled *Replicas* with my stolen dosh. When I picked it up in the record shop, the cover told its own story. Gary Numan stood, all in black with blonde hair, looking out a window into a cold park. The image said it all, chilly and withdrawn – just what the doctor ordered. I couldn't wait to get home to listen to it, and read the words of the songs like we all do when we get a new album. But for me, it meant so much more to me than it would to the everyday person. This man's voice did something for me that kept my troubled world from falling apart.

On getting home it was up to my room as fast as possible and on went the tape. The first song, *Me! I Disconnect From You* started and that was it. I was lost in the magic of it all. It was better than I'd imagined it would be. As I listened to it, I could hardly believe how much this man and his music meant to me. Hour after hour I'd sit alone in my cold, run-down room from then on with my stolen tape deck listening to the cold *Replicas* album.

Gary Numan's idea for the album was to adapt science fiction type of characters in the storyline, robots with human skin, and place them into a story with each song. But for me, it was far from that idea. *Replicas* came over to me as one person trapped in some kind of world alone, isolated and afraid, looking back out across at humans who just went about hurting other people all the time. I felt that person was me, for my whole life was one of pain and hurt and fear. But now, I'd found this very rare music that I loved with all my heart and the moment I put it on, I stepped into the world in *Replicas*. I took all the characters out of the album and put myself in the whole album as its soul person. Every time I put Numan's *Replicas* on, it was about me and my whole life and how I felt inside. Being in that world kept me whole and safe and feeling I was understood and would now be able to survive.

Some people may say that's all very strange and odd, but for this fifteen-year-old teenager, it was to become something that saved my life and nothing short of that. I'd be surprised if anyone else was sitting in their room all alone playing around with the *Replicas* album in such a personal way as I was, yet I'm sure someone out there had to do something like I did to keep from drowning in the sea of hopelessness. So, Mr. Gary Numan and his music threw me a lifeline, and I took it and held it close to my little world inside. I was no longer alone and it felt great. Even so, when I stepped back into this cold, real world the pain was still very real and people were still, to me, cruel and heartless. But in the coldness of the sounds of *Replicas*, I could step away from my fears and hurt, switch into myself, draw myself into the *Replicas* album and stay there alone hour after hour, night after night.

Soon Gary Numan's face was on every music magazine and all the girls' magazines. He became a star overnight, and *Replicas* went to number one in the album charts. I was just so proud of Gary; he was everything to me, and now his band was being hailed as the best new band on the music scene. It wasn't long before Gary Numan dropped the Tubeway Army band name for a solo career under just Gary Numan, a move that in some ways always seemed a wrong choice to me.

This shy, unknown pop star with the cold distant look in his eyes and the strangest voice ever heard in the history of rock music was not everyone's cup of tea, and hiding behind a band name for a while longer would have been a wiser choice, in my eyes. With his new solo career came Numan's next single, *Cars*, along with another masterpiece album, *The Pleasure Principle*, which in my books was every bit as good as *Replicas*. If anything, it was better suited to my life inside as its words and music sounded much more personal with such songs as *Me* and *Conversations*, which became lifelong favourites. Again, the whole atmosphere of the album fitted into how I felt as a young messed-up teenager. Both the single and the album topped the charts.

By the end of 1979 and on into 1980, I had sunk further into his make-believe world of ominous fantasy; yet nothing in either of the albums was sci-fi escapism – it was all very real and very moving, and it touched me in the deepest part of my soul. These words rang out across my damp, dark room, holding me together under the stress of the lack of any direction that was so apparent in my life:

> *Please don't turn me off*
> *I don't know what I'm doing outside*
> *Me and the telephone that never rings*
> *If you were me, what would you do?*
>
> *Me! I Disconnect From You*
> *Gary Numan, 1979*

Standing at the window wearing all black, I stared out across at the Old Mill Bakery as it stood in its own darkness. I couldn't but wonder would Gary Numan and his music be enough to keep me safe and somehow lead me to some normal life, or was there something out there waiting for my next mistake. I knew it would be safer to stay locked away with my music, but I was human and I wanted to climb to some normal level of existence, if at all possible.

*

In early 1980, I started to spend more of my time chatting to Tim Herron who lived on our road. Looking back, I'm so grateful for the time he gave me at that point in my life. No-one else found me interesting, so it was a breath of fresh air spending time chatting to him. Most of the time was spent talking about Irish road racing or as we called it 'Bikes'. Each year a road race was held a mile up the road called the Skerries 100 which I always went to along with just about every other kid from the town. Watching the likes of the great Joey Dunlop, Raymond McCullough, Steven Cull and Conor McGinn, it was to many around the town the greatest sport on the planet. To me, it didn't mean that much at all.

But over time, Tim drew me into the world of bike racing by giving me posters of the riders for my wall, and telling me stories of races gone by like the TT Races and the Northwest 200 and Ulster Grand Prix. Before long I had what they call the bug and I was hooked into the fast and dangerous sport of Irish road racing between the hedges on public closed roads.

Everyone had their favourite rider, most people's being Joey Dunlop. I had to be different and go for Ray McCullough, who still remains one of the all-time legends of the sport, now retired.

In 1981 Tim got me a lift to the Ulster Grand Prix. The buzz of knowing I would be at one of the biggest races in the world watching all the top riders and teams from the UK was too much, and I slept very little the night before. I got up three hours before we set off just in case they went without me or forgot about me. When we got there, the rain came down for the day, but it didn't spoil it for me. Just being there watching the likes of Mick Grant on a Works Suzuki and John Newbold, who was another of my favourite riders at the time, was awesome, along with Joey Dunlop and Ron Haslam on Works Hondas. I stood in amazement at the sight of all these heroes whose posters now filled the walls of my room.

Watching Tony Rutter and Roger Marshall, with their distinctive helmets flashing by at high speed around the famous Dundrod circuit in the pouring rain, was one of the very few happy moments that stand out in my otherwise troublesome life. I am forever grateful to my still close friend, Tim Herron, for all the time he gave me back in 1980 when no-one else cared enough to give me five minutes of their time. He is one of the true gentlemen who to this day still shares a spot with me on a bank at the races, a friend I found and a friend I never lost.

I'd found what was, in my eyes, the best sport on the planet. But in all truth, it fell way short of dealing with the growing problems I was facing and being controlled by every day of my life. Most of my time was spent locked away in my room listening to Gary Numan as if my life depended on it. A lot of the press and media had taken a big dislike to his music and his image. In his own words, all of his hopes and dreams of being a pop star and a success were very different from the reality. He felt battered and scarred inside and out, and was struggling to keep it all together.

With all this going on he released his third album, *Telekon*, which was a clear example of a young man whose dream had swiftly turned into a nightmare. The album with songs like *I Die, You Die*, *This Wreckage*, *Please Push No More*, and *We Are Glass* was put together to depict Numan's dealings with the press and media and the hurt he felt. But the album fell into the hands of a young teenager locked away in his own frightened little world, and became another stone in his life to stand upon in a sinking world that lay all around him.

> *They crawl out of their holes for me*
> *And I die, you die*
> *Hear them laugh, watch them turn on me*
> *And I die, you die.*
> *I Die, You Die*
> Gary Numan, 1980

These words screamed out from my tape deck, drawing me deeper into a world of my own oppressed anger at all those who hurt me down the years. *Telekon* was the only way I could safely tap into how I really felt and how I really hurt. Numan's music was taking on a life of its own in my life. That cold, amazingly distinctive voice seemed to reach the very deepest part of me. And I had now developed a very chilling need to get revenge on certain people that I felt hurt me in an unjust way. But I didn't want to just get them – I wanted to leave a mark behind that would never be forgotten, and that would one day be written about in a book.

*

In 1981 I was seventeen years of age, and like all seventeen-year-olds, I was very interested in girls. All my mates were dating and moving along nicely in their relationships. But things were not going at all well when it came to the opposite sex for me. I had no self-esteem or confidence in my looks. As far as I could see, everybody was better looking than me and better at talking to girls than me. But there were worse problems than just that. I had no idea what love felt like or how to show it. I had just spent all my life up to this point being abused and hurt, and all I felt was numbness inside.

It was a big surprise to me when, at a disco in the town hall in Balbriggan, I was told that a girl was interested in going out with me. I looked over to see what she looked like and saw one of the best-looking girls in the place staring at me with a lovely smile. Without thinking I said yes, and before I knew it I was up slow dancing with this cracking girl. By this time in my life my nickname was Sid, a name most people still call me today, after Sid Vicious from the Sex Pistols. The girl I found myself dancing with was called Anne, and the first thing she asked me was what my real name was. I came face-to-face with her and said 'Patrick'. There was a moment as both our eyes met close up. It was the first moment in my life I really looked into a girl's eyes this close.

My first thought was I felt like I was in some trance at the beauty I saw. Our faces moved closer together. My eyes dropped slowly to her mouth as her lips parted and her mouth slowly closed in on mine. The last thing I remember was those beautiful eyes of Anne's closing as our lips touched for the first time. I took my right hand and placed it on her face and put my left hand gently on the back of her head, and slowly got lost in the magic of my first real kiss.

My heart was racing and for a moment all my worries were lost forever.

Once the kiss was over, I was struck with all kinds of fears that kept me from going any further. Anne tried to touch the back of my neck with her hand, but my whole body froze and I pulled my head back. She put it down to me being just a bit shy, but it was far worse than shyness. At the time, I had no idea what the cause of it was, but in later years I came to realise it was down to years of abuse, mainly in St Laurence's and the blows to the neck and head which gave me a very nervous reaction when touched there. Anne wasn't put off by the setback though, and so I started dating her.

Like any teenager, I was smitten by this girl and found it hard to think about anything else when I was away from her. But it was all to end before it started. I just couldn't go beyond a kiss, and she got fed up with me and gave me the boot. I was left with a worse embarrassment when one of her mates passed on a message to me from her asking me would I ever get a move on and go further than just a kiss. That was the pattern from there onwards.

Girlfriend after girlfriend went by the wayside for the same reasons. Some girls I couldn't even put my arm around, let alone kiss. Some I found hard to talk to as my world had been cut off from all human contact or any kind of love or warmth for too many years. I felt like an alien to all human touch, and could do nothing to set myself free to be normal around girls. I only felt safe alone in my self-made world, yet the longing to reach out and taste the fruit and emotion of love from a girl was very real deep down, locked away somewhere inside my heart. What made it all the harder to deal with was I had a deep sense that I had a lot of love to give, which I found hard to understand as I'd never been shown any kind of love in any way from anyone all my life.

I withdrew from my relationship problems with girls to my own world again, alone with my music in my room. This time, I spent a lot of time listening to slow love songs for hours. I tried to imagine what it would feel like to have what they sang about. The more hours I spent listening, the more I formed a picture of what a relationship should be like. I imagined a relationship without games, or people trying to hurt each other, without one trying to make the other jealous all the time, a relationship where you'd stand by each other and have a fifty-fifty chance of giving love to each other. For me, there was no point in being in a relationship otherwise.

Maybe, in truth, I had fallen in love with the *idea* of being in love. But it gave me some light in an otherwise dark and lonely existence.

*

On the Gary Numan scene, he had brought out his fifth album, *Dance*, but not before playing three farewell gigs at Wembley. He was bowing out of touring because of the stress of being exposed to fame at such a young age. His idea was to back away from what had become a nightmare climb to fame. I felt that his experience was just like my own, but in a different way. I had withdrawn from just about everything around me into the only world I felt safe in, my room. I was still getting awful stuff said about me, and it hurt far more than I ever showed. I had to remain ice-cold to the world around me while all the time I was in a lot of pain and wishing my life was anything but what it was.

The cover of *Dance* showed Gary Numan posing in a gangster suit and hat, but he never lost that withdrawn feeling in his music that kept me fed with haunting sounds and words that fitted so easily into my cold little world.
She whispers, 'Isn't it odd?
You remind me of songs

That I'd rather forget
Like feelings I longed for.
You haunt me inside.'

Stories
Gary Numan, 1981

As 1981 closed behind me and I entered into 1982, a story was about to unfold that's been locked away in Skerries folklore for twenty-six years now. 1982 came with more run-ins with the law, with the prospect of facing my first term in a man's prison. But for me, I'll remember 1982 as the year the Black Cat struck fear into the hearts of all those who shared a place of authority in the town of Skerries.

Chapter Five

THE BLACK CAT

While an Irish nation lay sleeping and blind to the sexual abuse by Christian Brothers in residential institutions until it all came out in the late 90s, I knew about it, dating back to the early 1970s. So in 1982, I created the Black Cat to strike back against people who shared a place of authority over young kids and abused it.

Quote from *The Black Cat*

For the many thousands of people who have moved to the lovely seaside town of Skerries in the past twenty-five years, the Black Cat and the story behind him would be very much a hidden story that's been left in the archives collecting dust for all these years.

I was asked by many people from that time if I was going to write the story of the Black Cat into this book. I wasn't sure about it, as no-one has been able to track him down, and maybe some dark stories are better left in the past. But to my surprise, I got a call one evening from someone claiming to be the Black Cat. After a long chat with this guy and the tales he was able to tell me, I knew it was none other than who he claimed to be. He gave me the go-ahead to write about him, but only a shortened version of the facts.

On the bike racing scene, my love for road racing never slowed down. Another underdog at that time was Johnny Rea who was new to the racing world, and most of the guys who I went to the racing with said he'd never amount to much. So I stuck by him and trusted that one day he'd prove himself a winner at the likes of the TT races. I always looked forward to the local Skerries 100 Road Race that took place each year in the first weekend of July. The buzz would be there weeks leading up to that weekend before we'd take a place on the bank at the shady lane on a warm sunny Saturday afternoon to watch Joey Dunlop, Robert Dunlop, Brian Read and the great home favourite, big Sam McClements, a man everyone loved as their own hero.

It was one of those days when all your problems would seem a million miles away, and as bikes raced passed you at speeds of 160mph, it was hard not to be thrilled inside and out and feel like you'd never come down from the buzz of such occasions. But I always did, with a hammer blow at times.

*

I woke up one morning in 1982 with four cops standing over me with a search warrant. A lot of jeans had been robbed off clothes lines around the town, and I was top of the suspect list. Cop Morgan pulled about ten pairs of jeans out of my wardrobe and asked where I got them.

'In town,' I said. 'Why?'

'Ten pairs? I've only got two pairs of trousers,' said Morgan, 'and I'm working full time.'

I was taken down to the station and charged with stealing three pairs that they could prove and one pushbike wheel. A court date was set with the prospect of being sent for a term in a real prison – a far cry from the kids' prison that I was sent to in the 70s.

Lying awake in my unlit, damp room, unable to sleep with the fear of court the next day, I listened to the *Replicas* album until late into the night to comfort and ease my fearful heart. As I looked out my window over the cold rooftops into the dark of the night that hung over Skerries, I was unaware of another story unfolding in this small town.

A cold-faced boy with vengeful eyes was carefully writing two letters on fine-cut cardboard. Dressed in black with gloves and a mask with a single red line painted on one side, a symbol of the blood of all abused kids at the hands of those in authority in residential institutions, he slowly slipped out into the dark of the night.

Next morning while standing outside the courtroom with a few mates, two cop cars came into view coming from the right-hand side of the road, pulling up fast, doors opening before the cars had time to stop. One cop jumped out screaming as he came running in our direction.

'Who painted my house last night? Which one of you did it?' We were all pulled into a side room next to the main court-room. His mouth trembling with an uncontrollable rage, Cop Morgan shouted,

'Who is this bloody Black Cat guy who painted my house last night and left two notes pinned to my front door stating I'm his first victim? Let me see your hands now!'

He checked our hands for paint but none was found. He left in a state muttering under his breath,

'I'll catch him if it's the last thing I ever do.'

News spread like wildfire around the town of Skerries. Everyone was asking and trying to work out in their own mind who this Black Cat was and what was written on the two notes that were pinned to the front door of Cop Morgan's house. By the week-end it became the main talking point around the pubs. Old guys sitting over their pints down in their local pondered that story. If this was his first victim, who was next? The sense of mystery and suspense surrounding the story added something that kept the story not far from everyone's lips.

I wasn't surprised that I went to the top of the suspect list. I was seen as the only guy capable of doing something this far-fetched or thinking up something like the Black Cat. But would I risk something like that knowing I had a court date next morning? I laughed the talk off as very funny. Before long, rumours started to go around that people saw the Black Cat at the main grave-yard gates while they were coming home from the pubs. Just standing there watching people going home, dressed all in black – was this the Black Cat?

Within weeks of Cop Morgan's house being struck, the Christian Brothers' house was hit and left in an even worse state. Again notes were pinned to the doors of the house. The rumour at the time was that it was a pure case of exposing people in a state of authority who abused their role over kids. True or not true, one thing was certain, the Black Cat took what he was doing very seriously. It wasn't just a case of vandalism; the Black Cat had some hidden motive to why certain people were hit and others were not. No finger prints were left behind or any trace of evidence pointing to anyone. The cops questioned a number of people as to their whereabouts on both nights of the attacks, but no charges were made, so the Black Cat was still on the loose to roam around while we all slept soundly in our beds, plotting his next move, his next victim.

Meanwhile, my court case over the jeans and pushbike wheel came to a bad ending for me. I was expecting a fine, but on the day the judge passed down a one-year sentence in St. Pat's prison, next door to Mountjoy Prison. Before I could catch my breath, I was on my way to my first term in a real prison with cells and bars on the windows. All my buried fears of being locked up were unleashed, leaving me in my old state of com-plete fear of everything that moved around me.

Flashbacks to St Laurence's and all that happened to me there came back to haunt me. As I was taken through the main gates of St. Pat's into the hallway, I heard a deafening noise of steel banging and a multitude of voices sounding loudly together. It was the sound of inmates with steel teapots and steel trays coming down together to get their supper of a pot of tea and a bun. The sound is something I will never forget as it deepened all my fears tenfold.

I was taken down to a basement, stripped naked and checked for scars or birthmarks. I was showered and given prison clothes and taken to a cell on B2 block. The door was locked behind me, the keys turned and there I stood alone in prison with no weekends home. This was the real deal. I looked around at what you did your piss in, a pot with a steel lid. With just a few smokes, I puffed deeply on a fag to calm myself down.

Next morning I was awoken by the sound of keys, and for a split second I thought I was at home in my own house. Then it hits you like a ton of bricks that you're in prison, in a small, smelly cell, all alone and that you know no-one when you walk out to start your first day of your sentence. Down you walk with your piss pot to empty it and a bucket to fill for washing yourself in your cell. Standing there surrounded by hardcore inmates you don't know from Adam is a very frightening experience. I felt so alone, yet looking at some of the heads I saw, I just wanted to keep to myself.

You're locked up most of the time but let out to do a bit of work, and an hour at night to watch TV. The first guy that spoke to me asked me my name. After giving that to him I knew what his next question would be.

'What you in for?'

'Robbing three pair of jeans and a pushbike wheel.'

'You're joking me,' came the reply, 'And what did you get?'

'Twelve months,' I said.

'No way! For a couple of pairs of jeans and a wheel? That's mad!'

It became the biggest joke in the prison. My next encounter with inmates was when I was asked if I'd put my name down for the pushbike race in the Phoenix Park. I said no.

'Well, ask the Governor fast and get it down.'

So over I went into the main hall and asked one of the chief screws if I could have my name put down for the pushbike race in the Phoenix Park. I had just said it when I heard loud laughing behind me. The screw just laughed and said they were pulling my leg.

Back in my lonely cell, I found my only comfort was a small picture of the racers Barry Sheene and Kenny Roberts which I stuck to my wall with toothpaste. It was my only link to the outside world, to something I loved. A couple of Numan pictures to go alongside it gave me the two things I loved most in life. My hours in the cell were long and slow, and I pondered how I could sort my life out when I got out of this place before it was all too late.

My mental state took an all-time low on a Thursday afternoon when some guy picked on me and a row started. I was not a good fighter down the years as I've said, mainly down to just fear of people, so I took a good beating which led to me being knocked clean out. I sat watching Top of the Pops on TV that evening looking the worse for wear and feeling so low and so down in myself. I really needed a lifeline at this point to lift my spirits up again. With just a few minutes to go to lock up, like a ray of sunshine breaking through a cloud on a rainy day, Gary Numan came on Top of the Pops. His voice hit me just at the right time and, as if it was just planned to happen for me, Numan's words rang down from the TV into the prison and into my soul, and everything inside me just clicked back to normal again. I felt safe, and just knew I'd be OK and I'd get through this prison sentence.

One afternoon, not long after, a screw walked into my cell just as I was about to eat dinner.

'Mr. Bentley, he said, 'you're going home after dinner.'

If you have never been locked up, then you'd never understand the joy those words give. I could hardly eat the dinner as my freedom was just about to be given back to me in a couple of hours' time. Walking out of the gates to freedom is something you never forget. To be back home, even in a problem-hit family, is better than any prison cell.

*

It wasn't long after I got home that I started being served in pubs as I was now over eighteen. The well-known Gladstone Pub with its then famous small, smoky pool room became my local, where I started to drink a lot and play pool. The owner, Tony, became the only pub owner that never barred me, and to this day I have the deepest respect for him. I had about two rows that I can recall in the Gladstone, but throughout the years I had enough respect to keep my nose clean when drinking there. Most other pubs wouldn't serve me because of the name I had, or because they thought I'd start a row with drink on me.

News got out one morning in the summer of 1982 that the Black Cat had struck again. This time it was the head teacher Mr. Jones's house that was hit badly. Just like the previous occasion, notes were left stating that this was the revenge of the Black Cat. All the talk came up again around the town about who he was and why did he strike Mr. Jones's house. One thing

I was sure of was that he was never going to be caught, because the hits were all simply too well planned out.

After the head of a Kung Fu club's house was struck and notes were left, the Black Cat stopped forever. It's reported that seven victims were on his list, and all were picked with great care. The Black Cat disappeared into the night, leaving behind him one of the most talked about stories in Skerries history.

With the Black Cat story still fresh in the minds of everybody around town, my own life of crime went to a far more serious level. I picked up with a guy named Jay Hill who was great at picking off houses with money in them. We did a lot of houses and spent most of the cash on drink. Around the same time I started a relationship with a local girl, Jill, who I really liked and got on well with, but again I couldn't get close to her as my fear issues still haunted me. But at least we stayed together.

Just coming up to the Christmas of 1982, my ma got an offer of a transfer to a house in Balbriggan which she thought would be a new start for the family. By now, my relationship with Jill seemed to be getting closer than I'd ever been to another person before. But on the morning of our transfer to Balbriggan, I awoke with four cops standing over me again. I was arrested for the house jobs along with Jay Hill, and charged with at least five house break-ins. I was let out of the cop station that evening, and went home to my new home in Pinewood Green Road, Balbriggan. Not a very nice sign for the neighbours seeing a cop car drop me off at our new address.

A lot of the neighbours were out of work due to the 1980s un-employment problem, and seeing a family with the name we had arrive in their estate didn't go down well with a few. We were seen as outcasts, and tension overflowed many times with us shouting across roads at each other and cops being called to calm the situation. I dealt with it all by sinking into Gary Numan's new album, *I Assassin*, and smoking a few joints in our new surroundings in Balbriggan. I knew I was going down for another term in prison and had to block it out. I often took magic mushrooms to try to curb my growing fears of another jail term. I'd often taken them down the years, but had stopped after a terrifying experience where I took four times the amount I should have and was plunged into a trip that left me at the back of the harbour in Skerries heading into the sea. If it wasn't for a guy who just happened to be passing by, I'm sure I would have drowned that night.

*

When the court date came up, Jay Hill and I were sent to St. Pat's. We both got a couple of months for each house we broke into. We were taken out of court and the cops told us our sentence added up to nine months but when we got to St. Pat's the screws told us it was six months, so I thought that wasn't too bad.

We were given cards stating our sentence, and went through the same procedure of being stripped naked and being given prison clothes after a shower. Jay turned to me as we headed to our cells and said,

'I bet your girlfriend will be out dating another bloke by the weekend!'

'Not a hope,' I replied.

Saturday came and we both got visits. My ma came in to see me and Jay got visits from his family. As they were leaving, Jay shouted over,

'The news is out that your girl was out at a disco with another guy on Friday night, the day after the court.'

I knew he wasn't joking. My heart hit rock bottom. In a split second and for the first time in my life I felt the real hurt that can happen to you in a relationship. I went back to my cell in shock. I was stuck in jail and could do nothing about what was happening outside.

As I sat there, trying to make sense of the news, the silence was suddenly broken by a voice at the cell door.

'Are you Patrick Bentley?' said the screw.

'Yeah, that's me, what's up?'

'Well,' he said, 'there was a mix up when you came in the other day over your sentence. I'm afraid I've a new card for your door – you're not doing six months, you're doing nine months. Sorry'.

It was the last straw. I felt the room spin, and I started to sink and lose all control of my mind. Then out of nowhere, I felt a presence in the cell and a power came over my heart and mind, and I felt everything was going to be OK. To this day, I believe it was God, because at that moment I was truly losing my mind, yet the next minute I was OK and felt a power help me at my deepest point of need.

Alone in that cell I looked over how far my life had fallen, going all the way back to a young child aged two. You have a lot of time to think in a prison cell, and I gave some very serious thought to my life, maybe for the first time. Did I want this sort of existence, in and out of places like this for the rest of my life? I wondered would the cops back home in Skerries give me a chance to turn my life around, and would people leave the past in the past? Would I ever be able to have a proper relationship with a girl? In truth, I believe what was behind my break up with Jill was my inability to get close to people in an intimate way.

In my cell that evening, I made a vow to stop my wave of crime for good and never to return to this place again. For the first time in my life I felt this was something I could do. I knew my crime had started as a young five-year-old and that the habit had just stuck with me since then. But I was now nineteen years old, and I wanted to stop the crime and start to turn my life around. I hadn't a clue how I could deal with all my pain and anger inside, but I could start by giving up crime for good. I knew that I had something deep down that could start fighting to sort out my messed-up life.

The guy that walked through those prison gates never came out again. Instead a guy with a new hope emerged into freedom and the prospect of new beginnings. How he was going to do it he had no idea, but one thing he was sure of – he was going to stick to his vow he made that dark night in his cell, come what may.

Would he win? Would he lose? What would 1984 bring for Patrick Bentley?

> *Is this a feeling, or something I've found?*
> *This is a story, this is a song*
> *Any little thing I've told you is wrong.*
>
> *The Sleeproom*
> *Gary Numan, 1986*

Dad, Breda, Alex and Patrick
Photo taken down the lane in Lusk, outside our little house.

Ma and Dad.

Me age 7

The cover of the famous Gary Numan Replicas album, that became my own reflection and hiding place.

The lost 18 year old

*Gary Numan,
the picture that says it all.*

*Taken in Morne Grove Skerries 1987.
The smuggling love day's.*

The smuggler's cave. Photo by Dermot Carroll.

Baldongan Castle photo by Trish Halligan.

The two hideouts where forbidden love stories lay. Both linked with an old 16th century myth, and also linked in 2004 as I searched for my soul mate.

Smiles all the way!
On the tube heading to my 1st Gary Numan gig in 1988

The black cat.

The famous final race of the day 1985. Battle between Rea and Sam last lap coming out of Sam's tunnel. Spot me in the background wearing a white head band. Photo by Jack Corry.

The sparks are seriously flying in the shady lane as Sam and Rea do battle again in 1987. Photo by Myles Lally.

Gary Numan in the Berserker image that told more hidden stories in 1984.

My little Sister Fran , My Ma and My dear Grandma.

The back of the harbour in Skerries 1991.
The town got together as I gave my life to the lord Jesus.

The tormented soul.

Chapter Six

LOVE, SCARS AND LIES

I'm cold and corrupt
Looking for a heart
I'm trying to hide my scars
... I'm just trying to survive.

Scar
Gary Numan, 1993

1984 came, and my vow to keep out of crime was still intact. Yet inside I was still hurting and struggling a lot with the abuse of my past. Once I kept out of trouble with the law, that was the main thing for now. It always amazes me looking back at this time in my life at how many people who knew I'd given up crime weren't over the moon about it. You would have thought they would get behind you and be glad you gave up crime. But this wasn't the case.

I was the number one criminal around the Fingal area since I was a kid, and people had made the claim to other people that I'd never change or give up crime. So their statements were now being proved wrong, and that hurt a lot of people's pride. Plus in every town, people love to have that one person who they point out and say 'there's the bad guy'. Now that wasn't theirs to say anymore. It was slowly being removed, and instead of having the support of people, I had a lot of people hating this turnaround in my life and not wanting to give me breathing space.

*

At the beginning of 1984 I fell for a lovely local girl, Tina. I got on so well with her, but yet again my emotional problems of getting close to someone got in the way. This unsettled and frustrated me more with her than with any other girl. Maybe it was down to the fact that I really cared more about her than anyone I'd ever been with. I really wanted this to work out, and I knew I had a lot of love to give if only I could get free of the damage that controlled me on the inside and be able to reach beyond a mere kiss.

But it seemed the abuse of my past had far too big of a hold over my life and it meant I was always going to be losing any girl-friend I fell for. The frustration pushed me further into drink and further into my own safe world, but the nature of need as a human being seemed to push me into trying to make something work out with Tina. To me, she was someone who was far too lovely looking not to be snapped up if I didn't sort the relation-ship out fast. All this just created further stress until the bottom finally fell out of our relationship and she met someone else.

This wasn't like losing Jill; I was truly hurt over it ending. I felt a total failure in every way as a person. Seeing her around the town just added to the hurt I already felt. I just wondered when my life would ever be normal. I'd given up crime but felt my life was going nowhere. I turned to drink to try to block out the pain of losing Tina. But as we all know, drink just covers over a problem for a few hours, then when you wake up next morning with a hangover, the problem seems twice as big in your head.

I went out and drank a load of homebrew up in the house of Hego, an old friend from school days. I was pissed out of my mind in a disco and broke down in floods of tears and just couldn't stop. I knew my world was free of all crime but I was a total emotional mess inside. Everyone was moving forward with their lives, but I was paralysed and it just felt like I was going further downhill. I'm sure I was just looking for the love I never got in my life growing up and it was spilling out for the first time in front of everyone at a disco.

Looking back, it still stands out as a time I was starting to crack from an overload of emotions, being pushed past my human limits. But as if all this wasn't bad enough, one of the worst nightmares was about to unfold which I am now only facing up to fully. My life was on such a low that I was very vulnerable and unstable and was about to walk into the unthinkable.

I was out drinking one Saturday night in mid-summer 1984 and got a good bit drunk. I saw Tina that night and that just made it worse. After the pubs I headed up to a disco in a local sports club. I saw her go in ahead of me, but when I got to the door the bouncers told me I wasn't getting in. I walked away and stood outside. I turned towards one of the back windows and saw two guys looking out at me. They were waving, but in that moment I thought they were laughing at me because I couldn't get into the disco. Something just snapped. I drew back my right arm and put it through the window. Next thing I saw a gush of blood from my wrist, and I knew right away that the cut was bad.

Before I could catch my breath, five bouncers grabbed me and took me into one of the dressing rooms, and they all held me down as one guy tried to stop the bleeding from my wrist. As they stood over me with my arms and legs held, a guy started punching me in the face over and over again. I couldn't do any-thing to defend myself as I was being held down, so I threw my head towards him and gave him a head butt. I got him in the face, and next thing I knew he pulled out a badge stating he was an off-duty copper.

'I'm Garda James Nolan,' he said, 'and I'm charging you with assaulting a police officer and breaking a window.'

I was sent to hospital in Beaumont and stitched up. Early next morning, I had to walk with my wrist in a lot of pain and a bad hangover all the way home to Balbriggan. Words will never ex-press how devastated I now felt.

I knew I had broken a window, but I also knew I had acted in self-defence against this guy who turned out to be a cop. After giving up my life of crime I was now being set up for something I didn't do. I should have been me bringing him to court for hitting me while I was being held down and being treated for a badly cut wrist. That walk that morning is something I will never forget. I knew I had to face court again, and it seemed that all my hopes and vows to never find myself in this situation were all taken from me in a cruel way. But there was worse to come.

The day of the court case came, and I was on such a low that my mind wasn't on this planet. It almost felt like I had some emotional breakdown from the whole experience. James Nolan, the cop, got into the box, took the Bible, raised his right hand and vowed to tell the truth. But it was all lies. He told the court he showed me the cop badge outside after I broke the window. So that would mean I hit him knowing he was a cop. Nothing came out about me being boxed repeatedly in the face while I was being held down on the ground with my hands and legs being held. Under oath he lied to let an innocent guy be sent down. Yes, I broke a window which I would have paid for, no problem. But I was being set up, and what was worse was that I had no mental ability to fight this case.

That's how far down this whole experience had brought me. I sat in court and said nothing to defend myself. The judge believed James Nolan and passed a sentence of six months in Mountjoy. My world with its vows of not returning to prison was taken from me, and no-one seemed to care at all. What about the five guys in that dressing room that night? They knew the truth, yet they stood back and let this cop send down an innocent man. Up until this happened, the cops were right in bringing me to court and I had no bad feelings towards them. They were just doing their job, but this was unforgiveable. I lost all respect for cops and for the people who ran the disco that night.

Now I was losing my freedom again and facing another term in prison, and all my hopes lay in ruins. What probably made this latest episode so bad was the knowledge of my failure to stand up for myself in court that day, which gives you an idea of my whole emotional state – a condition that was fully taken advantage of that day in order to gain stripes for someone's climb up the ladder. But whatever can be said about it looking back at it from today, it still brings the hurt of the injustice to life again in a more hurtful way because at the time I blocked it out at the time like I did so many other things in my life back then.

So there I was sitting in the back of a cop car again, heading this time to the main prison, Mountjoy. All my efforts to survive in the world drained out of me, leaving me easy prey for whatever awaited me behind the cold bars of prison life. The atmosphere was, as I imagined, much colder with the inmates than it was in St. Pat's. You really felt like you were just a number. Plus the food was worse.

The first day I found I couldn't eat my dinner, and a strange weak feeling came over my body and I just slept a lot. The next day was the same. I was taken down to the doctor who took one look at me and called the screw back to the room. The screw took me back to the cell and just said,

'You're going to be OK. I'll be back.'

He returned and told me to pack up my things; I was being transferred to the training unit, an open prison at the back of Mountjoy Prison where there were no bars on the windows and you had your own room with hot and cold running water. You also got much better food and were out all day and not locked up until 9 o'clock in the evening.

I think, looking back to that day in the doctor's, that my health was going downhill fast. I can't recall much about the time, just that I felt so tired in every way and I'm sure the doctor told them,

'Get him out of here fast.'

Once in the training unit, I started to eat again and my health came back. I got on well with the inmates in the unit, mainly because they knew I was wrongly imprisoned. You had your meals together and I sat with a guy named Seanie who kept my mind off being locked up with his stories of jobs he had pulled off. He came in one day after a visit and handed me two tablets and said,

'Take them, you'll have a ball.'

I took them that evening without asking him what they were and woke up in the middle of the night flying out of my mind and couldn't get back to sleep.

Next morning, with my eyes popping out of my head, I walked into the main dining room and looked down at our table. Mike, one of the inmates, was hanging down the side of his chair banging his fist on the table to try to keep in the laughter. I did my best to look normal to the screws and sat down. Seanie just bent over the table with a smile, and said,

'Did you sleep alright, Patrick?'

Mike was flying and couldn't stop laughing.

'Shit, what was in those tablets?' I said. 'I'm out of my nut!'

'LSD and speed,' said Seanie. 'You'll be out of it for a couple of days – enjoy!'

I spent the next two days laughing my head off at anything that moved.

About ten weeks into my sentence I was having a meal at the table when just out of the blue Seanie looked into my eyes and said,

'You have nothing to look forward to when you get out of here, have you?'

The words shocked me back to the real world, and I just looked at him and said nothing. But deep down I knew he was right. I was totally lost and felt I could see nothing ahead of me whatsoever but failure. And I'm sure it was the same for everyone else, but I couldn't hold down relationships or get close to people, so I felt I had nobody waiting beyond the walls of prison life who would be waiting for me with any kind open arms, bar my dear mother.

I sat in my room and told myself, *It's not your fault you're in here this time; it wasn't you who broke the vow to return to this place.* So I retook my vow, and along with the vow I told myself to find some line of work and fight myself out of this dark place I'd found myself in.

I had walked into Mountjoy defeated by an injustice that nearly cost me my health. I walked out the gates with my new-found strength to prove anyone wrong and a vow to myself that I'd never return to prison again – a vow that stands unbroken to this very day.

The chance that I'd been searching for had come alive within me even though the scars of my abused life still gripped me in a constant fear that left my whole personality very much unknown since it had been lost by that frightened two-year-old child. But at last, I saw some hope ahead as I withdrew to my room to gather my thoughts after my jail term.

My new hopes were fuelled in late 1984 by Gary Numan's latest album *Berserker*, in which his own struggles with the rejection of the media and other sources really came out in his music. For me, the timing of this album couldn't have been any better. Numan stood with white make-up and blue stripes down each side of his face on the cover of the album, looking like he had been hurt in some awful unjust way. But now he had his own symphony of music and lyrics to capture his feelings, yet hide them at the same time with his coded expressions that left you thinking he'd never give up the fight against those who hurt him most along the way.

One song that stood our right away for me, and in many ways enforced all that I felt at the time, was the title song *Berserker*. It pinned down all I felt when I was faced with the negative things people said about my life. It was as if my eyes were being opened for the first time to all the people who hated me because of my past. What was worse was that I could see people who claimed to be nice to me, but in fact ripped me apart to others behind my back. But all their judgements were to be proved wrong because the actions of a person don't always reflect who the real person is, and that was particularly true in my case.

But for now I emerged from the back end of 1984 with the hope of finding a way that would remove my inability to get close to a girl and stay out of trouble with the law.

> *I've been waiting for you*
> *I've waited far too long*
> *Do you wanna come with me now?*
> *. . . I'll question everything*
> *I'll trade new dreams for old.*
> *Berserker*
> Gary Numan, 1984

I found myself very reluctant to go out to pubs and discos and felt unsafe around all people in general. The fear of being jailed again in some unjust way must have always been at the back of my mind. So I kept a low profile and just went out for a few pints but never took an interest in anything, even in girls. I had a push button around people that I just pressed and a shield went up. To be honest, I liked the sense of mystery that it left with people who found me a puzzle that was hard to put together. For me, that made me feel somewhat special. I loved the sense of being unknown. It was an image that I needed in many ways to survive and hold some sense of confidence while interacting with people.

*

It's amazing what sticks in one's mind and never leaves. A knock came to our door one day. I opened it to find this American guy standing there saying,

'I'm a Christian, giving out John's Gospels for free.'

I took one and let him talk away. He was so down to earth and just said,

'Listen Pat, I just want to share God's love with you.'

I looked up into that guy's eyes and saw God's love as clear as day, and it's something I'll never forgot. He sent me a lovely postcard when he went home. I knew that guy cared about me, yet he never met me before. You could feel it from him, yet it felt like a love not from this world – certainly, it wasn't a love I felt before in my life. I kept the small John's Gospel under my bed and read it through many times. Maybe it was a link in a chain.

But back in my world, I went out one rainy night for a few pints, never expecting much to happen. I went on to a local disco, and halfway through the night I noticed a lovely looking girl looking over in my direction. I pushed all my fears to one side and went for gold, and I asked her up for a dance. To my surprise, all my fears didn't seem to paralyse me like before. I felt free to draw close to this girl. I asked her name.

'Kate,' came the reply, as our eyes locked together for the first time.

From her eyes my eyes dropped down to look at her mouth. Her lips were wet from her last drink.

'Do you know who I am?' I asked as I drew her head that bit closer to mine.

'Yeah, you're the big outlaw Sid Bentley, but I think you're an OK guy.'

For the first time in my life I felt at home next to a girl, and looking into this girl's eyes I knew it was the start of my first real relationship.

We went home together, made love and from that night I was a different person. It was like being set free from a lifelong curse that was now broken. I learned from Kate how to love and give love and to this day I owe so much to her. We sat up that night holding each other, listening to love songs until early morning. She said she saw something in me that others couldn't see. For me, that was very hard to accept. I had spent all my life being told I was nothing and would never amount to anything. But Kate told me,

'You have so much love to give, and don't let anyone put you down because of your past.'

She gave me something I've never lost, and I was now beginning to find all the confidence that was missing in my life.

Kate and her family moved to Australia in the summer of 1985. Hurt as I was to see her go, she left me with a love in my heart that was never there before. I was on the right track at last, in all departments of life. I started to pick winkles, much to the amusement of some. A guy gave me a pushbike to go back and forth from Balbriggan to Skerries to pick up to eight stone, put them on the bike and ride five miles back to Balbriggan. I got slagged by those who saw me on this small red bike in the pouring rain riding home from Skerries. But I was on a mission in life.

My crime days were behind me, and the money I made from the winkles went into a bank account and I lived on my dole money. For the first time in my life I felt happy, and believed there was light at the end of the tunnel at last.

The local Skerries 100 Road Race 1985 was to go down as a day I would never forget. My rider Johnny Rea was out to prove he could beat the best. The showdown for the main big race of the day saw Johnny up against the local hero that everyone loved and wanted to win, Sam McClements. I was alone in rooting for the underdog, Rea. But this was to turn out to be one of the best races ever seen around the Skerries 100 track, if not the best. I was watching it as they came out of the Shady Lane, now known as Sam's Tunnel. From the drop of the flag both Sam and Rea swapped the lead on each lap as they battled neck and neck for the entire race.

Going into the last lap, Sam just held the lead, and 99.9% of the fans put their hope on Sam holding on to give them something to cheer about over their pints long into the night. We all watched with necks stretched out as the sound of two bikes in close company got nearer to the spot we were watching. My eyes peered down the empty road, my heart willing Rea to come into view first. Then two bikes appeared side by side coming out of the tunnel and passed us with just a little over two hundred yards remaining to the flag. Rea just edged his bike across and got in front of Sam to lead him over the line by half a bike's length.

I jumped up and punched the air with delight. As for the rest of the fans, they went home stunned that Sam the man was beaten in one of the best races ever witnessed around the Skerries 100 track. I did cartwheels home that day, and got drunk and went dancing that night to celebrate Johnny Rea, the young underdog who beat the people's champion. Johnny Rea went on to win a TT race in 1989, and before he retired he won the Ulster GP and numerous road races around Ireland.

As for Sam, he returned and was almost unstoppable around the Skerries track for the next few years. In 1989, in what was, according to rumour, going to be his last race before retirement, Sam the man was in a great battle with Philip McCallan. Sadly, when on the last lap and the last corner, Sam ran into line with a back marker and lost control of his bike, crashed and was killed. A great light went out in many people's hearts on hearing the news. He meant so much to the fans that followed the great man, and his loss put a hole in the local fan's hearts that remains to this day. He wasn't the first rider to lose his life to the sport, and wouldn't be the last.

*

I kept my head low and remained out of all harm's way. I remained very closed up to the world outside me, yet I saw, maybe for the first time in my life, hope. If I could now remain in a relationship with a girl and keep out of trouble, then sooner or later people would forget my awful past and I could start living a normal life. That was my single hope.

I started a relationship with a girl named Tara who one moment was all smiles, the next screaming at the top of her voice at you for no reason. But underneath all that lay a lovely girl who was just like myself, afraid to be hurt and was carrying a load of problems with her through life. It was another relationship that didn't work out in the end. But I just felt as I ran towards the summer of 1986 that my life was on an up, and that I was going to find my true love.

My heart was ready to give all my love to the right girl if I could find her. I wasn't interested in games of any kind. For me it was love or nothing. I had no interest in playing with someone's heart. I hated the whole idea of hurting people. I wasn't interested in trying to control a girl's heart or making her jealous. What was the point in that when you could just be putting everything into getting closer to that person?

But what started in the summer of 1986 was to become yet another great public battle. Only this time, it was a war and a fight for a girl's heart that I had fallen completely in love with. Just when I thought my grim life was going upwards, I found myself fighting for my heart and soul again. Fighting for love!

Chapter Seven

SMUGGLING LOVE

I've waited a long time
How I survived God only knows

I remember the feeling
I'll remember forever
How it all just came apart
I could tell you of horror
I could show you the pieces
But I just want to forget.

God Only Knows
Gary Numan, 1985

As the clouds of winter faded into the history books, the sum-mer of 1986 dawned with open blue skies and bright sunshine. I was filled with new hopes and new dreams going into that summer. I thought my dark, painful past was well and truly behind me at last, and the hopes of keeping my new clean-living lifestyle intact was something I kept a firm grip on, no matter what came my way. I kept very much to myself and worked away picking winkles on the seafront shores looking out across at the islands that sat in the open seas a short mile's walk from the surrounding south beaches of Skerries town.

I relished the simplicity of my new-found life and its daily rou-tine of picking for four or five hours, then returning home by bike to Balbriggan with my brother Alex. We were not the only ones who picked the shores that summer. There were a couple of other guys and a group of girls who took up picking there during the summer holidays from school. I never took much pass on anyone at the time. I'd come from a dark existence and had been training my mind to focus only on work and on keeping within the safe boundaries of what felt right for me. So, in a sense, I had withdrawn very much into myself.

The only other thing outside my work that was of great value to me was my heart's desire to find my soulmate one day. I am in no way afraid to admit that I was a pure romantic dreamer at heart. I was branded as one going all the way back to the times as a teenager when I'd sit alone for hours listening to love songs on a small radio in the dark, as there was never even a light bulb in our house back in those days. Looking out into the darkness from a damp, cold, unlit room, my dreams of fairy-tale romances became something I never lost sight of no matter what happened down the years. But it couldn't be just any kind of relationship; it had to be my soulmate or nothing.

I wanted the type of relationship that had no games – something true and honest, driven along by genuine love from both hearts, not just one. I saw far too many relationships back then where people just drew a person into a false sense of security, then went about attempting to control them for the rest of their lives once they felt they had taken full command of their hearts and minds. There were other people who got into relationships purely for financial gain, the security that they would never want for anything in life again while they were with someone who was climbing the money ladder. To be honest, watching people controlling the very person they professed to love drove me to go the other way, down the narrow path in search of true love, my authentic soulmate.

I had a taste of love with Kate, and it had given me the scent in my soul to search not just for a relationship, but for the one person I was born to love forever. For all I'd been through in the past, the one fear that never seemed to worry me in relation to life was the *What if you get hurt?* thought. I always felt you had to make yourself vulnerable to the powers of love if you were to get close enough to a girl to give you the right to state that you were in love, for real. So in my heart of hearts it was true love or nothing.

Yet looking back, such thoughts of myself stood in stark contrast to the overall image of me around the town. I was great at concealing my fears, but underneath, it was a frightening experience to see and feel how people still viewed me. To many I was and would always remain a loser, a person who would amount to nothing at the end of his life. A harsh tale of what can happen to one person if you didn't follow the right paths in life in a small town. But I kept my head down and slowly pushed on in the direction of my own destiny, and lived in hope.

*

One morning in mid-summer, I got up and hung round the house until midday waiting for the tide to go out so I could head over to Skerries to work. Alex wasn't in the mood to go winkle picking so I headed over alone. Under bright blue skies, I walked towards the seafront to where an old barn overlooked the small bank that led down to where we picked. As I rounded the back of the barn I heard voices, but before I had time to divert my direction, I found myself standing face-to-face with the group of girls who picked at the seafront. I'd never spoken to any of them, so I felt somewhat shy and nervous to find myself suddenly standing alone in front of them. After what seemed like minutes but was surely mere seconds, I pulled myself together and lifted my head up from staring at the ground, and made eye contact with one of the girls whose name was Cathy.

She was small in height with bright red hair. The moment our eyes met, it felt like a doorway opened up, and I was lost in what I can only describe as love at first sight. With our eyes interlocked I started to just chat away, trying to gather my thoughts under such a sudden rush of feelings. At times it sent me stumbling over my words but it didn't matter to us; we both knew something far bigger than words was taking place within our hearts at the same time.

I suppose we were like all couples when they first meet. Initially, there was that shyness and newness. I asked her did she want to take a walk up over the seafront, and her answering smile matched the beauty of her eyes. As we walked without saying a word, I slid my hand into hers and like magic, without words or sound, a bond was formed, a love was born, pushing all my past life's hurts and fears into what seemed now another lifetime. It felt like time had stopped for a single moment and God had changed all the bad luck in my life into a bright shining ending. My life of building my world from the bottom up now seemed to have at last reached a fairytale ending. As we walked back towards the barn I held Cathy close, kissing her softly on the lips for the first time.

Cathy was fifteen-and-a-half years old, but even then I had no idea of the consequence of the feelings that had come alive inside us both that day in the summer of 1986. I learned she came from a fairly well-known and respected family in the area. With the age difference and my background we both felt we should keep our relationship a secret for at least a while. We parted company for home and planned to meet again in a couple of days. I headed home on my bike feeling the world had just become a whole new place to live in.

The next couple of times we met were spent just getting to know each other, and from there getting closer. We smiled, laughed and held each other as the beginnings of love went about intertwining our hearts. We talked about music, and as it turned out she had a deep passion for music too. I told her about some of the past mistakes that had all but ruined my life. It was hard for her to place the person I had grown up to be with the person who stood looking down into her eyes that summer. A stark contradiction which was always a part of my life was on one hand you had a reckless ex-convict, and on the other, a warm-hearted romantic – a side of me that was previously only seen by Kate, and now by Cathy.

I cherish all the small things that made my relationship with Cathy so special. It was the running of my finger down the side of her face, the hours by the rocky seafront looking into her eyes, the holding of her hands and the long soft kisses that seemed to awaken feelings within my heart that I never knew existed until I met her. It was everything that we were when we were together that made up the simple truth that I was falling in love. As our love grew, the summer passed by. We continued to keep our relationship hidden from the world. There were warnings from a couple of close friends who advised me of the risks of being hurt, but to me love is worth any kind of risk. Finding Cathy felt like a reward for staying on the right path in life, so I wasn't throwing the love I felt for her away, no matter what.

*

In the meantime, my sister Laura was given a house back in Skerries by Fingal housing department. She asked me if I wanted one of the rooms, and I jumped at the offer. It gave me independence and another block in the rebuilding of my life, plus I'd be living nearer to Cathy. I took some money from my savings and went about decorating the room the way I wanted it to look. It was the first time in my life I had my own room, so I wanted it to be perfect. I bought myself a brand new stereo to listen to my music. There was never a prouder moment in my life when I had it all done and took a step back to view it all. At last, I thought, I'd made it to the other side of the dark waters I felt I'd been swimming across for years. Nothing could take it away from me.

With the summer turning to autumn, Cathy returned to school so we didn't have as much time to spend together. I wrote her letters and songs, and when we did meet up, mostly at weekends, I'd pass them on to her. When we were together we hung out in all the different secret hideouts that we had found during our summer together. One place which was particularly significant for us both was an old cave called Smugglers' Cave, which sat facing back out across the sea between Skerries and Loughshinny. We often set out for walks across the rocks and seafront cliffs until we made it to the cave. We'd sit inside for hours on end chatting and holding each other.

One Saturday afternoon we went there and it rained all day so we couldn't leave. It was one of those days I'll never forget. The sense of closeness we both felt was a moment that surpassed all others. Locked away in a cave as the rain fell slowly from the skies above. The place became a symbol of our love, from that day forward. A place where there was no fear, just two hearts reaching beyond to true freedom and love. I can still see us both making a run for home in the rain, through cow fields, over rocks, laughing our heads off like a pair of kids. Laughs of innocence and smiles of freedom. Like a last scene from a film, we stood drowned wet, face-to-face, the rain pouring down both our faces. I held her so close and kissed her goodbye until next time.

But just as my world seemed to be reaching the winning post and victory was in sight, a knock came to the door one afternoon while I was in my sister's house. I opened the door to find Cathy and her older sister standing there. I tried not to look at Cathy's face but sensed right away something was very wrong. Her sister did all the talking and came across very nice. She told me someone had called to their house and told the family about the relationship between Cathy and me, saying that she was dating an ex-con on the beach. My heart froze. The person had told Cathy's family that she was in great danger. I've never heard everything that they were told, but it was supposed to have been a long list of all the wrongs I ever did in my life. I told Cathy's sister we were just friends and managed to convince her that our relationship was innocent. Eventually she said that it was OK and left with Cathy.

As I closed the door behind me, it struck me that Cathy was being taken away from me at the point at which I really believed my life was finally turning. The nightmare was just starting. Soon, the news of our relationship was all over the town. Everyone was now finding out about the guy with the long record of prison crimes dating and in love with a girl and hiding it away down on the beach and in caves. Everywhere I went, I was being asked if it was true that I was dating a girl from such a well-respected family. I got warnings from Cathy's family not to see their daughter again. It started to sink in how much I was in love with Cathy, but now it felt like someone had run over me with spiked shoes.

After so many years of trouble, the only true and pure thing that had happened to me was now also viewed as something sordid. My past mistakes had now sullied the best thing to ever happen to me. Left to myself and my thoughts, all the old sinking feelings returned, opening up a deeper, colder anger at the injustice of the situation, and it began to haunt my life. Everywhere I felt eyes looking at me, judging me. I suppose looking back today, there is simply nothing that will cause tongues to wag so much as any form of forbidden love. I hated being in the spotlight again; it had taken me over three years to get away from all that. Being back in the public eye again now felt worse than before. I was trying to deal with being in love and losing Cathy, and trying to hide all my emotions and stay calm.

Most of the people gossiping about me and Cathy around the town were of the view that I must have been mad to think I could have a girl of the class of Cathy. I felt so claustrophobic, the anger and pain slowly pushing me back into my own shell of an existence again. There was only one place I could hide away, one place of safety where my hidden feelings could be reflected. Alone in my room, with the door locked, listening to Gary Numan's live gig *Berserker* which I now had on video. Alone in my silent world, I fed on the words to a song called *My Dying Machine*.

I can hear me scream
I've nowhere to run
I've nowhere to hide
I can only wonder why
Everything breaks down
Me, I'm trapped inside
Here inside this ends.

The coldness of Numan's delivery, his voice and the lyrics of the songs froze my feelings, providing me with a protective shield from the world outside my locked room. The music put an invisible wall around me once again to help me feel pain without the world knowing, and to lock my love for Cathy away where it wouldn't hurt me as much. It felt like a fresh war had now started in my life, only this time it was for the one thing I felt was most important to me, love! Cathy's family were adamant that they did not want me anywhere near her. To be fair, maybe I would have done the same thing if I was them. To hear their daughter, their sister was hanging around with an ex-con would set alarm bells ringing in anyone's ears, to say the least.

The person who went up to Cathy's house had set into motion an idea about my relationship with her that covered up the most important issue – how did Cathy and I feel about each other? It didn't seem to occur to them that we might genuinely be in love. All I was left with was going from being so close to a girl to now having it all run down and laughed at by people around the town. Even harder still was the knowledge that people held the power to stop a meaningful relationship in its tracks. What can a guy do who, for no reason, has someone he's in love with taken from him? You can't just switch it all off and move on with life.

I felt stuck in time, lost in a time warp of some kind. Alone with those feelings, I sank back into my own cold world as everyone else moved on with their lives, leaving me stuck in a dream of the times I spent holding Cathy, the smiles, the laughing, her eyes haunting me as the hours ticked by slowly.

> *This heart is empty*
> *I've barely hidden memories*
> *. . . I wonder does she think of me,*
> *I wonder, I wonder.*
>
> *Love is the clock law.*
> *Tick, tock, my heartbeat.*
> *I was a passion that passed*
> *Her spare time.*
> *. . . These quiet nights will slowly kill me.*
> *Don't leave me, don't leave me (I cried).*
>
> *Love is Like Clock Law*
> Gary Numan, 1983

You can't lock yourself away forever and I had to walk out my door to face people, but never without an ice wall of armour, a cold protective guard to shield me from that which I had to face in the world. All the hurt and pain were locked away behind an unemotional stare.

The weeks slowly slipped by. Sometimes I'd see Cathy around the town but could only manage a hesitant wave. Of course, this only served to make me feel somewhat worse. Soon though, I got a message from a friend of hers asking could I meet Cathy in one of our old hideouts. By now, it seemed the dust had settled a little and the watchful eyes of the town had shifted elsewhere. It seemed like the perfect time to meet up again. All of a sudden all my pain was forgotten and drained away, and was replaced by the excitement of looking into Cathy's eyes again.

The day came to meet her and as she came into view it was like meeting her for the first time all over again, only it felt my love for her was now stronger. I held her as close as possible in one of those moments when you just don't want to let go. We spoke briefly about all that had happened, but I didn't want to waste our precious time together on such negatives. Once we were back together, nothing else mattered in the world to me. We spent our time together talking about life and love, possibly with a greater understanding than what we had when we first met. Outside our circle the world seemed so cold and heartless, but once alone with Cathy I could open up about my dreams of just being in love and working and letting go of the memories of the past. Simple aims, but they were all I wanted, and it was these open chats that led us closer and closer.

Under the simple influence of the warm feelings of love, you never see beyond such moments. I was just so lost in the time under the stars sitting holding Cathy's hand with only God himself watching.

But more trouble came my way when word got out again that we were seeing each other. This time, all the love letters and songs were found and read by Cathy's family. I felt violated in a way as if they had read my very thoughts, my very soul. The talk around the town worsened and I felt under scrutiny again. I tried to remain calm and to hide my pain once again, and lived in a single hope that this war would be won by love itself. I felt love was the most powerful thing in this world and conquers all in the end, so it was the only thing left to trust in.

The void of losing Cathy was once again filled by Gary Numan. I comforted myself by buying his newest albums, *The Fury* and *Strange Charm*. Both albums had that same anger reflection about them which gave me two new fresh mirrors to air out my emotional state of being at the time. One song from *The Fury* played a big part in helping me through such dark moments as the one I was currently going through. It was called *God Only Knows* and is quoted at the start of this chapter. It had that whole air of someone trying to survive in the midst of something awful happening that has no end in sight. Listening to that song today still takes me back in a flash to those dark times.

One girl in the town pulled me aside to try to encourage me in the midst of all this.

'People have never given you a chance,' she said, 'because most of them don't know you've been trying to turn your life around. They think you're destined to repeat your mistakes over and over again. It hasn't occurred to any of them that you might transform yourself into what you are today. There are people who hate the fact that you proved them wrong. They feel they still have the right to judge your relationship with Cathy on the grounds of your past crimes.'

Her last words on the subject were,

'Never let the love you have for Cathy be seen as impure because of mindless gossip.'

Looking back now, people often asked me why didn't I just drop everything and go up and confront Cathy's family and tell them how much I loved her. The answer to that was down to one thing – fear. The old all-consuming fear of people who had the power to reject me or hurt me. I was in no way conscious of such fear; you never are when you've had it since you were a child.

The very thought of standing face-to-face with people who, in my mind, seemed so much better than me in every way would leave me sick with fear. As far as I knew, everyone was better in every way than me. That was the measure of self-esteem and confidence I was lacking since childhood. You sense a real shame inside because you can't stand up for yourself, and you feel people sense your fear of them and in turn can use it to their advantage to overcome you. So for all people said about me being such a strong-minded guy back then, the truth was very much the other way around. I just knew how to hide it so well.

Again in this story a lifeline was thrown to me, as Cathy wanted to risk seeing me again. My heart was resurrected from a painful state of being and again it was like the past never happened. Our hideouts had never been found out so they remained safe for us and we returned to them once again. On a Friday I could sneak her up to my sister's house and out from the cold of the night to watch TV and just have some normality.

Yet as we grew closer in love, so did the risks. In time, the inevitable happened and Cathy's family found out again, and the repercussions were worse than ever. People started to make phone calls to Cathy's house. People who knew it was a forbidden relationship took it upon themselves to stir up more tension for everyone. Things were sent in the post and the phone calls continued, causing greater upset for Cathy's family. The cops were now in the picture, trying to track down who was making the calls. All in all, it just made me look like the image of what's always been painted about me – I was trouble, or just bad luck no matter what I did, and it felt like I had brought all this trouble on Cathy's family. The people who made the calls were never found, but I know who they were – sick people who'd rather die than see people in love and happy.

I got a job in a fish factory in Skerries and started to work hard and try to forget the pain of losing Cathy once again. I'd often take lonely walks up to Smugglers' Cave and just sit there alone staring out across the calm blue sea, pondering what it felt like when I had Cathy here beside me, smiling, laughing, joking, now replaced with the sounds of just the waves softly crashing on the rocks surrounding the entrance.

*

Amidst all the hardship of that time, I was surprised to get a letter from Breda in London telling me Gary Numan was playing not far from where she lived and she'd buy the tickets for two nights if I arranged the flights. I'd never seen Gary live, so this all felt like a very surreal dream unfolding for the boy who lived much of the past nine years inside Gary Numan's music.

I left for London for a ten-day break away from all that was happening in my life in Skerries. Just before I left, I heard Cathy's Debs was coming up. Of course, I couldn't bring her – that honour was left to some guy from her school who barely knew her. So it was a relief as the plane ran down the runway into the open blue skies above to what felt like freedom, heading to stand and behold the one person whose music had served to hide and protect me. Words fail to describe the excitement of knowing that at last, long after seeing Gary on *Top of the Pops* on that first night back in 1979, I was going to see the man himself live on stage.

I arrived in London where I enjoyed catching up with my sister and how our lives were developing. She always was and still is a big part of my life. The night of the gig arrived. Walking through a sea of Gary Numan fans waiting outside the venue for the *Metal Rhythm Tour 1988* was amazing. I'd never chatted to a Gary Numan fan in the whole of the nine years I'd been into his music, so it was lovely to chat away and compare stories of how we had got into Numan's music, and what albums we admired over and above others. My anticipation mingled with the saddened memories of times spent listening to Gary for more reasons than just to hear him sing. Maybe this was to be a catharsis of sorts. The album *Metal Rhythm* was to become the album that in so many ways covered the theme music to this whole story and chapter in my life. It held an atmosphere that for me held up a picture of what I felt inside looking out that I never showed back home in Skerries. There was a lot of anger in the songs, statements of someone who had been hurt unjustly – that's the way I personally perceived the words and sounds within the frame of the album. Again I was putting my-self inside a Gary Numan album in order to survive the pain of rejection back home.

Once inside the venue, I really didn't know what to expect. The lights dropped down, and the fans began chanting,

'Numan, Numan, Numan!'

My own heart was pounding with expectation. On stage, a door of light came on with what looked like the silhouette of Gary on the other side. Slowly the door lifted and he emerged. Dressed all in black leather and looking every bit the superstar he'd always been, he walked slowly to the edge of the stage, his sharp, distinctive eyes glaring from side to side at the crowd as the intro music *Survival* played itself out. We all held our breath, and 'bang' – the stage exploded to life, lights flashing everywhere as Numan busted into a song off *Metal Rhythm* called *Respect* which just summed up the mood of the time.

> *You're so young*
> *Not one backbone between you*
> *But you think you'll make a hero*
> *Quite peculiar you're just boys*
> *You don't know what you've angered.*
> *Did you know you're talking*
> *To the heart of the machine?*
> *Welcome boys, welcome to the real world.*
> *You know me, I'm the smiling assassin*
> *I won't forgive*
> *And you know I won't forget!*
>
> *Respect*
> *Gary Numan, 1988*

For the next two hours, I was lost in the pure magic of the man and his music. Numan prowled around the stage pumping out songs that touched things inside me in so many ways. It gave me a sense of not being alone in the battle I'd found myself in back home. I'd been in the arena with the man and the music that was my one and only secret source of help, and it felt like it armed me with something for what lay ahead. I stood in my element as Numan thanked the crowd for coming and walked out of sight.

On the way home there was the voice whispering softly never to give up on love itself, to fight for it and that love would, in its own way, come back for me and reveal my soulmate.

*

When I got back home it wasn't long before Cathy and I got back in touch and reignited our love. With Christmas just around the corner I wanted to get something very special for her, something that would reflect the love I had in my heart for her. Just as destiny would have its way in the big scope of events in the story of my life, I just happened to turn into an art shop in Skerries one afternoon. There, hanging before me, was a beautiful painting of Smugglers' Cave by a local artist, Steve Hope. My heart almost stopped at its beauty. The painting was a portrayal from the inside looking out with the sun coming up over the sea. Straight away, I knew it was the perfect Christmas present for Cathy.

She loved it, and took it home that Christmas and hung it on the wall of her house. No-one knew what it was, or more importantly, what it stood for. In a way I felt my love for Cathy, my heart and my soul were wrapped up in the painting. Knowing it hung on the wall of her family home felt like I was in their home without them knowing I was there. I knew I'd never be welcome past the front door, yet what I stood for and who I was truly hung alone on the wall in silence among them.

As my heart slipped deeper into the bonds of love, I knew I would never give up on my feelings, come what may. Surrounded by the threat of being hurt, I felt it was worth dying for the love I held inside. I hoped with the New Year ahead that something would give, and that I'd get my wish and be able to walk hand-in-hand with Cathy down the streets of Skerries in full view of everyone without all this hassle. But 1989 was to prove much of the same, as time and time again I went from being so close to Cathy only for her to be taken out of my arms, leaving me fighting love's withdrawal again.

Adding to my problems was the ongoing nightmares of the stuff that went on in St Laurence's. I'd wake up sweating in the dead of night with the faces of my abusers looking down over me like it was all happening afresh. Such dark secrets lay so well locked away at the back of my mind, but when I was asleep, they had their own way of unlocking themselves and invading my dreams in the most frightening way imaginable. I'd sit alone in the dark, afraid to go back to sleep in case I'd drift back into such dreams. It was moments alone like this that my mind would ponder all the 'what ifs' about my life. What if I had never gotten into trouble with the law? What if I'd never gone to prison? How different my life would have been!

I'd pick up a Numan album and look at the words to his songs, frantically trying to draw some source of comfort to ease the fears.

> *I can't sleep*
> *All your words*
> *Seem to let me down.*
>
> *You told me*
> *Time makes it easy*
> *But you never told me*
> *Time stands still.*

Where are you?
Why don't you call?
It's been a long, long time.

I Still Remember
Gary Numan, 1985

One of the places I always met Cathy when we were dating was a road up near where I lived called Selskar Road. I'd meet her there most Friday nights and take her the back way into Mourne View where I lived. After we broke up I'd sometimes walk up there around 8pm on a Friday and wait for her in the cold of the night for hours even though I knew she wasn't coming, living in hope that just maybe she'd come walking into view. Love does funny things to us humans; it will make you stand in the frost of winter waiting for someone you know isn't coming, waiting for mere shadows in the night. People often ask the question 'How do you know you're in love?' Well, here's the answer. You know you're in love when the most important thing in the relationship is what you want to give rather than what you can get from the person.

The problem with someone who's truly in love is that if you're not with the one you're in love with, the feelings you have for them begin to cause you untold pain and you feel trapped as a person.

In 1990 Cathy and I got back together. I'd moved jobs and was working in a crab processing factory while Cathy was training to be a nurse. She was now able to drink in pubs and had her own friends. She was growing up into a woman from the teenager I walked the beaches with in the summer of 1986. For me, it was like someone had walked up to me that year, taken off love's blindfold and told me, 'You're in love up to your neck, boy!' With it came a new unease. I felt a danger approaching, but wasn't sure from where. I had a sense that something awful was coming my way and there would be no escape.

I remember keeping all this to myself, and headed to meet Cathy along Selskar Road one Friday. When she came into view, I threw my arms around her and pulled her as close to my heart as possible, holding her as if my life depended on it. I was treasuring our times together more now than ever before.

With Christmas approaching, my sister Breda came home from London. The two of us went on a pub crawl and ended up in a pub that Cathy's brother worked in. As soon as we walked in, we sensed the staff didn't want to serve us. However, Cathy's brother gave the OK, and we sat at the bar and ordered drinks. Not long after, Cathy walked in with some of her friends and walked over and sat at the bar beside us. I could feel all the eyes in the place peering our way. We chatted. It struck me as we smiled and laughed that this was the first time in the four and a half years of our relationship that we were sitting together in front of her family in public. For me, I saw how our relationship could have been had it been allowed.

As the drinks kept coming and the night wore on, that cold feeling that something awful was awaiting me crept in on me. Somehow things just seemed too good to be true. I tried to push the thoughts aside and just enjoy the night. All my instincts were flashing red alert as we went into the nightclub at the back of the bar. It seemed like a dream, walking in public with Cathy, but like all the dreams I've ever had it was short lived. Someone told Cathy's brother in the nightclub that we were still dating, and he approached me and asked me to my face was it true. I wasn't the type who would deny it, so I said,

'Yeah, we're dating'.

He walked away towards Cathy and that was the end of the party. Breda and I left shortly afterwards and walked up home.

The cold air of the night kept me awake long into the early hours of the next day, my mind racing up and down the years

101

spent fighting this war for Cathy. Now I was alone again, only this time it felt like the end – you always know when it's truly over. I felt helpless to do anything, to stop what now seemed like my last goodbye to our relationship. She once asked me why I was fighting for something I could never have. The answer was I never saw it as a war against people, I always felt it was more a stand for the love I felt inside for her.

The next day, I rang Cathy in work.

'Hi, Cathy. It's me.'

Silence.

'Everything OK?'

'Look, Patrick. I can't see you anymore. I'm sorry.'

'But why?'

'There was trouble at home again over last night. Look, I'm sorry. I have to go.'

All the awful feelings that had lain in the shadows of my mind suddenly came alive as I hung up the phone. The whole fear of being abandoned for good with such feelings for Cathy seemed to turn on me from the inside, and began to cut me up slowly like a jagged knife twisting its blade across every beat of my heart. Breda called in to see me that evening to see if I was OK after the night before. She went mad that this was all happening to me again, especially at Christmas time which always adds a deeper sense to people's pain if something goes wrong at such a festive occasion.

She suggested we go out for a drink just to get out from sitting alone in my room thinking too much. I probably wasn't up to it at all, but dragged myself along anyway. Once we got to the pub, we ordered drinks and stood just inside the main doors. Shortly afterwards, the doors opened and in walked Cathy with a couple of her friends. We all chatted for ages, but I kept up a good front compared to what I felt inside. As it was near closing time we all left and went outside to what was now my moment to say my last goodbye to Cathy and to our relationship face-to-face. I was in no doubt that this was the final chapter in the story of my struggle to hold on to the girl I loved.

In all the time I had known Cathy I stood up for her and never hurt her feelings. Anytime she was down I was there to hold, love and comfort her. I knew she had put up a brave fight to try to get people to see I wasn't what people made me out to be, yet here I stood in what seemed the cruellest of endings, facing my last intimate moment with her. A fight fought for love now in its closing scene. I walked up to Cathy and looked at her intensely. Slowly I lifted my right hand and placed it on her heart saying softly,

'I will always be here if you need me.'

I held her close for the last time as all our close moments to-gether flashed across my mind, all the good times, all the kisses, hugs and laughs we shared together.

Within minutes Cathy was gone, and in her place was the un-bearable pain of her loss. The temptation was to run after her and beg her not to let our love end. But I kept walking until I reached home.

After a disturbed night's sleep, I woke to my first day of begin-ning the fight to try to get over losing Cathy from my life for good. Breda headed back to London a couple of days later. I left her off at the airport and hugged her goodbye. It was so sad watching her walk out of sight, I felt like everyone that I loved was slipping away from me forever.

Over the next few days, my mind retraced every aspect of my life from a young kid trying to fight to survive without schoolbooks to gain a proper education to being locked up at the tender age of nine, to the abuse suffered in places like St Laurence's, to years finally struggling after prison terms to rebuild my life and trying to make it to a place of ease and true stability. Then just when it looked like I had beaten the odds, broken to freedom and found true love with Cathy, it was taken from me.

The only comfort in my life was Mr. Numan's music and the whispering soft voice that touched my heart so many times throughout my relationship with Cathy, promising me one day I'd be gifted by love itself and led by the heart to find my soulmate. Whether that voice was God's, my soul or just wishful thinking, it did provide me with the comfort I needed in this moment in my life.

Come New Year's Eve, I headed out to the pubs alone. I ended up at the local rugby club disco. Most of what I remember of that night was feeling that I was in some strange, numb trance. I noticed all the couples enjoying each other's company as I stood with my back to the wall, hardly able to manage a smile. As the night closed into a New Year, I headed home with the cheers of 'Happy New Year!' ringing in my ears, but all I could wonder was what this New Year would hold for me? The air was so cold that night, the frost was out and the roads and paths sparkled brightly from the shine of the cold ice. In other circumstances it would have been a beautiful sight, but all I could see was the image of Cathy turning over and over in my mind as I walked past cheering crowds singing in a New Year. I tried to look cheerful and break a smile as I walked by.

Sometimes in the days ahead I'd meet or see Cathy around the town. I hardly knew what to say. We would speak for a few moments, and I would feel lovesick saying goodbye to her as we parted. I'd record the moment and sit in my room playing it over and over in my head. I was told she was dating a guy from her workplace. I can't say I wasn't hurt by the news, I was, but I had the respect for her to stand back and let her get on with her own life, plus after seeing them together, he looked like a really nice guy who you just knew would take good care of her.

I remember giving the air about me that I just didn't care what happened or what people still thought of me, but deep down I did care, a lot more than I'd ever admit at the time. I really wanted to prove myself to people and to prove people wrong. But I felt I'd lost something inside by losing Cathy under the watching eyes of the whole town. I took one last look over my shoulder at the past few years before making the first tentative steps into an uncertain future. All I took with me was the knowledge that I was still alive and breathing and willing to learn how to keep myself out of harm's way. Despite temptation, my life remained clean living, and for that I was thankful.

It's a chapter in my life that was kept together by the one man and his music, Gary Numan. He was my silent voice who kept me sane throughout the whole time. He was like a friend whose music took me to safe places that only his voice could. Many a night he spoke into my painful world and helped me feel OK about being misunderstood in so many ways. I suppose Gary's own struggles mirrored my own, and in the music there was this amazing touch that delved into the lowest places where my heart often fell to, and sat with me in those dark moments until daybreak came and I found my way into the light of a new day.

I took one long walk in January of that year up to where, for Cathy and me, love was truly born, Smugglers' Cave. Sitting alone into the late afternoon, hours watching ripples in the waves, I was unaware of all the history that was linked to this cave. In the 17th century, Luke Ryan (born 1750, died 1789 in a French prison) was one of the main characters who used Smugglers' Cave to smuggle goods to and fro. But more interesting was the 18th century Jack Connor, who was seen as a romantic character himself and who practised his trade from Smugglers' Cave. Connor had himself mentioned in an 18th century ballad in a particularly richly worded verse.

> *The lover may sigh*
> *The courtier may lie*
> *And Croesus his treasure amass*
> *All these joys are but vain*
> *They are blended with pain*
> *I'll stand behind field and my glass.*

These men from the past left their mark on the cave because they smuggled goods. For me, I used Smugglers' Cave to smuggle something of greater value than all the treasures that Luke Ryan or Jack Connor possessed; on a sunny day back in the summer of 1986, I started to use Smugglers' Cave to smuggle love from my heart to a girl's heart, under the sole guidance of the voice of love.

As I sat that afternoon with my heart torn within from the pain of losing the girl I loved, little did I imagine that another old 16th century myth covering Smugglers' Cave was to uncover a story that would interlink back into my heart to fulfil love's promise that one day love itself would unfold my soulmate into my arms to love forever. But until then, I sat alone in the cave looking out into another uncertain future. Yet I couldn't possibly have known that within a couple of short weeks of sitting alone and broken at the mouth of Smugglers' Cave, the greatest love a human heart could encounter in one's life was heading my direction to bring me to No Higher Love.

Chapter Eight

No Higher Love

He predestined us to be adopted as his sons through Jesus Christ, in accordance with his pleasure and will.

Ephesians 1.5

As a new chapter in my life opened before me, with it came deep uncertainties and the dreaded possibility of some worse pain than that which I was now trying to come to terms with. I was still very much in the first stages of losing Cathy, and the feelings were still so raw and painful. It always seemed to be at its worst at night. Trying to get her face out of my mind and trying to get to sleep seemed to drag on well into the early hours of the next day. It felt like there was a never-ending tape playing all the times we spent together, surrounded by the stars of the night skies. What I wouldn't have done to hold Cathy for one single moment to take away the awful pain that gripped me on those nights. I'd sink deep into self pity until I drifted off to sleep.

In the days that were to come, people kept stopping me to ask me if it was true that Cathy was seeing someone new, and how I was taking it all. I remained in a calm state of mind around people and told them,

'Well I hear Cathy's new boyfriend is a really nice guy, and I respect them both and I know he'll take good care of her.'

But deep inside, it was a hard pill to swallow. Inside I kept asking what he had got that I hadn't, and all the questions that go through any guy's head after a break-up.

I liked the town of Skerries, but what I never showed was how I hated the so-called self-righteous people who found it hard to accept that my life of crime was over and that they were left with no-one to point the finger at. For me, it was a matter of pride in such people's minds. Who wants to be proven wrong when all along they stated I would never amount to anything good? It hurt all their preconceived ideas of how my life would turn out. In a sense, I wanted to prove the whole world wrong and make something of my life. It meant so much to me coming from my background to shake off the name I still held in Skerries. How I wished my life had started in some different family. How I wished I had the start other kids got in life. I knew if I had all that, this wouldn't have been happening in my life today.

All my life I wished I was adopted as a kid into a warm, loving family, but all that was just wishful thinking that filled the gaps in my mind as I struggled through another day without Cathy. Within a week of early January 1991 the walls around my heart started to come up, and somehow I was able to freeze my feelings and hide away deep inside my own world somewhere. I suppose it was either that or lose my head and go up to Cathy and beg her to come back. I knew that would just cause more pain than I already was experiencing. Something just closed down inside me, and I was now back in my cold self-made world that I created long ago as a kid. It was very much like going back in time and closing all the doors to the outside world, yet with it came the sadness of a failed attempt to be someone different than a cold-faced, lifeless human being with a bad name to go with the stone-cold face.

My nights from this point onwards were back in what I imagined in my mind to be a glass cage with this invisible wall of glass to keep the world at a distance from me. If I mistrusted the world outside in the past, then this time around it was a complete mistrust of all the people who played their part in pushing me back into my cold cage again that formed a wall of justified anger. All I felt I had left in the whole world to hang on to was my music. It was the lighthouse that kept my world above the stormy waters. In the eyes of the townspeople I seemed like a cold, calm human that was dealing so well with his loss, yet you always sensed some people were waiting for the blow up that would prove them all right, that some people never change.

In my silent pain I kept my head and let the suffering take place away from all who knew me. The side effects were always made worse if I bumped into Cathy down the street. I recall one occasion meeting her outside a shop. I didn't let on I saw her. Seeing her again was like seeing a vision. Her bright red hair and fair skin shining in the open day, making me fall victim to all I tried to hide inside for her.

One promise I did hold myself to in that time of pain was that I vowed to love again and to find an ever deeper love next time around. I knew that somewhere, somehow I'd find closeness and love with a girl that would surpass even my love for Cathy. To stop and give up on finding my soulmate was to give up living. Even in the midst of all this uncertainty and pain, something inside seemed to whisper the words *You won't find love – love will find you. Love will come back for you.*

*

A week later, John Fold and I took a walk to catch up on what was going on in each other's lives. We bumped into a local Born Again Christian named Peter Heart. It wasn't the first time I had chats with him about God and the Bible. I always found him and his brother to be really nice people. I'd go as far as to say they both always left me with a sense of amazement at the things they told me about God. I had no interest in religion, but they said that God is not religion – rather that what God wants is a personal relationship with anyone, not a form of religion or a place where we go to once a week for an hour.

I found myself chatting for hours to Peter this day with my friend John Fold – we were standing outside the Gladstone Pub for two hours asking all sorts of questions. He kept explaining that by dying on the cross, Jesus paid the full price for sin so that we could get into heaven as a free gift, but that we must give our lives to Jesus first and repent from our way of sin. He also explained that Jesus died because God had to punish sin because he is a holy God as well as a loving God, and that he can't pretend sin hasn't happened and turn a blind eye to it. So if I'm a sinner, my sin must be punished, and the Bible says that God sent his son to pay that price to the full so that I can be saved and go to heaven. Simple enough maybe, just too simple to accept as real.

But as Peter said, it's simple to get into heaven only because it cost God everything by sending his son to the cross to make the way in which he could forgive us and make us his children. We went into the pub and the chat kept going. It wasn't just the words that Peter spoke that were catching my attention. As he spoke, I felt a power coming through him that I never felt before. It struck me in my heart and left me hanging onto his every word. When he went to the toilet I said to John,

'What do you think of all that he said?'

'It's all very interesting,' he said.

But to me, this was far more than interesting. He told us loads more and said that there was a Bible study the following Thursday and asked us would we like to go. I said I'd be there and John said he would too.

Come Thursday, we met Peter at his house and off we went to see what all this was about. We got to the house, and a guy named Sean opened the door and welcomed us into the sitting room. There were around twelve to fifteen people, all Born Again Christians, in the room. I found them all really nice and down to earth. They all just had the same story – that Jesus came into their lives at different times and that they had a personal relationship with God through Jesus. They could go into his presence at any time because they had the Holy Spirit living inside them all.

The study went OK. Then they all started to pray, one after the other. I could feel that John was finding this too much and knew he was trying to hold in the laughing. That got me started. I've no idea how we both didn't run out of the room, but we held in the laughter and got through the night. On the way home we asked Peter loads of questions about God, the Bible and how it had change their lives. He asked us if we would go again. We said we would.

The next day I sat in my room pondering what was said in the conversation with Peter. It all made so much sense that there had to be a God behind the making of this world, and if so I'm sure he wants us to know him, be in contact with him and know him personally. I saw something of that in Peter and the rest of the Christians at the study. There was no doubting that they had something I hadn't got or that I'd seen in religious people, but I wasn't sure what it was I saw or felt when I was around them. All I knew was that they made the Bible seem so clear to me, and nobody else ever made that kind of impact on me before.

Within the week leading up to the next Bible study, I still had the darkness of moments reliving the early stages of my lost love, Cathy. It was still just a handful of weeks since we'd broken up and the pain was still so raw and open before me, like a great open wound bleeding with the uncontrollable need to be close to her and to hold her close to my wounded heart. The need was so unforgiving, leaving me with nowhere to hide my pain or to go to for a moment's rest. But I struggled through the week until the next Bible study with John. Peter called and off we went again to see what this was all about.

Peter was so relaxed, and I just loved listening to every word that came out of his mouth. We got to the study and got a very warm welcome from the Christians who showed up that night. This time, however, there was no laughing or anything of the kind – we just listened as they talked openly about the Bible. After the study, as we were all chatting, a sense of something too wonderful for words came over me. I had no idea what it was, but it was starting to really become clear to me that I wanted Jesus in my life, that I wanted him to save me.

I didn't say a word about how I was feeling but when I got home and Peter dropped us off, I told John that we needed to get right with God. He seemed to agree that these people had the truth, and what they told us about Jesus and his death on the cross was all true. We said we'd talk more the next day about it, and I left for home.

Next morning, I woke up to go to work with Pete. I got into work around 9am. As I started my day's work, I noticed something very strange happening inside of me. I tried to fight it off and get on with my work, but the more I tried to fight it, the stronger it was getting. I wasn't afraid of the feeling, but for the life of me I couldn't understand what it was. It got so strong that I ended up ringing Don Stafford, a Christian from Balbriggan, who knew my brother Ray very well. I told him what I was feeling and asked if I could go and talk with him after work. He was very nice and said,

'No problem, Patrick.'

I got out of work at five, headed to see John and told him what I was feeling. I told him I was going to see a Christian pastor after tea and asked if he wanted to come along. He said,

'No, I'm heading out to the pub.'

So, alone, I changed out of my work clothes and got my dinner down, and away I went to chat to Don, the pastor of Balbriggan Baptist church. Again, I got a warm welcome and sat with him over a cup of tea. I told him I'd been to Bible studies and that this strange feeling had been growing over me all day long. He smiled and said,

'Patrick, that's the Holy Spirit drawing you into a relationship with Jesus.'

He told me that Jesus said, *No-one comes to me unless the Father draws him.* He said the feelings I was feeling was God drawing me to his son so that I could be saved through his death on the cross. The more he spoke, the clearer the picture of the cross became to me.

He asked me did I want to ask Jesus into my life. I didn't know what to say. I didn't say no and I didn't say yes. I ended up saying that I just needed to go home and think this through a little more.

I thanked him for giving me his time and warm advice, and left his home. It was eleven o'clock by the time I got home, and I felt tired from a day's work and just wanted to sleep. But the feeling of being drawn to something or someone grew stronger with every passing minute, keeping me restless and unable to drop off to sleep. With time ticking on into the next day, I found myself still awake at 2am on Saturday morning. I became more and more restless, and the sense of someone drawing me seemed to just slowly get stronger until 4 in the morning.

Lying alone in my bed, I suddenly opened my mouth and asked Jesus to come into my life. No sooner had the words left my mouth than I fell into a deep sleep. I awoke around 11am. I opened my eyes and sat up in the bed. I pulled back the cover and stood to the floor. I knew something was so different inside me, but I hadn't a clue what it was. I just knew it felt so different, like something had come into my heart that hadn't been there the night before. I got dressed fast and headed down the stairs, looked at my sister and told her I was heading down the street to get some shopping.

It seemed so surreal as I headed down, as if I had just come to live in Skerries – everything around me seemed new and different. The change inside didn't scare me in any way, but just amazed me as my mind went back to the night before when I asked Jesus into my life. I could feel a love racing in my heart that I never felt before, a love far greater than any love I could ever imagine would exist or could be felt in a human lifetime. The whole experience was so wonderful that it had left me in a state of some kind of shock. As I walked to the shop and home again, it seemed people even looked different to me, yet everything was the same as any other day.

I had time to gather my thoughts in the afternoon, and I decided to head over to Peter's house and tell him what had taken place the night before and how I was feeling since. As I rang his bell, he answered the door before I had time to say a word. A smile came across his face. He knew before I spoke a word that I had asked Jesus into my life. I sat for ages telling him what had happened and how I was feeling. He told me what I was experiencing was being born again, that a new birth had taken place that now enabled me to have a personal relationship with God in a perfect manner. He said the Holy Spirit had come into my heart and that the love I was experiencing was God's love coming through the person of the Holy Spirit.

We talked for ages, and everything seemed so clear to me as it never was before. I could now talk the same language with Peter even though I knew very little about the Bible. One thing I did know was that I had never dreamed such a love could be felt or be mine. I had known so much about human love with Cathy, and that to me was the greatest love anyone could feel in a lifetime. But this love was so pure, so beyond words of human language and to think God was showing me this love, a person with a background like mine, was something that was so hard to take in.

Peter told me that if I ever wanted to go to a Christian Church he'd be glad to give me a lift anytime. I asked him when it was on. He said it was on the following morning and I said I wanted to go. I left Peter's and went home. I didn't tell my sister what had happened – I just kept things to myself for the time being. The next morning, Peter took me for my first visit to a Baptist Christian church. I was met with kind words and smiles that made me so welcome. People from the Thursday night Bible studies who had met John and me were so glad with the news that I had given my life to Jesus, and they couldn't encourage me more with their kind and friendly words. The service was great. People just sang songs to thank God for what he had done for them. Some prayed out as if they were talking to God directly, and it all seemed so deep and personal. But what seemed to me to be the most wonderful thing of all was this deep, real sense of the presence of God in the midst of it all and inside my own heart.

When the service ended, we made plans to go to Rush on the Tuesday night for a Bible study, which I couldn't wait for. I got home that day and opened a Bible I got from Don the Friday before. As I started to read it, everything made more sense than ever before. I couldn't think why I couldn't see all this before; it all seemed to open before me in a new and blinding light. A powerful sense of joy raced into my heart as I read the Bible. It all just seemed so new, as if I was asleep all my life and had now woken up from a twenty-seven-year bad dream to the real world. That there was a God, and he was now real to me and in my life. No human words could explain the joy I felt at all that was happening to me. All I wanted now was to get to know more about the Bible and Jesus.

I felt I had found the key to the meaning of life, and it wasn't just religion that I had found but a deep and personal relationship with the living God himself. I couldn't wait for Tuesday to come so I could meet the Christians again. But if things were great at this point, nothing in life could have prepared me for what took place on Tuesday afternoon.

*

That Tuesday, I woke up and went downstairs for a cup of tea. My sister Laura was cleaning out the fire and asked me if she could ask me something.

'Sure,' I said. 'What's up?'

'There's something different about you the last few days,' she said. 'What is it?'

Without thinking, I just said,

'Laura, I became a Christian last Saturday morning. I'm a new person – my old life is over.'

With that she started crying, and said,

'What the hell are you talking about? Where's the other Patrick gone?'

I got a bit of a fright and tried to calm her down, saying,

'It's OK, I'm still the same person . . . I'm just a Christian now with a personal relationship with God.'

I could see fear in her eyes as she tried to make sense of what I was saying. I calmed things down the best I could and told her everything would be OK.

I left to go to Balbriggan a bit shaken and still trying to make sense of what had just taken place – not what had happened with my sister, but with the way the words came out of me with such power and conviction. I started thumbing a lift and, as if God had planned it, Don Stafford, the pastor who talked to me the Friday just gone, came along the road and picked me up. I told him I had become a Christian and that Laura was upset and at home crying about it all. I said,

'Don, this change is so amazing, but I don't understand much about it all.'

He was so understanding and took me back to his house for a coffee, a meeting that will stay with me for the rest of my life. Don sat me down and started to explain something to me. In a gentle voice, he said,

'Patrick, everybody is searching for what you have now. The whole world is trying to find that something that's missing inside their hearts.'

He continued,

'When man fell at the beginning of time, he lost the spirit of God that linked him to God and made him whole and complete. That spirit came into you last Saturday morning, and that's what you're experiencing inside.'

Don had a Bible open in front of him as he was speaking to me. Without any warning, the room lit up for what seemed like a split second and Don's words seemed to stop. He wasn't aware of this at the time, but suddenly a rush of what seemed like a river of love flooded my heart to such an extent that all I remember saying was,

'I have to go, Don. This is just too amazing to take any more in.'

I could hardly stand up from my seat as the full power of God's love raced into my heart leaving me without enough air around me to breathe. I just had to get out into the open air. Don knew something from God had taken place in that moment and knew I was in safe hands. I left thanking him best I could, telling him I found myself trapped in the most amazing unspeakable moment of my life. I knew I was God's child, that God loved me and was pouring his love into my heart at this moment in a way that no-one could ever explain. If God had come down and appeared in front of me it didn't seem it would surpass the assurance that I knew God loved me and he was real.

The experience was so powerful that to this day it's still a haze how I got back to Skerries that day. But when I did, I went to find John, who was working in a house near the Coast Inn. I walked up to him and said,

'They were right, John.'

'What do you mean?'

'I gave my life to Jesus. And everything they told us at the studies is true.'

The look of fear ran across his face. He could see something had taken place in my life, and he knew he had seen it in me at the last Bible study we went to together. I thought he would see it the same way I did but of course all this was after happening just to me, not him or anyone else around me. He said he'd talk later, so I left and met my brother Alex.

I told him I wanted to chat to him over a cup of tea. He came along to the nearest coffee shop. I told him everything. He just looked at me as if to say, 'I haven't a clue what you're talking about, Patrick.' It became clear to me that no-one could see or understand what I was talking about, or what had taken place in my life. It seemed so clear to me, yet it just seemed strange and very odd to everyone else around. I left Alex and headed home to get my dinner and head to the Bible study.

Peter picked me up, and I explained everything that happened to me throughout the day. My big question was why no-one else could see what I could see. He said,

'Pat, God has come into your life. He's opened your understanding to let you see this new life he's put in you. But your friends are still in the same place – their eyes haven't been opened, so everything you're telling them doesn't make sense. But if they turn to Jesus, their eyes will be opened.'

It began to dawn on me that all this was just happening to me and not to any of my friends. I found it hard to understand, as it seemed so clear to me.

As we got to the study and prayed and read through the Bible, I got talking to other Christians about my day gone by. Everyone seemed to understand what I was talking about and told me to just keep reading the Bible for myself, and to pray and that they'd all be there for me. After the study as we arrived back in Skerries, Peter asked me into the house for a chat and a cup of coffee. He was so helpful in any way he could and always had great patience with me. He was always willing to give me all the time in the world with any questions I had, and I seemed to have an endless amount to ask him.

As we sat talking, he made a statement that will stay with me until I leave this world. Still to this day I can recall the moment as if it was yesterday. Peter read a verse from the Bible that can be found in Ephesians, Chapter 1, Verse 4 that contains the following words:

For he chose us in him before the creation of the world.

The statement means that God had already picked me before this world even started to be saved and to go to heaven when I die. No sooner had this statement left his mouth than the truth behind his words hit so deeply into my heart, that God loved me in spite of my life and all the bad things I'd done in the past. In that moment, everything else in life seemed so small and unimportant to me. All that life had to offer me seemed like dust falling through my hands as I beheld that God had this big plan going on behind this world we see around us, and I had just been drafted into the light of this plan and this new life. The sense of the presence of God just seemed to fill the room as Peter spoke, and for the second time that day I had to cut someone short and head home.

There are some things in life that truly amaze us all. There are people we hail as our heroes, in music, sports, great heroes of war, people we love, who we worship, our own kids whom we love down to the last hair on their heads. Then there are things like drink and drugs that a lot of people love because of the buzz they get from them. As humans, we all crave the pleasures of love, money, sex, drink – the list is endless of what we desire and what makes us tick. We all have secret needs that we have to fill at all costs. That's life for all people.

But on that night, I beheld something that left all the pleasures of this world and the fulfilment of them so empty when held up next to the pure love of God when tasted for real by a human heart. For the second time in one day, God showered down that love to overflow into my heart to the extent that while I walked home from Peter's house, my legs almost gave way from under me as wave after wave of God's love raced into my heart.

There are words we use to tell a tale like the greatest moments in life. This moment will never be explained with human words, nor will the moments that took place throughout that Tuesday in January 1991. All my life up to this point was nothing short of a secret quest for true love, the true meaning to who I was and what my life in this world was all about. All the questions were now answered in the most amazing ways that baffled all reason and human understanding.

There's no point trying to reason out God. He's so powerful, so pure, so holy and above all our small preconceived ideas of him. We can't at the best of times understand ourselves, this world, life itself, yet we all think we can, in a blink of an eye, explain the God who made all things and holds all things in his power.

The only way to know God is to come to him as a child, bend the knee to him and confess we're all wrong, request his forgiveness and ask him to come into our lives and to save us through his son's death on the cross. And let's be honest, that's the one thing nobody wants to do. It strikes at our pride and makes us all angry with God. So we back away into our own worlds, which in truth leaves us hanging in a terribly uncertain future.

If you were to meet me today and ask me what part of life I find most interesting, I'd tell you in a flash: Death! It's not a subject anyone likes to talk about; we do our best to avoid bringing it up, yet it's coming to us all at some point. People never stop for long enough to find out where they are going after this life. Some people are honest enough to say that nobody knows, so why spend time on the subject? The only answer I'd give is this: the Bible states very clearly that if you have Jesus as your personal saviour, you have no fear of death and the grave. The Bible states that if you have Jesus, you have eternal life already.

Nothing is more dreadful in my eyes than to think of a human lying on their deathbed, helpless, going out of this world of time without the peace of knowing Jesus and that everything he did on the cross is enough now to give the dying person a free entrance into eternal life. Nothing in all of life put together is as important as having Christ living in a real way in your life and taking you across the river of death into your eternal home in heaven.

All this truth was now completely understood in my heart and mind as I made my way home that night from Peter's.

Never had I imagined a human heart could feel such joy, love and peace. All I could mutter in my own words was thanks to God for his great mercy towards a person like me. I'd come from the backdrop of losing Cathy at Christmas to entering into a greater love that no man could take away from me. I felt truly saved in all respects, and words failed to explain the joy of this new-found life God had given me freely.

When I got home, my sister was waiting up for me with a load of questions about what I'd found in my life that had caused such a big change in such a short space of time. I sat up for ages telling her as much as I could. She listened to every word I had to say without getting afraid or angry. I showed her some leaflets about how a person becomes a Christian. She looked at them, but said she couldn't make any sense of it. I just told her she needed to ask Jesus into her heart, and if she meant it, he'd come in. I left her and went for a much needed night's sleep.

*

Over the next few days, word got around Skerries that I'd gone off my head and was reading the Bible and going to studies. A lot of people put it down to the break-up with Cathy, saying that I had snapped under the pressure. But there was no getting away from the fact that something had taken place in my life that was making me happier than at any other time in my life. The mixed views around town that had again drawn me back into the spotlight didn't bother me in the slightest way. I was so proud of God and what he had done in my life, and if people wanted to make a laugh of it all, I didn't mind. My life had changed so much, but I was still human; I still missed Cathy and remained very much in love with her. But I supposed God's timing and his love took up so much of my thinking and time that it covered over much of the pain of losing the love of my life.

As I read the Bible, things became clearer and clearer to me about how real God was, what he had done for us and what he wanted for my life from here onwards. Without doubt, the biggest and most gripping thing I found out in those days of my early Christian life was the full understanding of what took place on the cross two thousand years ago. I had always thought that the Jews and soldiers killed Jesus, which, on the face of it, seems to be true. But the facts point to something bigger than all this when you read the Bible with God-opened eyes. It states that it was God himself who put his son to death. That God was punishing sin in Christ so that he can now forgive someone like me by dealing with my sin, but laying its just punishment onto the soul of his own son.

This truth points back to the Garden of Gethsemane when Jesus sweated drops of blood. He knew a moment was coming when God would, in a sense, turn away from him on the cross because he was bearing the sin and its just punishment. In other words, there was this awful moment when there was a split in the Godhead between Father and son. Something that never happened in all eternity or would ever happen again. That's why Jesus cried out *My God, my God why have you forsaken me?*

We will never know the full extent of the suffering Jesus must have felt losing the sight of the face of his Father, and in the next moment feeling the pain and suffering of hell being let loose on his body and soul as he bore the wrath of a Holy God's just punishment of sin. This whole truth had such an impact on me – again, words fail to express it. God had done this to his only son so he could forgive me my sin, give me the gift of eternal life and make me his child.

I went out and got books on sermons on the cross and read everything I could get my hands on to take in such a truth as this one that seemed hidden from me all my life. Christ dying on the cross stood out for me as not only the most important point in the history of this world, but as the only event that will still hold meaning after this world passes away. The fact that the son of God died on a cross in such a manner to save fallen mankind should make us all stop in a sense of wonder and amazement for the rest of our natural lives. That's all I wanted to do from this point forward in my life – to go to church, Bible studies, prayer meetings and to tell as many people as possible about this new life Jesus gives if you turn to him in simple faith.

The next year and a half was to be the happiest time of my life, and nothing could take my joy this time. I'd found God, or he'd found me, and I felt as safe as anyone could feel. I had met lots of new people, new Christians. My sister Laura became a Christian, as did my brother Stuart.

*

It's maybe the biggest heartbreak of my life to tell you that my fairytale story of becoming a Christian and living happily ever after was to come to a dark end. What lay ahead was to turn into years of darkness, pain and hurt that couldn't be matched by anything as painful from my years growing up. I thought the silent pains of my childhood years of neglect and abuse, with God in my life, were all water under the bridge and my fairytale new life with God and Christians was going to last forever. Looking back now, I can see how naive I was. The reality couldn't have been further from a happy, everlasting fairytale ending.

Something lay waiting in the dark shadows of my past, waiting to tear my whole world apart again. I'd found true happiness in all respects of my heart's needs in my relationship with Jesus. He had filled the empty place in my heart in a way only he could. I had beheld the greatest love any human could find in a lifetime, only to watch it all slip away. Finding myself pushed all the way down to the point of rending a name of one found guilty of cosmic treason.

Chapter Nine

DARK LIGHT

With my new-found faith growing stronger with the passing days, one remark was made by a Christian named Steve that's worth noting in the context of my story. Steve called to my house for a chat, and halfway through a warm talk he asked me how Gary Numan fitted into the scope of my new life. He said,

'Now that your life is so fulfilled, do you still listen to him?'

I paused before replying.

'Why, is there something wrong with listening to Gary Numan?'

'Of course not, but do you need his music now as much as you did before you found Jesus?'

'I've given up drink, smokes and nightclubs, and more importantly, there's a great change inside me towards people that in the past I hated. But the one thing I will never drop is Gary Numan. He's more of a friend to me than most people I know, and I'd never turn my back on his music for the world.'

With that talk still in my mind, I got in touch with my brother Ray and told him I was planning to go to London to see Gary who was playing in the Outland Tour that march to promote his new album *Outland*. Ray said he'd come with me as he'd love to see Numan play live. Plus it was another opportunity to see my sister Breda again. She was staying in a small bedsit, so we had to sleep on the floor of a room upstairs that Breda had a key to. To say it was cold was an understatement, but it was all worthwhile to see Mr. Numan play again, this time in the Hammersmith Odeon.

We got to the Odeon early and treated ourselves to some *Outland* t-shirts, and mixed in with some of the fans. As this was Ray's first Numan gig, I was dying to see what he thought of Gary live. We settled down into our seats six rows from the front and got ready for Numan's entrance onto the stage. After the intro music faded and the chants of Numan's name died down, out he walked as cool as ever to the screaming roars of fans.

Gary, with his unforgettable staring eyes, ran up and down the stage to each song with his distinctive voice and body movements. The show went down a storm, and stands out to this day as one of my fondest memories of seeing Gary live. Ray loved every second of it, and we went to the closing show next night to top off a wonderful holiday in London. I had a great time with my sister explaining all about how I became a Christian. She was happy to see me in high spirits so soon after seeing me in a mess after my break-up with Cathy.

When we got back home to Ireland it was back to work and to Bible studies and church life. My happiness seemed to be growing, and I never once got a feeling of being bored with my new life or bored of talking about Jesus to Christians and people I knew. You didn't have to ask me twice to explain my life with God. It just flowed out as naturally as eating or sleeping. I was never in any way put out when people made a laugh of it or said I had gone off my head, which was said a lot to my face, on a weekly basis. I never felt embarrassed in any way in front of my friends if I got slagged off, mainly because God was so real to me and I felt it was the greatest honour to ever befall a human heart to say you're a child of God. God had saved me and shown me his love in the person of his son. Jesus was willing to die on a cross in my place, so why would I feel ashamed of him? He stood up for me so it felt a great honour to stand up for him even if it meant being misunderstood or sneered at by those close to me.

The more I got to know God, the more I seemed to talk about him. The joy of it all overwhelmed me at times to the point of not being able to speak clearly to people about what it all meant to me. I still had my down days along the way, but I never lost the sense of God's peace. A lot of trials came my way, like the times when I'd let the memory of Cathy take up my whole day with thoughts of how much I still loved her and wanted to see her, but I got over those days and moved forward into another day.

I found that praying was the best part, mainly because the moment I started to pray, I felt God moving very close to me and my heart being touched by his love. If you have never felt that in your life, you simply have missed the greatest feeling in the world that the human heart could possibly experience. After such prayer times you would feel your face glow with an unseen reflection of God's Holy presence. You felt you could walk on water, so to speak, and the overwhelming sense of this nearness would stay with you throughout the day.

With Laura, Stuart and Ray now Christians, family life changed in so many ways. We started up Bible studies of our own and kept in close touch with each other.

*

Another big interest I picked up at the time was an old set of books by a preacher by the name Martin Lloyd Jones, who had died in 1981. He was known by all just as The Doctor because he was a famous doctor in the 1920s, before he got saved and became famous for his preaching at Westminster Chapel for thirty years from 1939 to 1969. The first book I read was entitled *The Cross*. The book was all in sermon form as he preached it from the mid- 1960s. The book had a bigger impact on me than anything I'd ever read in my life. He explained the death of Christ in ways I'd never heard before, so I went out and kept buying his books on sermons from different parts of the Bible. So the Doctor became a bit like what Gary Numan had been, someone I looked up to and admired. He was a man with great passion, yet very humble and down to earth. Some Christians reckoned he was one of the greatest preachers in the history of the Christian church. For me, he was the best – he could move me to tears and spellbind me like no other preacher could do or has done ever since. I sent away to get his sermons on tape and they were even better than reading his books.

So life couldn't have been better, and the smile on my face was very rarely missing. During the summer I was baptised at the back of Skerries Harbour in front of two hundred people, most of them lifetime friends who I grew up with. I stood before them all and openly explained how I had become a Christian, and that day I was baptised in the sea. It was a day like no other day. I felt so close to God, and nothing felt as good as openly stating to the whole town of Skerries that I was a child of God, and that I belonged to him now and forever.

There was a mission team over to help out with the church from Wales at this time. I got on with all of them so well, and they helped me grow and encouraged me in the new life I was now living. One of the team that I got on particularly well with was Brian Davies. I could really talk freely to him, and we seemed to hit it off the moment we met. He was another guy I really looked up to and had a lot of time for. I kept in touch with him when he went back to Wales.

As I moved along with my faith, people asked me one big question on a daily basis, which was what the difference was between what I believed and other religions. In a simple way, I'd explain that all other religions and faiths put their trust in getting into heaven by living a certain life based on good work. In other words, when they die and face God they hope that having lived a good life will be enough to gain them entry into heaven, but you can't be sure if you have done enough until you get there.

But when you read the Bible, it states very clearly that getting into heaven is a gift from God on the grounds that Jesus did all that was needed to gain eternal life for everyone by dying on the cross. And you must turn to him and give your full trust to his work alone on the cross to gain eternal life. In that way, God gets all the glory and good work comes after you're already saved. But works have nothing to do with getting into heaven, they come as a result of being saved. People got saved first in the Bible, then good works came as a result of being in a relationship with God. And it is God who helps them work by changing things in your heart to make you the person he wants you to be.

A lot of people I explained this to couldn't believe that it's all the work of God. To this day, people reject his free offer of eternal life and are trusting in good works of some kind in place of what God has done through the death of his son. If you try to work your way to heaven, you'll have little joy in your life because you'll never think you've done enough, or that God has forgiven you anything bad you've done in the past. You'll never have true peace of mind that when you die, all is OK and God is waiting for you with open arms and that your sin is all paid for in full by Jesus's death. I never got tired of telling people this simple truth, and I always had time for people no matter the time of day or night. I was always glad that people would turn to me and ask me such questions, and I felt only too happy to be there for people whatever the need or questions might be.

*

With time passing and things getting better all the time, I saw nothing that could spoil my happy life. I loved the church in Swords where I went. I loved all the people who went there and they went out of their way no end to help me in all kinds of ways. I never dreamed at this point in my life that anything could step in my way and take all this happiness away from me.

I can't tell you adequately in words, but I'll do my best to explain the plain truth of how my happy life was slowly torn apart. Most of what happened was all my own doing, and it's to me alone that I must point the finger of blame. Yet behind my downfall was something I was very blind to at the time, and it all took me from a kind of blind side. I didn't see it coming, yet it was right in front of me all the time. Of all the mistakes I've made in my life that are written about in this book, this is by far the biggest mistake, and one that I regret with all my heart.

I had become friends with so many new people, all of them Christians, and I had no reason to distrust any of them. One person was a Christian woman named Annie whom I got on very well with and started to meet up with at her home for prayer and Bible studies. She was a separated woman with five kids, all of whom I liked. There was nothing in the line of a romance between us, just great friends with the same faith in God who wanted to learn more about him together.

As time passed, the prayer meetings and worship took on a deeper meaning and the closeness we felt in the time together drew stronger than any of the time I had known with God before. With this happening, I noticed that when I went to church it wasn't as good as the times I was having with Annie, and it started to unsettle me a bit. I went to the pastor and told him the church was missing out on better things with God, and that the worship was a bit too dry and laid back and that we should do something about it. He was very understanding, but I'm sure he was a bit concerned at where I was heading with all this.

In my own mind, I started thinking that God was showing all this to me for a reason and I needed to let people in the church know something was lacking at the meetings, so I explained it to whoever would listen. But some of them thought I should just enjoy whatever God was showing me in my own prayer times and not to worry about what was happening in other people's lives. Great advice, looking back, but I didn't listen and kept pushing my views and in part became more unsettled, as did Annie.

My pastor came to me and asked me to preach a sermon, my first one in the church. I was overjoyed at the thought, and went to work on the death of Jesus on the cross. I worked hard to get it just right, and come the Sunday, I stood up in front of a packed Christian church and gave what everyone said was a powerful word. I was so overjoyed to think I was used by God to preach a sermon. But from that high point in my Christian life came the beginning of the end of my happy life with God.

Within two weeks, Annie and I made up our minds that it was time to leave Swords church, as it wasn't going the way we both felt it should. We both gave letters to our pastor telling him we were leaving and felt we should start having prayer meetings and studies at Annie's home in Lusk, Co. Dublin. The upset caused by us both leaving was widely felt, and a lot of people who had stood by me were very hurt at the news. My pastor was shocked and tried to reason with me, but my mind was made up and I thought I knew better.

In a short time, a few young Christians started meeting with us. My brothers, Ray and Stuart, and a guy named Rory Wilson came to start up a group with us. I did the Bible studies, ran all the meetings, did all the sermons on a Sunday evening and led the prayer meetings. In other words, I put myself in the role of pastor of this group – something that was far too much for me to take on. But I thought I was doing right by God, so it didn't matter when people told me otherwise.

Peter called up, and as always was very kind, and spoke of his concern for me. He explained that I was too young as a Christian to be overseeing a group without being under a pastor myself and having other Christians supporting me. His words fell on deaf ears and I wouldn't take his advice to heart. As far as I was concerned, our meetings were great and for me to stop now would go against God's plan for the group we had.

What I didn't see at the time was that I hadn't time like before to just enjoy my everyday time with Jesus. My time was spent running this group and working. Slowly, I started to see myself go downhill. My joy wasn't the same, I was stressed out and worrying if what I did was a big mistake. I had a chat with Annie about it, but she remained confident it was all going to work out in the end and that God was going to do great things through our small group. At times I felt everything was working out, but most of the time I felt very low inside myself. But life must go on, and I pushed forward.

As news got around other Christian churches that we just upped and left Swords church, I felt old fears from the past starting to rise up inside of me. I rang Brian Davis in Wales whom I got on so well with and looked up to. His wife answered the phone and said that Brian was very upset that I had left the church. I asked how he knew, and she said that someone had phoned him. I asked to talk with him but he wouldn't come to the phone. Something inside started to snap at the thought of losing his friendship. It felt like my old life was coming back to haunt me all over again. I stumbled over my words as the fears of rejection flooded my heart. I hung up the phone and turned to Annie and filled her in. My mind was in torment, and all I could feel was hurt racing through my whole body.

Annie asked what was said to him.

'I don't know,' I said, 'it sounds like he was told I just left the church. He was also told I was passing judgment on the congregation.'

He was the last person I expected to turn away from me, and looking back now, it was a small problem that could have been sorted with another phone call to him a day or two later. But in the heat of the moment I rang the airport and booked a flight to Wales for the next day. This seemed like something I just couldn't let go, as his friendship meant far too much to me.

I headed to Wales the next day on my own with just his address in my hand. After I arrived in Cardiff airport, I travelled by train to a town near where he lived. It took me five hours to find his home. I booked into a B&B, then went up and knocked on Brian's door. The door opened, and Brian stood there, a look of shock on his face. To make matters worse, he was in the middle of moving house. He brought me in and by the time I came to explain what I was doing coming over to Wales to see him, my reasons seemed so stupid and embarrassing. What was I doing coming all this way because this man wouldn't talk to me on a phone? It all seemed so surreal, and even I couldn't make sense of it.

Looking back now, it seems so clear that I couldn't handle his rejection; it was too much to bear, so I flew over to look for his acceptance rather than explain why I left the church. It started to dawn on me just how stressed out I was as I talked to him and tried to explain why I left. But my words didn't seem important even to me at this point. I was starting to go down a road inside emotionally that was now pulling me slowly apart. Brian was very kind, and I stayed with Christians from his church for a couple of days then headed back home to Ireland with nothing really sorted, just feeling worse for wear.

Back home with the group I struggled on as best I could, asking God for wisdom to help the group and to keep things going.

*

On a lighter note, as my life ran on into late 1992 I took Ray and Stuart to London for two Gary Numan gigs at the Hammersmith Odeon. Gary's tour named the *Isolate Tour* was playing the last two shows of the tour, and it was another opportunity to get away for a while from people back home. We stayed in Brixton with Breda again and had ourselves a great time just being together as a family. This time Breda had a bigger house with loads of room to bed us all down.

The first night of the gig was Gary Numan at his best. He just seemed to get better each year I saw him, and the light show was even more amazing than at previous gigs. Before we left the second night to see him, we got talking about how we could share the Gospel with Gary. I had taken some Christian tracts with me, so we came up with the idea of sticking them to a teddy bear and throwing it up onto the stage halfway through the gig. We got some elastic bands and fastened some of the tracts to it, then set off on our mission to get this teddy to Gary.

As we got to the main doors of the Hammersmith Odeon, one of the door staff asked me did I not think I was a bit old to be throwing teddies up at Gary Numan. I told him there was Christian Gospel messages attached to the teddy and we were here to share the Gospel with Gary. He gave us an even stranger look after that statement. Halfway through the show when we were about halfway back from the stage, it was left to me to have a go at throwing the teddy towards the stage. I stepped out of my seat onto the walkway, and took a run and threw the teddy as hard as I could. When I got my balance back and looked up, I was amazed to see that the teddy had landed at Gary's feet. He was at the end of singing *Cars* at the time. He looked down, and you could tell he noticed something odd about the teddy. Slowly he bent down and picked it up, and walked over and sat it down behind him on the stage. It was the only teddy he picked up that night. Ray turned to me and said, 'Mission accomplished!' with a big smile on his face.

Gary's next album, which came out in 1994, was called *Sacrifice*. My brother Ray, still to this day, reckons the teddy played a part in Numan writing about God from 1994 onwards. I'm not convinced of that, but maybe we'll ask him some day does he recall the teddy with the Christian tracts from Ireland.

*

As we went into 1993, I moved out of my sister's house in Skerries to a flat in South Shore Road, Rush to live alone for the first time. The place was cold, but it gave me my own space and it was time to move on with my own life. My dad, who lived in Rush, began calling down for cups of tea. It was the first time in my life I actually got to know him. As time passed, I started to develop a relationship with him, and looked forward to his visits. I didn't go into the past with him – we just chatted and joked together. He'd ask me about the Bible from time to time and even came along to a couple of Bible studies.

I had the feeling that with time we could get closer, and we eventually even started talking about the past. But I wouldn't push it – I was just so glad that we were starting to feel relaxed around each other and opening up a bit. Sometimes I just looked over as he drank his tea and wondered what he was thinking about. He told me stories of years ago when he was growing up around Rush town. I knew I had loads of time to get to know my dad for the first time, so a lot of the time I'd just listen to his stories and take in the moments we were spending together.

Life stayed pretty much the same, but deep down I was moving slowly into a dangerous place as I felt the stress of single-handedly trying to run our small group. I was losing touch more and more with all the Christians outside of our group. Within the group most, if not all, of us had lots of hang-ups from our upbringing, which only led to a bigger problem for me to try to give advice on how others should cope with problems of this nature. I prayed to God for wisdom to give the right advice, but as time passed, I felt deep down that this group and I should be in a main Christian church, not trying to do it alone. But Annie again stated that we should remain out on our own until God showed us his plan for us. Looking back now, it was the wrong advice to take.

I was too young for all this, and was in great need myself to just be stress-free and under a pastor, so that I could take time out to be alone with God without the burden and stress of helping other people week in week out. So the fall was coming, but in what way would it come? I was watching out for any danger that would take me down and out of my faith. But when it came, I didn't see it coming, as is always the case in such things.

I began helping a girl called Tara who had just broken up with her boyfriend. I worked with her for a while and got on really well with her. I spent time talking to her about God and the need for her to be saved. As time passed, I asked her down to my flat for tea and gave her all the time and advice I could. She was a really good-looking girl with a great personality to match it, and it was only a matter of time before something happened.

Tara came down one evening in November 1993, and, to put it mildly, passions took over and she spent the night with me. The next morning I opened my eyes to face the dreaded shock that I had let God down, not only to myself but to this girl. As a Christian, sleeping with someone outside marriage is forbidden and I had always been careful not to step over the line, but this time I had fallen into the trap. Looking back, if I had any cop on at all I should have just repented, got myself into a church and carried on with my relationship with God. But the blow hit me so hard that I felt I had betrayed God. I felt like a Judas. To make it worse my boss picked me up for work and Tara walked out with me. I felt the whole world knew that I betrayed God and slept with a girl.

I can't put it into words, but the pain of what I felt only got worse as the day went on. All the preaching I did on the streets seemed hollow to me now. Looking back, the truth was I'd made a mistake – I'm human just like the next person. What I failed to see was that God still loved me just the same and wanted to forgive me and leave what happened in the past. But I lost it big time, and all I kept thinking about was the cross and all he did for me. The pain just overwhelmed me to the point of losing all sight of God's love.

By the time I got home from work that day I was fit for nothing. The hours into the night were spent sitting looking into my gas

heater, crying. The one and only good thing that happened in my whole life, I had messed up. I felt so hurt and empty inside. I felt God had left me, yet the truth was I had left him and he was standing with open arms to take me back. But my heart and mind were overtaken by guilt and shame and I couldn't see my way through what I had done. As far as I knew, my Christian life with God was over forever. I had gone too far, and with the added pressure of the group, it was the end of the road.
Things didn't go any further with Tara.

So I now told the group that they should get into a Christian church as I wasn't taking any more part in running the group. Everyone was very upset, but I explained I shouldn't have been running the group to start with it.

Now I was alone, living in a flat, with no friends, and my relationship with God in tatters. I had nowhere to turn, and with Christmas just around the corner everything seemed so dark and hopeless. All the wonderful times of feeling God's love and the light that shone all around my life were now slowly being replaced with a kind of dark light. Nothing or no-one could console my broken heart. To lose God is something that words cannot explain.

The Christmas of`1993 was spent up with my ma. The only light that shone that Christmas was that for the first time since my ma and dad had broken up, my dad was coming to my ma's for his dinner. It was so nice to be getting to know my dad and then seeing him sitting with Ma eating dinner on Christmas Day together.

As I made my way home Christmas night to sit alone in my flat, I wondered where my life was heading now. What lay ahead in the next chapter of my life became the main reason why I wrote this book. No words could ever capture the hurt and pain that lay in the dark shadows waiting to strike the two hammer blows that would send my life into what I often call an emotional coma.

Chapter Ten

Too Much Too Soon

Sitting alone in my small flat in Rush, I thought back over my life and pondered all that had gone wrong up to losing Cathy. And now, worst of all, I had been found by God and had found an unconditional love to fill my life with, only to see it all slip away right before my very eyes.

What made this so bad was that everyone started to talk about how my Christian life was washed up. I was once the guy who stood on the streets of his own town preaching the Gospel and telling people the answer to life was to be found nowhere else but in a relationship with Jesus, that through him and his death alone you could have a brand new life and the hope of eternal life. But now all the talk was, 'He's given up on God, and it's all over.' Words fail to explain how bad the rejection and guilt and shame felt over my heart and soul.

Another aspect that added to my growing misery was the knowledge that so many Christians had warned me of the danger of trying to run a group on my own without proper help and encouragement from more mature Christians. My whole theory that God had this big plan for me and the group lay in complete ruins around me.

All around my life, the echoes of my own words seemed to come back like pointed blades from every claim I so proudly spoke about and cut me in places I didn't realise I could feel hurt. In my heart of hearts I really wanted nothing more than to live my life for God for the rest of my life. But unknown to me at this point was that I had come into Christianity a very messed-up young man with very serious mounting problems and insecurities that were far more in control of my life than God was.

In those first couple of weeks after my breakdown with God, I'm sure it felt something like what Peter felt when he betrayed the Lord three times. He went away and wept bitterly. I had now spent two years away from the world of drinking and nightclubs, but it was just a matter of time before I'd slip back into my old ways again.

Now, looking back, I wish I had had the sense to stop and just go back, to realise that God was standing with open arms to take me back and forgive me, that his love for me hadn't changed in the slightest way. Just because I'd fallen didn't mean God was now disowning me. The problem lay with me. I just couldn't see past all the mistakes I felt I had made. I felt God and the Christian church could do better without a guy like me around. So off I went into yet another unknown future filled with a sense of uncertainty and darkness without any feeling any sense of belonging inside my heart and soul.

> *So I close my eyes and drift into sleep*
> *But something is here*
> *In the dark, in the dream*
> *Like a cruel wind clutching my heart.*
>
> *Deadliner*
> *Gary Numan, 1994*

I awoke, gasping for air after yet another nightmare, my heart filled with a sickening, empty feeling. It was at this place in the dark of night I felt the first pains of really missing God. He had filled my life with such peace, and now all I felt was an empty space surrounding the places he had once touched on a daily basis. In the dark of night I felt an anger rise up inside my heart at the people who sneered and laughed at my latest fall in life. With nowhere to turn, could my old faithful friend Gary

Numan come to my aid once again? Could he throw up yet another album that could suit my present situation like he had been doing ever since I first heard him way back in 1979?

Almost to my disbelief, Gary brought out an album called *Sacrifice*, which I referenced in the last chapter. It contained a song called *A Question of Faith*, with such words as:

> *I dare you to judge me*
> *Now God has disowned me*
> *I've come to you to be saved.*

> *They say I sold my soul*
> *And we all reap what we sow*
> *I'll shine for you.*

> *Burn if you want to*
> *You'll be the prize of my pain*
> *They say I've lost my way*
> *I'll wait for Judgement Day.*

> *A Question of Faith*
> *Gary Numan, 1994*

What a perfect picture of my life now, I thought, as I listened alone to those words, me, a man condemned by everyone and now feeling even God didn't like me anymore. It was so strange that Numan had been bringing albums out down the years that always fitted each new change in my life.

I am sure Gary had his own ideas on why he wrote certain albums. I was just glad that in some amazing way, each image mirrored out how I was feeling year after year, right on the button. I started to hit the pubs with my old friend John Fold, who was such a great guy to help you in a time of need. He was always there to hear what you wanted to talk about, and never passed judgement on you.

We all went to the Pier House Disco for a late drink and dance. As I walked through the doors, my eyes spotted a lovely girl dancing in the middle of the dance floor. She was small with short fair hair and I felt drawn to ask her for a dance, but as she was talking to a guy, I put the thought out of my mind. At the end of the night I was walking towards the bar when I found myself standing behind the same girl. She turned around and we got chatting. I told her I was going to ask her to dance earlier that night, and she said she was surprised I didn't ask. I told her I thought she was with someone. But she explained he was a cousin of hers. I asked her her name, she said it was Karen Webb. I told her mine.

We clicked right away. I found her very warm-hearted, and she had a great romantic touch to her personality which would be right down my street. Without having any dodgy stuff up my sleeve, I asked her if she would let me walk her home. She agreed, and we got a taxi home to Rush. As it turned out, she lived a few yards away from my flat, so I asked her in for a coffee. Nervously, she went along with me. I put on some love songs and asked her for a dance. We danced slowly, and gradually I moved around to her mouth and lips and softly kissed her. From there I walked her home and asked her could I see her again. She agreed. I knew that this was the start of a relationship right away. It just felt so right, and the feelings I had from the first night we spent chatting and slow dancing told me that it wouldn't end there.

With Dad dropping down a lot and our relationship getting closer all the time, I pushed everything else to the back of my mind and planned to meet Karen at the same disco a week later. I remember getting to the disco well before her and waiting for what seemed like forever for her to get there. At last she walked through the door with her friends, and our relationship continued from that night forward.

In the forthcoming days and weeks, our love grew into what I'd consider to be a very deep and meaningful relationship in every department. We spent time doing what most couples enjoy – going out for a drink or discos, or staying in and watching a DVD and getting a takeout. I met her ma and three brothers who I found to be very nice and very easy to get along with. On the whole, everything was going great and being in love with Karen kept the memories of my past well and truly to the back of my mind. Anyone who knew us sensed the closeness was very real, and it stood out in public.

As this was my first relationship since my break up with Cathy, I was amazed I didn't cause any walls to form around me with Karen. From time to time, an awful sense of missing God would cloud over my days. Deep down, I was unknowingly trying to fill the place in my heart that only God could fill, but I justified it away by telling myself how badly it had all gone in the end as a Christian, and I didn't want all that pain again.

So I found ways to push all the past out of my mind and move on with my relationship with Karen. I talked to her all about my past life, and told her that I was a Christian and how it had fallen apart. She always seemed interested in everything I talked about, and it was part of our relationship that we both enjoyed being able to talk openly and honestly about our past.

Karen's dad had died a short time before we met. She would talk about him and her memories of growing up as a kid around Rush town. Our love grew stronger with the passing of time, and my relationship with my own dad also grew to the extent that I now felt I was getting close enough to talk a little about the past so that we could try to get some healing in our relationship.

He would come down more often as time passed. He'd keep me laughing with his stories of growing up in the days when money was short and life was so much harder than it was nowadays. We'd drink our cups of tea and he'd head off until next time.

It was only plain to see I was now forming my lost childhood bond with my dad and was the closest in the family to him at this stage.

As we moved into June of 1994, dad dropped down for his cup of tea and chat. As he walked in and sat down he didn't look too well – he was a bit yellow in the face. I wasn't overly concerned but asked him was he worried about how his health was.

'No, I'm grand,' he said. 'I'll be OK.'

I pushed the thought from my head.

By July, my dad was in hospital with what was now liver and heart problems. Everyone went in and out to see him. I had this idea dad was grand and he'd be home soon. No worries at all. I didn't take any notice of what was going on at all and told everyone to stop worrying. Then on the 19th July, I was told the family had been called to the hospital. There were no mobile phones back then, so I was the last to hear as I lived a bit away from everyone else. The moment I heard, it was like I woke up to the fact that dad was really sick. It just hadn't dawned on me at all before, or maybe I just hadn't let it. But now my heart felt strange, and panic started to hit me.

I jumped on a bus and made my way into Beaumont Hospital. I couldn't get there fast enough. All I kept thinking was why I didn't realise dad was this sick. All our warm chats over cups of tea raced through my mind – all the things I was planning to chat to him about.

When I got to the hospital I raced to find which ward he was in. I followed the signs, rushing past people. I asked two nurses where Patrick Bentley was. They looked at each other, then asked me who I was.

'I'm his son.'

Again, they looked at each other. The older one leaned towards me and spoke in a subdued tone.

'You do know he passed away an hour ago?'

My whole life flashed before me.

'No, no,' I said. 'I didn't know.'

'I'm sorry.'

I found myself backing away from them and turning and walking away. I walked aimlessly up and down the corridors and staircases in a daze, not knowing where I was going. When I came to my senses, I made my way back to the ward to find my ma and sister in a side room, crying. It was so surreal. This couldn't be happening to me. Not Dad. Not now. Not when I was just getting to know him for the first time in my life.

I walked down to where he lay with the curtains pulled around him. There lay the lifeless body of my dad, eyes closed forever. The pain sank in that I never came to the hospital to see him because I thought he'd be OK and come home to pick up where we left off in our relationship, in our last conversation. How wrong could I have been? The shock just left me numb all over. I walked back towards the room where all Dad's family and my ma were. I was too shocked to comfort my ma or anyone else. I felt my world closing up around me and I just wanted to be on my own.

I left for home with the awful truth hitting me that dad was gone forever and there was nothing I could do about it. It was the first time I'd ever lost anyone in the family, and it was the strangest feeling I'd ever experienced. It all seemed to sink in very fast that my dad who I'd just spent the last year getting to know, had been taken away from me just when I was getting close to him for the first time in my life. It all seemed so cruel and before its time as Dad was only 54 years of age.

The story was that his heart gave up and his liver packed in. Back at home, I sat alone turning the awful loss I felt in my heart around in my head. Karen had heard the news before I told her. Rush is a small town and my dad was well known, so the news was out that he had passed away.

Karen and I sat in that evening as families came and went, and funeral arrangements were made for Dad to go to the church the next day and be buried the day after in his home town of Rush. Everything seemed like a dream, and I drifted through the next day until I was picked up in a car carrying my ma, Laura and Ray. We all drove together to pick up my dad's remains from Beaumont Hospital and take him back to Rush church. I can still see my dad's lifeless face and body dressed in a suit, with my ma bending over the coffin and giving him a kiss. People started praying, but my eyes never left my father's face for a moment.

Waves and waves of hurt ran through my heart to the extent that I couldn't reach out to my ma who was hurting far worse than anyone else at that moment. I had never lost anyone this close to me before, and the feeling was like nothing I'd ever experienced before in my life.

Looking back now, I'd give the world over just to reach out and hold my ma at that moment and tell her how sorry I was for what she was going through. But it was another moment lost with my ma. I still recall getting a lift back to the church behind the hearse. My dad's sister's husband was driving and watching me in the mirror. For me, my dad's death was yet another downfall that was pushing my life towards a much bigger disaster in the unseen future that lay ahead.

As we got to the church I felt a numb feeling take over from the pain I had experienced at the hospital. Everyone was very nice, coming over as they do at funerals to pay their respects. With Karen by my side waiting at the church, I felt pretty much OK for the rest of the night.

The next day after the church service, we put my dad to rest. The sight of his coffin being lowered down into a hole in the ground seemed the cruellest way to say your last goodbye to the dad you never really got to know. My last thoughts standing over my dad's grave were *If only things were different. If only we had the time to really get to know each other. If only we could have travelled back down the years to try make sense of how it all went so wrong and how he really felt as a human being.* All the questions I wanted to ask him, but now they all died with my dad.

As I walked out of the graveyard, I made a promise to myself that somehow I'd make inroads into getting close to my ma after this all blew over. But for now I just wanted to do what I did best, block out this pain like I'd being blocking things out all my life. In all truth, I couldn't handle my dad's death. It was too much to take in that I wouldn't see him again. All those lovely days when he'd drop in for his cup of tea and a chat was too much of a loss, along with all my other losses down the years.

Yet even in this painful time, I never once blamed God or was angry with him. As far as I knew, God gives life and God takes life away, and he had his own reasons that I never once questioned.

As people and families went to different pubs after the graveyard, I didn't mingle for long and went home early with Karen. We had booked a week-long holiday in Courtown, Co. Wexford. So we started packing stuff for what was a very timely break away from the highly painful emotions of my loss. The holiday gave me time to get closer to her, and by the time we got back, our relationship had become deeper than ever and it helped me push my dad's death further to the back of my mind.

*

We talked about moving in together, which seemed a great idea as the relationship was very strong, and living under the same roof seemed the best idea for us both. We found a house near Main Street in Rush up for rent. It was pretty old-fashioned but we took it. So, I moved out of my flat and we set up home together, and from the time we moved in we got closer and everything just got more meaningful in our relationship. We did what all couples do who live together. We had our ups and downs, but more ups than downs.

But lurking in the background of what seemed like a nice break-through in my life lay a nagging empty feeling and a longing in my heart for my relationship with God. I often sat alone re-membering how much it all meant to me and how it all just fell apart on me. I could see how immature I was in thinking I knew so much better than everyone else and in letting myself go it alone without realising I was very young to it all. I could see my mistakes as clear as day now, but I felt everyone was better off without me around.

Another nagging pain that I kept very much to myself, was my love for Cathy which was still very much part of me inside. I hadn't noticed it myself for a long time, but then one day while in Skerries shopping, I noticed myself looking around as I shopped from one place to the next. It seemed everywhere I went I saw someone with red hair, and my heart would jump, thinking it was Cathy. I never let it upset my love for Karen in any way, but it was there and there was still a lot of feeling very much alive, racing around from time to time. In some ways I'd never dealt with losing her the way I did. But I was so good, as I said, at blocking things out and moving on. I'd been doing it since I was two years of age, so I was a true professional at hid-ing my feelings away from the world around me.

*

As we moved into the Christmas of 1994, my first Christmas living together with Karen, I wanted it to be a special time for us both even in light of the fact that it was the first Christmas without my dad around. I made up my mind that it was time to begin building a meaningful relationship with my mother. After what had happened, I needed to try to sort out the rejection I felt from her as a boy growing up. I knew a lot more now, and realised that a lot of what happened between us was down to her struggles trying to rear eight kids on her own. The reality was that there were so many hurts festering inside, some I didn't even know about, that were outside my problems with my ma. Inside I truly longed for the mother I never fully knew or got close to. In the aftermath of the loss of my dad, I knew my road back to understanding our troubled past lay open.

Christmas came and went and we all enjoyed it as best we could. I spent a lot of my time having little words here and there with my ma. Nothing too deep, but doing my best to start down the same road as I had done with my dad.

My relationship with Karen seemed to be getting even deeper and nothing seemed to be holding us back from growing closer in our love for each other. If we had any rows, we were very good at sitting down and sorting them out before they went too far. The only thing I didn't bring up were the things locked away about my past hurts, and the moves I was hoping to put together to make inroads into my past with ma. I felt it was something I didn't want to unlock to anyone around me, not even Karen.

As the end of January came, I heard Ma got a claim from an accident that happened a couple of years before in which she had broken her arm, and she asked me would I go into town for her to get curtains for the house. I gladly got the things she needed and set about dropping up to the house to put them up with a new curtain rail for her. Alone in the house, we chatted away. I started to advise her on what she should do with the money from the claim she got. Like all accident money, it's bad luck and this wasn't any different. I didn't like her plan of just leaving the money in the bank. I said she should take it out and give it to her kids – after all, we never got a thing as kids growing up.

Looking back, I was so wrong to say what I said, but that was my relationship with my ma. Far too often I snapped at her, but it was because of something that went far deeper into my past with her. I left that day not speaking to her and headed home. A couple of days later I dropped over to see Laura. Ma was there. I hardly spoke to her.

Then one afternoon I was sitting at home when this feeling came over me from nowhere to go down and make up with her. I got up and got a bus to Balbriggan. When I walked in the door, I saw my ma standing over the sink peeling spuds. She had her back to me. I said,

'Listen, Ma, I'm sorry about what I said.'

And that was the end of it. We got on really well and joked and laughed.

As I was leaving, I did something I hadn't done before. As I was heading out the door, I stopped and turned around, and gave her a hug and said I loved her. It was the closest I'd ever felt to her in my life. With both our faces smiling at each other, we parted company on great terms and I left with very high hopes in my heart that, at last, I was getting close to my mother. I was on an unusual high over the fact that we got to sort things out and clear the air. What I wanted now was to talk to her about Dad's passing and how it was affecting her inside. I hoped this would be a further step towards getting even closer to her.

A couple of days later it was coming up to February 14th, Valentine's Day, so she sent me a birthday card with some cash in it. It was such a nice card and I planned to drop down some days later to thank her and chat with her.

On February 23rd, I went to bed at midnight and slept well. Karen was up early to head to work. I was due in work with Pete around 2pm as the crab boats were out on an early tide. Around 9.30am, I heard knocking on the front door. My first thought was the boats went earlier and Pete wants me in earlier, something that was common in my line of work. I didn't move to get up. Then I heard Alex shout in the letterbox,

'Patrick, it's me.'

I thought he must have got drunk in Rush and stayed in some girl's house, and wanted me to get him breakfast. So down the stairs I went, opening the door slowly. Before I opened my mouth, Alex stepped in. In a quivering voice he said,

'Pat, Ma's dead. I'm sorry. She was knocked down by an artic lorry last night in Balrothery.'

The blast of the shock of his words in that awful moment was to become the last blow to my life. I grasped for words as I got dressed as fast as I could.

'What was Ma doing up there?' I asked in a frantic voice. 'What the hell happened?'

'She went up for a last drink alone. She rang a taxi and was waiting at the bus stop for it and stood too far out on the road.'
It felt like a nightmare was unfolding inside me as we headed to Pinewood Green in Balbriggan, to my ma's house. When I opened the front door I was met with the awful sight of my sister, Laura, sitting on the stairs looking like she'd been crying forever. I entered the sitting room to see Ray crying on the sofa, holding Ma's bag. Alex turned to me and said,

'Ray had to go in to identify Ma with the cops and her brother Paddy and sister Lily.'

Simon was sitting there, the pale look on his face betraying very little emotion.

I made my way across to Lily's house and rang Karen in work. She was sent home in a taxi. I asked did anyone ring Breda in London. I was told she was on her way home. I sat down to try to gather some of what I was feeling and what was happening together. I looked around the room as people broke down in tears, one after the other. But it just wouldn't sink in with me that my dear mother had just been killed right at the point when I was setting out to get to know her.

Just like with Dad, she was taken away in a flash, and everything inside me felt numb. I felt nothing, just an awful frozen feeling right through my heart and soul. I couldn't cry like everyone else. I kept myself going by being there for the rest of the family. As one after the other cried, I stood there and comforted them all.

Before I knew it, funeral arrangements were being made and a trip down to the cops was planned to find out how the accident happened with the lorry. As in all accidents involving a death, the family was looking for someone to blame. I had a look at the report, and felt it was just an accident. At the end of the day, nothing was going to bring my mother back, so I was not going to start blaming the lorry driver. Harsh as that may seem, considering that it was my mother who had died, I felt that that was what Ma would have wanted. No point putting a life sentence on a man's head when I felt he wasn't to blame for what happened.

And then it was time for the dreaded removal of my ma from the hospital to Balbriggan church. When we got to the hospital, Alex and I were asked to take a look at Ma laid out before the family came in. We both walked in, and right there the memory came flashing back that only seven months ago I had stood with my ma looking down into a coffin at my dad in the same spot as I now found myself. I turned away as I just couldn't take it.

My ma wasn't disfigured badly from the bang she got, bar a bad cut to the head. We agreed that she looked OK, and then the rest of the family came in to pay their respects. I still remember looking at people breaking down in bits crying, but all I felt was a cold, numb feeling that seemed to stay with me day and night.

When we got to the church, I was overwhelmed by size of the crowd, as face after face flashed in front of me and people shook my hand. I always feel so sorry for those who come up to people at times like this – they know there's nothing they can say. So I'm always grateful to people who do come up.

We carried our mother into the church and went through the service. My only sound memory of the funeral was carrying my mother's coffin out the next morning and near the back of the church, standing crying, was my mother's former boyfriend, Fred. I put my hand out onto his shoulder as we carried the coffin past him. My heart went out to him, but inside, nothing was sinking in at all. As we all walked behind the coffin to the graveyard, I stood half holding my brother, Ray, as he wept.

I took a last look at my ma's coffin as they lowered it into the ground and out of sight forever. No words can or will account for the aftermath of losing my mother like this. My mind flashed back to when I was that two-year-old child left alone in a cot, reaching through the bars for my mother to come back. But this time, she was never coming back. She was gone forever, just like my dear father. I was left numb inside and out and torn to the bottom of my soul with grief.

From this point onwards it's been said of me that I became un-loving and uncaring as to who I hurt or what mess I left behind me. In all truth, no one has ever known what losing my mother did to me, and the reality is that some people just didn't care. But what unfolds in the next few chapters comes mostly out of the loss of my mother.

Something broke inside me that cold morning Alex told me Ma had been killed, and out of that awful experience came what you are about to read in the following chapters.

Chapter Eleven

THE RINGING OF THE DIVISION BELL

The crowds slowly disappeared back into normal everyday life after my ma's funeral, and I watched the rest of my family struggling to come to terms with the loss. Even though I hadn't shed a tear since hearing the shocking news, I felt that I could just step back into my little world with Karen and put it all behind me and get on with my life, just like after my dad's passing. I found myself taking a walk in the town a week later only to be stopped by a sudden rush of pain that seemed to darken even the very light around me. All the warmth that had kept my world alive inside just seemed to go out in an instant. A sickening feeling hit the pit of my stomach. The shock of this experience took hold of me without any warning and set in motion a string of events that gradually tore my world apart in a slow and devastating way.

Everything that had taken place in my life that caused so much pain was, in a silent way, pushing me closer and closer to a full emotional breakdown. I'm sure looking back now that my mother's death was the final blow, but at the time I had no idea what was taking place inside. All I knew was that I felt a devastating feeling that I had never experienced before.

In my relationship with Karen, she did what most girlfriends try to do to help out with my loss. But what can you say to a person who's just lost their mother in such unfortunate circumstances? I never told Karen about my experience while out walking in the town. I thought I'd be OK and things would start returning to normal. Little did I know my life was slipping fast out of all human control. I had little knowledge that I was barely hanging on, while underneath me was a dark and bottomless abyss.

With this came undealt-with stuff that up to this point I thought I'd left well hidden in some safe place at the back of my heart and mind. All my feelings for Cathy that I thought were gone came flooding back as if I'd just lost her yesterday. The abuse and beatings in St Laurence's and all the fears that came from being locked up in such a place flooded back afresh into my world. I felt more helpless now than at any other time in my life.

With my growing problems came a strain on my relationship with Karen, who was trying to talk to me and get me to open up, but I was lost in what I could only describe as some kind of emotional coma that left me closed up and cold in body, heart and mind. It must have been very hard on Karen, who slowly but surely went from being so close to me to being as far away as one could be. This led to rows in the relationship, which was understandable from Karen's side, but from my side that was the last thing I needed. Some nights I sat alone and smoked a few joints to try and relax, but of course it never helped in the long run.

One friend at the time gave me a tape of Pink Floyd's new album, *The Division Bell*, which summed up with its lyrics how I felt inside at the time. It became the album that I often sat for hours listening to for comfort. One song, *Wearing the Inside Out*, painted a picture of someone who was numb on the inside. That resonated with me.

No-one around me knew all this was going on inside me. The signs were that I was just getting a bit colder to people around me. But really, I had started to retreat from the world around me just like I had done back as a young teenager sitting alone in my room listening to Gary Numan's *Replicas* album.

But over and above all this, there was nothing as bad and nothing that hurt me as much as losing the ability to love Karen, or just the ability to love, full stop. That was the very thing I held as priceless in my life and something I had had with Kate and Cathy. And to find even that was being stripped away from me, leaving me cold and a mere shadow of my former self, was beyond bearable.

The only thing left to do was to attempt to cope the best I could with my total lack of feelings and try to hold on to the relationship with Karen, which I found a further strain because trying to maintain some kind of warm feeling was causing pain from within me. It felt like a splinter tearing into my heart with every attempt to get back to normal living. Some people often tell me today that I was grief-stricken over the death of my dad and ma, and couldn't cope with it and closed down from the shock. Whatever term is used to describe my condition, all I knew at the time was that I was in a living nightmare that was only in its first stages. Mixed with this growing problem was the shame that I had turned my back on God, and this shame had never left my heart and mind. A day would not pass by without me thinking of how happy I was in my relationship with God until I let it slip out of my hands in such a foolish manner.

Some Christians did come to me and told me God was waiting for me with open arms to come back. I was told I was being far too hard on myself. But that was me. I'd lived a life of being told I was nothing, and it led to terrible guilt trips. I just couldn't forgive myself for walking away from God even though in my head I knew he forgave me. I still had a fear of going back and having it all go wrong again.

But with time, as my life went from bad to worse, I told Karen I felt God was calling me back into a personal relationship with him. Karen knew all about my faith from talks we had over our time together, so it wasn't news to her. But I told her it meant I was moving out of the house and back to my mother's house. Two weeks later I returned to my relationship with God, and within days, Karen explained she felt God calling her to himself. So with us both now living the Christian life, my life seemed to be on the up for the moment. I was so thankful that God took me back and felt a deeper closeness to him.

The small group I left had by now joined a main Christian church but still held prayer meetings to which I went along to for a while. However, I felt I didn't want to go down the wrong road of trying to run prayer meetings and take on far too much too soon. Plus I felt a couple of people in that group pushed too much on me and that was part of my downfall, so I kept closer to the mainstream Baptist church in Swords. The people there couldn't do enough to help and support me after my return to God.

On the outside, I suppose things started to look like I was heading in the right direction. People around the town of Skerries who knew me heard the news that I had returned to my relationship with Jesus. On the surface, my relationship with Karen improved. But underneath, I was very much crippled by the loss of my mother. I pushed all of that as far out of my mind as I could, but inside, the problem of my fear of people in general was growing. I felt uneasy and unsure around anyone who seemed to hold a place of authority or who had strong personalities, as I always had in the past. I spent time asking God to heal the problems that were messing me up inside, but I don't think I knew enough about them at the time and nothing really changed inside my heart.

*

In May 1996, Karen and I got married. I stood up and made this great speech about how people were always breaking up but that God was in this relationship and it would last forever. Looking back now, I was in no right state of mind to make such a decision so shortly after the death of my ma. But in my heart of hearts I really wanted this to work out. I wanted my lifelong problems to go away. I wanted to live my Christian life with Karen as man and wife and to be happy. I went into the marriage hoping this was the start of great things ahead. I pushed all the pain and hurt out of my mind, but again looking back, I don't like the person I see myself as that day. I was still very much in an emotional coma that was unseen by me and all others who lifted their glasses to wish us the best for the future.

I would say that out of all the chapters I've written, I found this one the hardest to reflect upon and write, mainly because no words could account for how low I was at the time without anyone really seeing it. I often felt sick trying to draw this time in my life out and pen it down. Most people who get married within Christianity go on to live great lives, and I had messed up my life so many times I could only hope I'd survive any tragic pitfalls that seemed to dog my life throughout the years and make a good go at making this relationship work out.

But to my horror, I wasn't long into married life before I found that my inability to open up and get close to Karen was causing rows. Some members of my family began to think I was just not trying to make it work. But I had no choice; I had no control over what was going on inside me. Even worse than that was that no-one was linking my problems to my ma's death. Not even me. The rows just led me to closing Karen out more and more. John Kennedy, a friend from Skerries, once said to me, 'There's three things you can do when you're trapped in a row relationship. One is fight back, the other is run, or the most painful, which is to play dead'.

I took the third. I never said much because I was in too much pain.

In one row we had, Karen was just trying to hold on to the relationship by asking me why I was the way I was. I couldn't answer. So to avoid hurt, I played dead, or lay low and just hoped the rows would stop. My fears went through the roof as I felt trapped in a relationship I wished I was free of. But we struggled on in spite of our troubles. We tried to get help, but I couldn't open up for the life of me in front of other people when Karen was there. It's not that I wasn't willing – I just wasn't able.

As the relationship continued to fall apart, I came under a lot of criticism from people who stated I wasn't putting anything into saving it. That just pushed me further away from Karen and people around our lives. The problem was that no-one understood how hurt I was and all attempts to help me were now leading me further away.

*

On the bike scene, I kept up a keen interest and took trips up North most years. In 1997, at the Northwest, I took a very keen interest in one rider who not only had great skill on a bike, but was one of the most unique and charismatic personalities I've ever heard talking. I could listen to a man like him all day long. His name was Owen McNally. Such a lovely warm, down-to-earth human being, who could ride a bike very fast as well.

Coming in to the Northwest in 1997, Owen wouldn't have been given much hope of winning but in the last race of the day, he beat the best around to win the 250 race, and behold, a new star was born in the racing world. I went to the Ulster GP that year mainly to see him race. I went to a place called Deers' Leap on my own and sat in a ditch to watch the first 250 race. On the first lap, Owen came around leading, and it was the first time I really saw the riding skills that won him the Northwest that year. He went on to win the race and was leading the second 250 before he broke down. From that day forward I found someone to replace Johnny Rea as my favourite rider.

Back on the home front, I started to do some street preaching, on a one-to-one, sharing my faith in God with people. On St. Patrick's Day, Ray and I took a board with a Gospel message and stood on the streets of Rush and handed out Christian tracts. Some people who knew me often asked me did I not feel embarrassed standing with Bible text on a board in a town where everyone knew me. I always felt nervous at first, but never embarrassed about standing for God.

People often gave me stick, but in my mind, representing God was always a great honour, and even though I fell away from him, I felt over the time I was walking with him that there was no greater honour than to be sharing such an amazing message of what Jesus did for sinners on the cross. You must always remember we are all going to die some day and meet this God face-to-face. So why would anyone feel it's somehow odd to be out telling people about him? I'm sure when we see him, we'll all feel he was the only one worth talking about, rather than wasting our time on the things that we can't bring with us after this life.

Back in my personal life, things only seemed to slowly worsen which began to pull my life with God down again. My greatest fear was losing my relationship with God. Once was bad enough, but I couldn't bear losing it for the second time. On top of that, I was riddled with a sense of guilt and shame that my relationship with Karen just wasn't working out. The fact that I couldn't show love like normal people was slowing eating me up as a person. Deep inside, I felt it was only a matter of time before any grip on life I had would soon break, sending me into that unknown dark abyss that I always sensed was awaiting me.

Surrounding all my problems were all those who were fast to point the finger of blame at me. People who never knew what I was struggling with. All they seemed interested in was how I should be putting more into my relationship with Karen. All they were really doing was helping to push me further under.

*

But despite the problems surrounding my life, Karen became pregnant in late 1997 and in May of 1998 our son, Aaron, was born to the world. Any mother or father who has kids under-stands how amazing the natural bond is between parents and their kids. Aaron became the only person I felt close to in an otherwise cold existence. But it wasn't long after Aaron was brought home that we discovered he had colic and other prob-lems with his digestive system. These issues led to him scream-ing day and night and to frequent trips to doctors and hospitals, but nothing worked.

I had just started a new job in a steel company which was close to being a Nazi camp. You couldn't stop for two seconds to talk to someone or you'd have someone shouting down the back of your neck. I take my hat off to Karen who bore most of the minding and caring for Aaron when he was sick. Every night for eighteen months, Aaron would be up screaming his little head off. The only way to get him to sleep was to wheel him around the block late at night, even in the rain. However, this never stopped a deep bond developing between us, and he became my pride and joy.

*

The whole of 1998 and into 1999 was spent away from the bike racing, and with Aaron sick I missed the 1998 Ulster Grand Prix, but saw the highlights on TV midweek. Owen McNally came good again, winning the second 250 race, thus enforcing himself as one of the top riders in Ireland. And there he was after the race being interviewed with his smiles and his unique way of going on. I promised myself I'd get more race meetings in the following year, with my main interest to watch the rare Owen McNally's rise up the road racing ladder.

I got to the 1999 Northwest 200 and watched Owen take second place in the 250 race and witnessed a new racing star emerge to glory with three race wins, the great David Jefferies from the UK. Owen took a second place at the TT races, and was winning every week on the smaller road racing tracks around Ireland. So next up was the Ulster Grand Prix in the August.

By this time I'd left the steel company, as I had seen enough of younger workers cursed at every day to work harder and treated like cattle by supervisors who should have held lifetime jobs in slaughter houses. I went back to processing crab meat under a new boss, as my old boss, Pete, had packed it all in. The new guy running the business was Joe Duff, who was only too happy to have me, one of the best at the job, working with him.

It would almost seem on the surface that things were starting to improve, but 1999 was to prove to be the year I lost all grip on my life and slid into what I can only describe as the darkest time up to this point in my life, and undoubtedly one of the most misunderstood periods by all who claim to know me.

Aaron was by now just getting over his sickness, yet my relationship with God and Karen seemed to be hanging by a thread. Inside, I felt like a man that could do nothing right in anyone's eyes. A growing sense of shame at my failure as a human being seemed to grow around the endless pain that by now had blinded me from linking it back to the tragic death of my mother. All that was needed now was one last push or shock to completely push me over the edge, and it came in the August of 1999.

I got in touch with Tim Herron to book a lift to the Ulster Grand Prix. It was always a great time to just put all my problems in a box and get away for a great day at the bikes. There was no doubt who I was there to see: Owen McNally and David Jefferies, who had won three TT races in the June of that year. The weather was lovely when we arrived at the famous Dundrod track. The day kicked off with the first 250 race, but to my disappointment, Owen broke down on the first lap. The same happened in the 125 race. But the racing was some of the best, if not the best, I've ever seen at the Ulster Grand Prix.

Halfway through the meeting I took a walk on my own into the pits for a look around. I passed Owen McNally's truck where his bikes stood. Owen came out of a caravan next to his bikes, so I asked him to sign my programme and with a smile he replied,

'No problem'.

I asked him had he sorted the problem with the 250 for the last race of the day.

'Ah yeah,' he replied. 'All sorted.'

So it was back to Tim and the boys for the last event of the day, the 250 race.

We stood on a high bank looking down into the riders' helmets at the famous Quarries Bends that sweep towards Dawson's Bend and on to the Start and Finish line. After such a great day's racing, my fingers were crossed that Owen could top the day off with a win and send me home a happy camper. As the noise of the bikes screamed towards us, Owen McNally was first on the road with Ian Lougher second, and the Race 1 winner, Patterson, in third place. On Lap 2, Owen was pulling slightly away on his rivals and looked like he wanted to make up for the disappointment of breaking down in two races earlier in the day. By Lap 3, he held a two-second lead and looked to have broken away from the chasing pack behind.
As Owen came around Quarries to end Lap 3, you could see down into his helmet, and you could tell by his eyes that he was trying hard. As he rounded Dawson's Bend I took my eyes off him for a split second to see if the gap to the chasing riders had gotten any bigger. In that split second, there was a huge gasp from the crowd as Owen lost control of his bike, hit a bank and landed halfway across a field, suffering major head injuries. The only thing I saw was the bike in mid-air and Owen lying across the field. He never regained consciousness, and sadly passed away a few days later in hospital.

I was numb inside and out, and we left the track to head home. Down the years I'd seen riders I knew lose their lives to the sport time and time again, but this time it was very personal. When we got home I asked Tim to drop me off in Skerries, where I picked up some beer and fags and sat down on the beach alone. I hadn't drunk in three years. I'd tried to keep a front that my Christian walk with God was doing OK and that my marriage was doing OK. But alone on an empty beach, trying to come to terms with seeing Owen McNally's crash, I knew my own life was crashing and slowly coming apart. The pain inside was so bad that night that I wished I could just go to bed and sleep and never wake up again.

Owen McNally passed away on the Friday of that week, and everything was set in motion that would lead me into the most painful and darkest time of my life.

Some weeks after Owen died I was working late, cooking and processing crab meat. On my way home on a mountain bike I lost control on a footpath and woke up to the flashing lights of an ambulance and a cop asking me if I knew my name and where I lived. With blood running down my face from two bad deep open wounds to the side of my head, I said I lived with my mother in Skerries. I tried to lift my arm up to my head, but found my collarbone had been broken in the crash. I was taken to hospital and released the next day. I still don't remember much about the crash.

For weeks afterwards I suffered strange side effects from the blow to the head. I woke up one morning and thought I was back in the time when I was dating Kate. I suffered from dizzy spells and found it even harder to be around people. On the eve of Christmas 1999, I sat alone in my room one afternoon holding three photos, one of dad, one of my mother and one of Owen McNally. The division bell had been ringing out the warnings all around me, but my pain had all but blinded me to how torn apart my world was becoming.

I woke up on January 1st, 2000, the first day of the Millennium, after coming home drunk the night before and having a row with Karen, and I moved out of the house in to my sister's that very day. The only person I felt close to in the world was Aaron, my son. But I left because as a person I had nothing to give any more. No-one had a good word to say about me or to me. I felt if I couldn't show love I was better off alone. There wasn't another time in my life when I felt so hurt and angry. Behind me stood the only door I could see in the midst of the pain, and waiting for me on the other side of that door was the painful story of the pure white line.

It came for me at night
And took me dream by dream
To where everything is dark
And no-one hears you scream.
Took everything I loved
And turned love into pain.

Exile
Gary Numan, 1998

Chapter Twelve

PURE WHITE LINE

I'm scared to sleep, I'm scared to dream
I'm scared to wake up in case I scream
I'm scared to whisper one word
That's all it needs.

I'm scared to look, I'm scared to see
I'm scared of mirrors in case it's me.
I'm scared of memories . . .

. . . I'm so scared
I just can't breathe.

I Can't Breathe
Gary Numan, 2000

Since I was fifteen years of age, I would sit alone night after night listening to Gary Numan's Replicas album, and each album down through the years had become something very personal. They were almost like a great orchestration of music that reflected all my feelings and hurt and anger at the world outside of mine. But as my relationship with God slipped out of my hands for the second time, and as my marriage to Karen slipped away with it, I was left standing yet again in the public eye of all the people who knew me. My unstable life had reached a place where I felt nothing inside but a cold, hurtful pain that seemed to hold me in a terrifying grip.

I stayed with my sister while I went on the hunt for a flat or house that I could rent. I felt I was being depicted as a failure by just about everyone who saw my marriage come apart. Inside I was truly devastated. Since 1986 when I was with Cathy I had always been able to hold down a relationship with a girl, and now seeing that part of my life being torn away from me left me, I think it is true to say, in the darkest place I'd ever found myself.

If there was ever a time I needed something to expand the place I now found myself in, it was now. I needed a mirror that would help reflect back to my mind what I was feeling, as these emotions were so new and different to anything that I'd felt before. That came in the form of Gary Numan's album Pure, which became the central theme of how it felt to be in my skin that year.

Numan's point of view, as expressed in Pure, wasn't anything to do with where my life had fallen to, but it was musically and lyrically perfect to set up as the grand picture, a grand symphony of sound for everything I felt inside my heart in 2000. There were many references on Pure to Gary's own views on religion which I wouldn't have agreed with, but in order to fit such songs into my own frame, I saw them through the eyes of someone who had fallen from a relationship with God. I now felt sure that I would never find my way back to him and that I stood as one who had failed him in public, and I felt that I was going to be haunted by the thought forever. I was guilty of some awful cosmic treason of God. This seemed to be the final nail that pushed me into the painful world of Pure.

The lyrics of I Can't Breathe reverberated mercilessly inside my skin, inside my body back then. The world of people stood still all around me, and it seemed even Christians had now given up hope on me. In my own mind I was beginning to see very clearly who the people were that truly cared about me, and there were very few.

The one guy at the time who never gave up on me was John Fold. He and he alone kept close to me and never saw me as a failure in life. He'd spend not hours but weeks talking to me and I am forever grateful to the man, who is a true friend forever.

*

I started to go out to the pubs and nightclubs again, and it was in a pub in Rush that a guy introduced me to the world of ecstasy tablets. I'd heard all about them but had never taken one. I took one that night – it cost me a fiver. I dropped it with a mouthful of beer and waited to see what all the talk was about. Around fifteen minutes later a rush of heat went up my body, and my face felt like it was burning. An hour later I felt untouchable, and all the pain that enveloped my life was gone for the moment. I felt I could talk to anyone about anything right then. I felt I had all the answers and just wanted to go to a nightclub and dance my heart and soul out. To have all that pain dissolved from my body and replaced with hot rushes of love for everyone you meet seemed the answer to all my problems.

Next thing I remember was heading to a nightclub, and by the time I got there I was fully up on the E and just wanted the dance floor. Once on the floor I felt I was in an arena or some crucible where I could let out through the music how I felt being locked up in my emotions for what seemed like years. The only thing missing was Numan's music, but maybe next time.

The next morning, I woke up with a hangover the size of the moon. For the few hours it dazzles you with its chemical buzz, ecstasy takes its toll with a hangover ten times worse than with drink. It takes up to three days to get back to normal. By then you're thinking of the next night out, your next E. It was the start of my plunge into the world of Class A drugs. A week later it was the same, only now I took a Numan CD with me so I could dance to the one person's music that I felt bore all the hallmarks of how I felt inside. I was much more comfortable on a floor when I could get Numan played, a floor all to myself, because no-one else would dance to him.

The very first beat of a Numan song opened up everything I felt deep down inside, and everything that had happened to me seemed to race through every move of my body, yet somehow my mind was careful not to make it noticeable to anyone watching. I suppose it was a form of therapy that even I didn't know at the time. I was expressing hurt and pain but also I suppose I was making a statement of my survival as a human being.

But it didn't take long before the talk was, 'Sid Bentley's dancing out of his head to Gary Numan!' No one saw beyond what they wanted to see. A fallen Christian, from a broken marriage, dancing on his own on ecstasy to Gary Numan. It couldn't get any more shameful than that. The whispers caused more hurt and pushed me further away from people and into the Pure album, as it became a deeper antidote to the torment in my mind.

Like the two-year-old child who carefully structured a safe world to protect himself and had been continuing the same pattern ever since, I was carefully building a true picture of who I was, yet I knew deep down no-one would be able to understand it or even try to grasp how I was able to take this man's music and use it in such a way that it would convince me that what people said about me was not true, and that they had not grasped all the facts of my life.

If I had no real understanding of the person underneath all this hurt and pain, what chance had anyone on the outside? I may have seemed very reckless and carefree as my life was slipping into a dark pit, but in reality I was feeling a deep sense of shame and a dreaded sense of fear that seemed to be reflecting out of every mirror at me. I felt abandoned by everything good I ever held close to me that was real. Alone in a room, another song from the Pure album summed up my overall feelings about how it felt looking out from my world at some of the people around me.

You could hurt me
Take my breath away
Would you like that?

You could rip me
Leave me torn and cold
Would you like that?

One more sin makes me unforgiven . . .
All I feel makes me unforgiven.

Torn
Gary Numan, 2000

The weekends of ecstasy and drinking went on, and with it came a deeper sense of being lost.

In June 2000 I moved out of my sister's house into a flat in Bath Road in Balbriggan. I closed the door behind me, and in a sense I opened another to close out all other worlds. I sat the first night in my flat wondering how my life always seemed to go so well and then bang – the awful crash into some lonely existence. When you're alone, your life starts to flash before you. All the 'what ifs' and trying to make sense of one's life. It just didn't stand to reason how in one moment back in 1991 I was enjoying God's love, and now I was living alone with just my music to keep my head afloat.

A couple of weeks after moving into my flat, I bumped into a guy I'd often got ecstasy from and he asked me had I ever tried cocaine.

'No, never,' I said. 'What's it like?'

'Well,' he said, 'it's very different to ecstasy.'

He left the thought with me, and that's all it took. A week later, I got a bag from him worth €50. It was the start of another chapter in my life.

I took it home, rolled up a €10 note, chopped the coke and banged it up my nose. The feeling was very different, but not as strong as E. I lay back with the headphones on and smoked a few joints. I sank into a different world. All my pain and worries sank away, and I let Numan's Pure album take me away with my feelings. There was a song called Walking Shadows about a person in a coma.

> *All my life they've been here*
> *Waiting for you patiently.*
> *All they want is your heart and soul.*
> *All they want is your tears to fall.*

In my coked state of mind, I thought about how I'd felt all my life – people wanted feelings from me, people who, deep down, were ashamed of my past life and my upbringing. I felt somehow my search for a soulmate was still going on.

I put on a song that night I'd never heard before. It was Aslan's Dreaming of Dreams from Goodbye, Charlie Moonhead. The music and the words sent a shiver down my spine as Christy Dignam's voice rang out.

> *I'm dreaming of your dreams*
> *Your never-ending schemes*
> *I'm shattered and unseen . . .*
>
> *I'm falling down into the depths of your soul.*
> *And it's cold, so cold in the rain.*

Somehow the music spoke to me, of illusions and visions . . . the present, the future, the before . . . I may have been coked out of my head, but for me somehow I had a future that was going

171

to be no mere illusion. I had a dream in the back of my head, and as Christy Dignam's song was played over and over that night, one small spark of light illuminated a jigsaw that formed a picture and story. You'll have to wait for a later chapter to see how it unfolded.

*

If my life wasn't the pits enough, it was now about to take another untimely blow as coming into 2000 the stories were unfolding of the sex abuse scandals in state schools run by Christian Brothers. In 1999, Bertie Ahern, the then Taoiseach, made his speech to apologise to all victims of abuse. For me, I had locked all my abuse in St Laurence's to the very back of my mind. But before long, news started to emerge that victims of St Laurence's were coming forward and making statements of the abuse by Brother Mark and some of the housemasters.

The cops from the area of St Laurence's had a full investigation underway, and were asking for victims to come forward. I rang the detective in charge and had a long chat with him. It emerged there were over one hundred victims who had come forward, and that sadly three had taken their own lives. After that phone call, I made up my mind to come forward and take a case for my own abuse in St Laurence's.

I picked a local solicitor from Skerries to head the case, and he started proceedings against the State as well as the religious order. I knew I was doing the right thing, but the timing of opening such past hurts couldn't have come at a worse time for me. On the outside I could keep up a front that I was OK, but taking up this abuse case pushed me further over the edge with the drugs. I was now taking three E tablets when I was out nightclubbing, but my real problem was the cocaine, which I never took when out socialising. It was a drug I loved to take alone, listening to my music. I loved being with my own self-made buzz away from the world.

In Ireland today, as we all know, cocaine has taken over as a social drug and nearly everyone, in my circle at least, has taken it at some stage. Coke is a drug with a mind of its own, which is something that I hope to explain before the end of this book. It is a very creepy drug that slowly reels you in and keeps you thinking you have it under control. It's not like E which you drop, fly for five hours, come down and go asleep, then take it next week. Coke is a drug you can't keep until next week. Once you have it you'll take a line, then that's it – you'll take whatever else you have.

The immediate buzz for me was the very smell of the drug. I loved that smell. I loved the routine of breaking up the lumps and with a blade, slowly cutting it up real fine into lines, then rolling up a note . . . those first few lines hitting the back of your neck, and slowly you're flying and everything seems so nice and all your problems are gone . . . but for a moment in time. The next morning, your problems come back, only now you have a depressing coke hangover to add to everything. I'd spend up to ten hours alone in my room at a time snorting coke, smoking joints and texting a couple of people whom I felt safe to text.

When I was on coke I saw no danger. I always felt you could trust the whole world, but all that was nothing but part of the illusion that comes with the coke buzz. I started using it more than ever. My close friends, like John Fold, knew about it but not how bad the habit was. It became my own secret world of me, my feelings, my coke, my hash, Gary Numan's music, and added to that now, the music of Aslan.

I spent night after night alone with a head full of coke and my headphones on, texting people stuff I felt deep inside at the time, stuff I'd usually keep to myself if I wasn't on drugs. I felt so isolated in a world that was going from bad to worse. While I was out of my face, my mind wandered back to God and the sunshine of his peace and love that was so much part of my every day. But all that seemed to be from another lifetime that was one million miles away from where I had now found my-self. My God-given halo, pure, smooth and white, was now a jagged halo, with its sharp edges slowly cutting my life apart.

I'd drift away on the coke and think about my dad dying and my mother being killed. I'd hang onto every word of another song from Pure.

One perfect lie
Was it told too soon?

. . . Cold mercy
I kneel down by your grave
I kneel down torn and guilty . . .

I kneel down by your side
I kneel down scared and helpless.

One Perfect Lie
Gary Numan, 2000

I wrapped my painful world around every beat, every sound, every emotion of that song and played it out over many a dark night into the open skies outside my window, trying to reach a clear picture of my mother, but none ever came. I couldn't con-jure up a clear picture of her face no matter how hard I tried, and if I had a photo of her in my hand I just couldn't look at it for more than a couple of seconds.

*

On the first weekend of July 2000, I made my yearly trip to the Skerries 100 Road Races. For a few hours that day I forgot my problems and enjoyed the greatest sport under the sun, as bikes flashed past me at 160mph on small country roads. I went out that evening and met a guy who was selling E. He told me that they were very strong and to only take a half. But I took a full one, and after twenty minutes I was out of my head. I dropped another one about 11 o'clock. I don't remember much after that – most of the night was a blank. My next memory of the night was being in a taxi heading out to an all-night disco and band in the Man O' War just outside Skerries. I dropped another E when I got there and before I knew it, it was 9 in the morning and I was standing there telling some guy my whole life story.

I fell asleep in someone's house and woke up around 3pm. I was supposed to be at the Church in Skerries at 3pm. to stand for the baptism of John Fold's first child. Another messed up situation, another friend let down. I made my way home and got in the door and turned on the TV. The programme was interrupted by a newsflash that Joey Dunlop had been killed in a crash off his 125 machine. It sent the whole world of bike fans into deep mourning. Joey was everyone's hero. He'd taken all the risks in winning twenty-six TT races. Now, at the age of 48, after winning the TT just four weeks before, he was gone from all of us forever. The father of road racing who we all expected to retire and grow old with his family was taken from us, and the shockwaves have never fully left us all. Sixty thousand fans turned out for his funeral and it was broadcast live on TV, showing just how many people truly loved the man.

I went out to face John Fold that evening feeling the world couldn't get any worse than this. I ended up in the Stage disco out of my face on E again and woke up with yet another depressing hangover that lasted well into the week. From then onwards I sank deeper into myself, with only Aaron as a comfort in my increasingly depressed state of heart and mind. It's a small miracle I kept up a very good relationship with him with such troubled life surrounding me. I took him for stayovers and minded him up in Karen's during the week. The money I was making processing crab meat was simply being blown on coke, and as Christmas 2000 came, I was slipping deeper into the addictive world of cocaine.

We planned to make sure it was going to be a great Christmas for Aaron, and Karen and I put our differences to one side. I stayed in her place on Christmas Eve and all went great on Christmas Day itself. Karen had laid down a rule – no Gary Numan, to which I agreed. But I was dancing to a CD with Aaron, and when I put on the next CD, I mistakenly put on Numan's Cars. A row broke out, and that was the end of Christmas 2000. I left and got a taxi home to Balbriggan.

8pm. Christmas night alone. Again.

I rang a guy and picked up €400 worth of coke and some hash. I closed the door to the world outside and sat down at my table with my music and headphones. I opened all the coke and put it onto two CD covers.

Outside my cold window, people were gathering with friends and family to enjoy a drink and each other's company and party the Christmas night away. I sat chopping up fine lines of coke and rolling joints. Alone. Everything I loved or anything of any value to me seemed gone as I snorted line after line, and drifted further into my own closed world where it felt safe. The pain of failure, the pain of shame, the pain of people's cold opinions, replaced by tapping into who I was under all the pain and hurt. Numan's voice screamed song after song that surrounded my soul with hope and the familiar clear picture of understanding that kept me hanging onto his every word as the hours slowly slipped by.

By 1am I had half the coke up my nose and a few joints in my lungs. The phone was ringing to invite me to parties, but I never answered any calls. Looking back now I realise that I never took coke to go out to parties and mix with people like most people do today. My sole reason was to sit alone and listen to Numan and to every beat of my feelings as hour after hour was spent drawing from the man and his voice for comfort. In some ways it was like a night spent conjuring up a film in my mind –

the people around me who hurt me were one day going to meet the real me, but for now I was just a shadow man, an unknown person trying to survive and hide from the world. Terrified by just about everything in my life, terrified of my past, terrified of my mistakes.

But as the coke went up my nose, line after line, everything seemed so wonderful. The pain goes and the buzz takes over. Your mind seems so clear. The beats of the songs that race across your mind sound ten times more powerful, and you feel nothing can stop the high you're on.

8am. A twelve-hour night taking coke and hash was behind me, and once you've taken your last line, the party is over and you're already coming down to earth. All the nice feelings are replaced with what we call 'the horrors'. It's bright outside, and like a zombie you crawl into bed and try to fall asleep. If you're lucky you'll find sleep and wake up around 4pm dying with a coke hangover that is awful beyond words. For twelve hours my life seemed amazing, but that's coke. It opens up feelings that seem so amazing but they are counterfeit, nothing short of illusions. You think you have a handle on this drug, but it's got a terrifying mind of its own that will play with you bit by bit until it takes everything away from you – your mind, your soul, your life!

You may think you are one of the lucky ones who says, 'Well, I only take a few lines now and again.' But as you'll find out before the end of this book, there's no such thing as playing small with cocaine. If you only take a few lines at the weekend, you're in a trap with those who take one hundred lines at the weekend. My Christmas was spent hiding in the shadows of this world. Coke opened up my back door away from what I'd become. I sat that Christmas night coked out of my head. I thought about God, about my marriage break-up, my past abuse as a kid, my memories of sitting with Cathy on the beach surrounded by love, my dad's and ma's deaths. I thought about my son, Aaron – had I failed him as his dad?

Was this going to be my life from now on? Drugs? Would I ever be able to love again? Was there any way back from the pure white line?

Owan McNally.
He was the life and soul of everything he touched.
His death still affects me deeply today.

Myself & Kevin O'Malley
Author of his own book called Inside.
Plus Kevin also proof read The Jagged Halo.
We remain great friends.

My soul mate and the greatest woman in my life.

2006, The breaking down years.
Talking to Gary Numan about his Jagged album
Photo by John Outlander

Gary Numan the Jagged tour launch gig. Photo by Adrian Foley.

The Jagged image that speaks of hidden stories
Photo designed by a member of Gary Numan's Fan club.

Darren Lindsay, a big kid at heart.
He will never be forgotten.

Martin Finnegan
Just as I was writing this book , both Martin Finnegan &
Robert Dunlop lose their lives within two weeks of each other
to the sport they loved.

Robert Dunlop

The greatest fairytale story of all times.
Michael Dunlop winning the race on the Saturday at the
northwest. Two days after his Dad Robert was killed in the
practice for the same race. Photo by Paul Woodlock.

Overcome with emotion after the race.

Paul Hunter
I followed his snooker carer, but was more impressed by
his amazing personality. Like Owan McNally's death I never
came to terms with Paul's death

My Ma

Taken after I completed writing book "The Jagged halo"
with my new identity intact.

Chapter Thirteen

HOPE BLEEDS

'You came into my dream last night with that smile that
always held me like a lover, rocked me like a child. All
I remember from the dream is a feeling of peace. I woke
up with that feeling and tried to keep it alive as long as
I could. I'm writing to tell you that I'm on a journey to-
wards that peace and to tell you I'm sorry about so many
things. I'm sorry I didn't take better care of you . . .

'So you never spent a minute being cold or scared or sick.
I'm sorry I didn't try harder to find the words. To tell
you what I was feeling. I'm sorry I fought with you. I'm
sorry I didn't bring you more compliments on everything
you wore and any way you fixed your hair. I'm so sorry
I didn't hold on to you with so much strength that even
God couldn't pull you away.'

Letter from the film Message in a Bottle (1999)

In early 2001 I sat watching the film Message in a Bottle starring
Kevin Costner, about love found and lost. A reporter finds a bottle
washed up on the beach with a love letter from a man who, in his
grief, had sent a message in a bottle to his dead soulmate.

In so many ways it gave me a spark of light and hope that somehow, some way I would find love again. One day I'd find a love
greater than I'd imagined. If I could love Cathy the way I had
loved her, would it be asking too much to just be free from all
this pain, to be able to open up and love that deep again? But
I was still so lost at sea, in a dark world where drugs and pain
came swimming into my life weekly.

You couldn't look at a newspaper anymore as stories of abuse were on every page. As the stories started to come to light that so many kids had been sexually and physically abused in such horrific ways, it all just kept adding to my own struggles to write about St Laurence's as letters from my solicitor to further my own case came in the post. Statements of the abuse had to be handwritten in great detail. In short, my past hurts were being opened up like a can of worms, and it felt like I was being exposed to not only my own abuse in St Laurence's but to the abuse of all the kids who must be now facing the same horror from their past. I thought of the children who had lost their lives in those schools, whose bodies lay in unmarked graves. It could only make us sink down into ourselves and try to find new hiding places.

*

One great joy that became a glimmer in the midst of such darkness was the news that Gary Numan was coming to Dublin for the very first time. He was down to play Vicar Street on the 17th February, in what was named the Pure Tour. I rounded up a few mates to join me. The numbers grew into a small gang. John Fold and Tim Herron were among the mates that came along to the show with me.

Before the gig took place, I started up what I felt was going to be a soul-saving relationship with a girl I got on very well with as a friend. I met her through John Fold. She was so interesting – and great-looking. We had so much in common, and while out drinking and clubbing one night I bumped into her. Her name was Gemma. Lovely smile, eyes that went into your soul with every striking glance. I really felt I was starting to come back to myself when I was around her.

We headed back that evening to John Fold's house and laughed and joked, then we fell into a deep sleep beside each other. We woke the next morning and we met in the silence of the room where our lips touched, and it seemed like time stopped for one moment, it seemed like a kiss with a mind of its own. It seemed like it was never going to end.

I felt awoken for a moment in my otherwise dark existence in this world. It felt like two people were passing through a time in life, and a new breath of life was being passed within each other's souls. It never felt just like a kiss – it always felt like something far greater. It was the start of a deep relationship that seemed like it was going to last forever. A fairytale feeling surrounded our time together. For my birthday, she gave me a beautiful statue of a silver bird. Very surreal. A week later we watched Message in a Bottle together, and I wrote her a letter and left it in a bottle for her when she came home that day.

What seemed so romantic and real became only short-lived as once again my past hurts, my messed-up emotions came in like a storm from the sea and washed me away from Gemma. It wasn't her fault. At the time I seemed whole to her. She never knew the full scale of what was happening underneath my smiles, my kisses, my love. Looking back, I see again now with clear eyes just how messed up a person can be and still hide it from the world. From that relationship breakup I had lost one of the best friends I ever had, and though I never showed it at the time, I felt so guilty for starting it. It was another nail in my soul. I so wanted it to work out, but I was dead inside and found myself alone again.

As I stood in Vicar Street, the music started to throb up through the floors. It had been so long since I had seen Gary Numan live, and never did his music seem to reflect the torn-up world of one of his fans as it did now. Numan walked with that distinctive walk, that sharp, cold look that you always felt was hiding a small smile of pleasure underneath that just sometimes crept out from underneath all those angry glares. The scene was set for a moment that all Numan fans love, the intro to a gig. But for me, all that the Pure album had meant in such a personal way was going to rain down from that stage into the unseen brokenness of my heart.

The opening song, Pure, set the tone for one of the best Numan gigs ever seen. He was at his finest, walking around, pumping out his own personal feelings to what the Pure album meant to him. But down in the crowd, one fan took it all deeply personally and left that night holding another shadow of light that was always fading, as Numan coolly thanked the crowd and walked away until next time. We left Vicar Street, Numan's voice still ringing loudly in our ears. We headed in a mate's car to Stage, the disco in Lusk. I dropped an ecstasy tablet when we got in the door and danced the night away.

But again there's always the next morning, and the hangover from ecstasy. My life had been given a dark reflection of how far down I was falling seeing Gary Numan's Pure album played live. It hit stuff and places inside me that I could never explain to my friends or even to myself. But after that gig, my life started to rock and wave like a ship lost at sea. The storm was blowing and the wind grew stronger. People added to my pain by running me down for walking away from Gemma. I was made to feel I had just used the girl, but nothing could have been further from the truth. I did care for her, but the drugs and the state of my emotions just made it impossible to love anyone, let alone be in a relationship.

To top everything else in my life that was collapsing all around me, I had a row with my boss over bringing bits of crab meat home, a row that led to that job going down the drain. The only person I now felt close to in the world was my son, Aaron. But I felt like I was such a failure to him. I kept in touch with Karen and in close touch with Aaron but only as a hand touching the side of an endless cliff as I fell further down, never knowing how the story was going to end.

My nights became more isolated as my coke habit took over my life. Nights sitting alone were my bread and butter, snorting coke, smoking joints, trying to catch all the lost moments of holding a girl so close, my clear eyes looking deep into hers. Sweet kisses, fading memories, fading moments replaced by a deep drag on another joint, another line of coke up my nose, another Gary Numan song screaming down the headphones.

> *If you are my shepherd*
> *Then I'm lost and no one can find me.*
> *If you are my saviour*
> *Then I'm dead and no one can help me.*
> *If you light my darkness*
> *Then I'm blind and no one can see me.*
> *If you are my comfort*
> *Then nightmares are real and deceiving.*
> *If you are my answer*
> *Then I must have asked the wrong question!!*

> *A Prayer for the Unborn*
> *Gary Numan, 2000*

It's a terrifying experience to be so hurt and broken and to feel even God must be ashamed of you for walking away from him. I often felt God had the right to strike me down dead and that he would be truly justified in doing so. I felt my life was nothing short of a total disgrace to God and to the world. Yet somehow, something kept telling me not all this was my own fault. I would look at the front pages of newspapers with the news of all the abuse in state-run schools and ask how much all this shit had affected me.

The coke going up my nose numbed the pain. It stopped me thinking too far back to growing up as a kid. I pushed those feelings far from my mind and replaced my picture with another to set my mind upon. I had a way of putting aside all the words of people who even claimed to love me but spoke nothing but hurtful stuff about me. Those who even wanted a part of me but ran with the crowd and inside were ashamed of what I had become. It all left me feeling I was the victim of a very real and painful betrayal. I felt so overwhelmed with a frightening sense of being abandoned by everyone, bar Aaron.

If someone did claim to want me, it was always at a price. I felt such a sense of anger in my heart. I spent hours after hours at night snorting coke, smoking joints and just racing my mind over such feelings. I felt I wanted to scream back at all my critics but knew it would only expose me to further hurt. I was the one taking drugs, I was the one whose life was in a mess. I sank back into my coked state of mind, drawing another drag from a joint and tried to draw the perfect picture of how it felt looking out from my painful state into this sea of people's faces that I could see so clearly, drawing back into the sea of the sounds of Numan's music.

It wasn't until Gary brought out the Jagged album in 2006 that a song called Fold gave me the perfect words and sounds to capture such dark moments of hurt and how I felt towards so many people at the time, those who had a secret need to expose my sins to the world in an attempt to hide their own.

> I fold your letters
> All lies, all cold.
> I fold my memories
> My life and soul.

> I fold compassion
> And vengeance bleeds through.
> I fold forgiveness
> And wait for you.

> I fold all reason
> Screaming your name
> I fold your heart and
> Feed on your pain . . .
> Fold
> Gary Numan, 2006

My life screamed out.

And one evening, as I drifted further and further into hurt and pain and coke, the face of my little boy, Aaron, flashed in front of my eyes. Like a ray of light, his love for me and my love for him coincided. Next day, I had to pick him up. My love for him was always growing, like any dad's love for his son, but in one moment a deeper bond for my kid took over my heart and slowly I came back from the brink of being lost forever in the dark world of cocaine, hurt and pain.

On top of this came the news that Karen had been offered a house in Balbriggan in Pinewood Green Estate. We talked a few things over, and felt something could be saved in our relationship. I gave up my flat in Bath Road in the summer of 2001. I gave up all drugs and went about trying to salvage something – even if it was only for Aaron, it felt the right thing to do at the time. I hoped things would work out as I moved the last of my things out of my flat and set up home with Karen again.

On the surface it looked like things were on the up for me, and for myself and Karen as a family, but before long the old familiar problems of not being able to open up or get in touch with my emotions started to result in ongoing rows and hurtful things being said to me. It hit me hard that I'd made a mistake coming back into the relationship. I felt the old familiar pain that I was trying to hide to make something work between us. But my bond with Aaron was different. It was growing stronger. The love I felt for him gave me enough reason to stay in the relationship with Karen.

*

In July, I started a new job for a cleaning company in a northside shopping centre, a job I loved. My brother, Simon, worked for them as well and got me in along with my brother Stuart. We all worked hard, and again on the surface my life seemed a million miles away from the days of drug taking and self-destruction. But inside told a different story. I felt a stranger to Karen. I felt guilty for being the way I was to her. I longed to be the way I was at the start, to be the way I was with Cathy. I longed to feel normal about my past growing up as a kid. So many things, so many hurts seemed to grip me on a day-to-day basis that most of the time I couldn't see where they were coming from. I just felt all wrong as a person. I was simply a shadow of my former self. But I knew how to hide my fears so well.

The only light that filled my otherwise dark day was knowing I was going to see Aaron's face when I went home. He'd be the first to meet me, running towards me for a hug. It's a very hard thing to explain a father's love for his child. If you're a dad, you'll understand what I mean. So, my life was my job and Aaron, and my very distant relationship with Karen. It wasn't that I wanted it to be this way – it was just that I felt nothing and even trying to feel romantic caused me hurt. If anything, I felt it was getting worse as even being in the same room was becoming a problem when we were alone. I was worried – was this it for life? Was I one of those people who just stayed in a marriage because of the kids but remained so unhappy?

Things were now so bad I couldn't go and sit with a counsellor for help with Karen because I couldn't open up in her company. I fell into just going through the motions of life like too many people do. My hope of loving again was like an unattainable dream, something that swept over my heart and soul all the time. It never left me no matter how cold I felt inside. I hoped to be set free from what seemed like a deadly spell that was cast over my world. I held hopes, I held so many hopes – in love, in God, in being free from the hurt, but they were always bleeding in some way until I was left empty-handed. All I could see was failure hanging over my head.

It wasn't Karen's fault, it wasn't something that was down to just our rows – it was something far greater that was pulling my life apart bit by bit. At night I started sleeping alone in the box room as the dark shadows raced over my heart, a sharper cut each time. My life started flashing before me.

That's when the dream started.

The dream of one single kiss
To feel free from this prison
I'd found myself in and
To be able to kiss so freely
No pain, no hurt, no fear.
The Dream
P.B.

*

Despite all my hopes bleeding around me, I experienced another great moment – when God touched my life again.

It's very hard to explain in words what that means. A touch from God. It just means feeling God's love, peace and joy for real. It felt so amazing, mainly because I wondered why God would touch me after all I had done in his name. I felt so undeserving and so full of shame that God would come near such a person that had shamed him so deeply to the world around him. I tried to pick up my relationship with him and started to go to church and mix with other Christians in Swords Baptist church. I was always made to feel so welcome by everyone. They couldn't have been nicer to me, but inside I was afraid of what people would think of me if they knew the full truth about the person I was and what I had got into.

I knew God wanted to heal things in my life, but I pushed it away as all my fears took a firm grip over my life again. Sitting in church, the shame I felt that my marriage was in bits was huge. It was that old problem of worrying what people thought of me, wishing, thinking of a way that I could prove to them all that I was an OK person, that I wasn't as bad as the stories would lead them to believe.

The pastor tried to make me feel at home by asking me to give a small talk one Sunday, which I did and it went down great. That's what sort of people they were – always open arms, always trying to love you and be there for you. But my problems ran so deep that it was only a matter of time before I withdrew, yet again, into a small shell where only my son and I lived. The reality was that I felt like they were too good to have someone like me around. I always maintained the greatest respect for them all but I felt less pain when away from people, alone where God could get on with other people who hadn't got the problems I had. Again, God was gone like the time before, and my life just tiptoed along life's road waiting for the next downfall, waiting for what always seemed like another drop off a great cliff, waiting for me in the dark shadows of my tomorrow.

*

I kept up my keen interest in bike racing. I was very much drawn to yet another favourite rider by the name of David Jefferies, an Englishman who had first caught my eye at the 1999 Northwest 200 having taken three wins on the day. By the end of the 2002 TT Races Big Dave, as he was known, had won nine TT Races and held the lap record for the TT course, and had become just about unbeatable around the famous 37½-mile track. As always, I went for something other than the fact the rider was great to watch on a bike. I was drawn to David's personality, his wit and the fact that he was just so down to earth. I wouldn't say he replaced Owen McNally, but he did give me the same buzz to watch racing.

On the work front, my job was working out great and I was given a supervisor's role over the cleaning, a job I did well. Luckily, I found the skills of dealing with people under me came naturally. I treated them all with great respect, which led to a harmonious relationship with all my fellow workers. Any problems I had with anyone, I sat them down and talked one-to-one with them with great care until we got all the problems sorted out. I kept the work standard up and kept the peace between all the cleaners at all times.

I suppose, looking back, my job did help me to forget my growing problems at home with Karen. It kept my mind preoccupied and I enjoyed a time of some self-worth as I took pleasure from the responsibility I had been entrusted with.

If you had met me at this stage in my life, you would never have imagined that under all those smiles at work such a different story was going on. When we meet people, we don't know what they are suffering from and what they're hiding from the world outside theirs. You hear someone has just taken their life and everyone saying you'd never think that anything was wrong in the person's life – they were always smiling, working, everything seemed so normal. Yet underneath the smile, the laughing, there could have been deep pain that controlled and hurt them most of the hours in their day.

I'd fallen into that place. I went to work, smiled all day long. Went home and held the love of my life, Aaron. After dinner, when he fell asleep, I'd sit in the back kitchen while Karen sat in the front room watching TV. I'd listen to Gary Numan and Aslan and drift off into a daydream. A daydream that helped me cope. My mind would race back to when myself and Karen were happy but by now my love for her was drained away by things said, things done, by rows.

So my mind would race back further to the one place in my life I knew I felt the closest to a girl. Smugglers' Cave with Cathy. I'd sit alone hour after hour trying to draw on thoughts of sitting on rainy Saturday afternoons holding her close to my beating heart, trying to find a link back to those moments, hoping they'd lift up my dead heart and bring back to me a love that I'd lost touch with.

I hoped it would help awaken me to life again, something warm that would save me from this cold, lifeless, painful existence. I'd give my own life for the freedom of a kiss. Just one kiss, without feeling trapped in this pain. I imagined a girl's mouth slowly coming close to mine, our lips touching and being awoken to touch again. I don't know what other people think about in a dead relationship but that's where my mind was spent night after night as the weeks and months passed me by.

*

My hopes were slowly fading as the year ran into 2003 and there were more visits to my solicitor over the abuse case. It was now put to me that I should think about going to get some form of therapy, as the State had now set up therapists for all the victims of state-run schools where abuse had taken place. I had a think about it, but wasn't ready to open up to talk about it just yet. I had just about been all but swallowed up with a sense of failure within myself and was just about hanging on to my time with my son and job to keep me from going under and never returning.

By May of 2003, it was time to take our yearly trip up North to the Northwest 200. This year, I talked my brother Stuart into coming with the gang as he had never gone up North to a race as big as this. We enjoyed the day and it was priceless watching Stuart's face when he saw the high speeds at which the riders passed him. He's been hooked ever since and has gone to more races than myself. He left the Northwest a fan of David Jefferies as well that day. A week later the TT Races 2003 were on, and like most race fans we tuned in on Manx Radio to hear the races live each year.

On the Thursday afternoon of practice week, I headed to see my solicitor in Skerries. As I sat in the waiting room, my phone beeped. There was a text message from Tim Herron. It just read, 'Sid – Jefferies killed. Tim.' The room spun around me as

I tried to take in what I was reading. Before long the phone rang and the full picture came together that David Jefferies had been killed at a place called Crosby, at a flat-out left-hander, taken at 170mph. David had hit a wall and died instantly. I left the solicitor's office in shock.

It was the same feeling all over again that I felt when Owen was killed. Some people say it was oil on the road, but a friend of mine who had been over for the races went to the spot but told me he found no oil marks anywhere. My own opinion is something happened to the bike, a view not many fans would agree with. It was yet again a very untimely blow to me that felt like someone in my family had just died. I just couldn't get over it. I just couldn't get Dave's face out of my head. He was just so good a rider, a person, and now in a flash he was gone forever. The unforgiving sport had taken another great light and left race fans with that sense of being helpless to come to terms with the loss. If that didn't push me over the edge, something lay waiting around the next corner that would.

I reflected on my obsession with the sport of road racing. With its addictive attraction, maybe it was a close parallel to my own years of drug taking. The adrenaline. The rush. The thrill. The euphoria. The danger. The dicing with death. The list of casualties. The devastation and havoc it wreaks on family and friends.

*

After the loss of David, my health started to get worse, and in work I had been handed the full supervisor job, as cutbacks meant the head supervisor plus a couple of other staff had to be let go. The boss in the cleaning company over the contract for the shopping centre, Joe Hoey, came to me and asked would I take over the writing up the rosters, ordering in the cleaning stuff and taking care of all the staff's everyday needs. But with the cutbacks he could only give me €20 a week extra to do both my job and all this extra work. I told him I would, as I wanted to help out after the cutbacks.

I did my job very well and kept the show going without any mistakes. Then one morning in October, Joe met me with the news that he had a girl to work with me to help with the supervisor's work. I welcomed the news and went to meet her. Her name was May West, and I spent the next few weeks training her in and helping her to get to know the place better. At first she seemed like a nice woman, but everything was about to change in the most horrific way I could have imagined.

I had just made my mind up to go into therapy for my past abuse in St Laurence's, but in order to go ahead, I needed every Wednesday off work as it was the only time the therapist could fit me in. So I told Joe that I needed this time off and felt safe to explain that it was very important and to do with abuse in my past in a school. I informed May as well, as I felt Joe would tell her anyway. I took up my first therapy class with a woman just outside Swords, and after three sessions I felt it was very hard going and was opening up all kinds of closed doors. I felt very down in myself, but I never let it interfere with my work. I suffered from panic attacks on and off after each session but kept up my visits as I felt in the long term I'd benefit from them.

But one afternoon in November 2003, I had just come into work on a moped bike I was now using to get back and forth from work. I headed to one of the yards to clean it up when I turned to see Miss West walking towards me. She started to order me about, telling me to put on a pair of wet bottoms if I was cleaning up the yard, to put out the fag I had in my mouth and to move my bike because it was in the wrong place. I had been led to believe that she was just working as a co-supervisor, and was not to give me orders. I was already feeling down that day, and out of the blue I had a panic attack and felt I should go home, which I did.

I returned the next day to have a meeting with Joe who took me aside so that I could explain what happened the day before and why I left my workplace. I relayed what happened with May and how I'd been going through a hard time since taking up therapy. He told me to keep my problems at home and that I was being given a warning for leaving my workplace. I apologised for what happened. I left the meeting with a deep sense that I was being pushed out of my job to make way for Miss West to take over.

On 20th November, shortly before noon, I went to Argos to buy a Christmas tree and a sitting room table. I had no way to get them home on the bike, so I put them in one of the cleaning stores until I could get someone to pick them up with a car. With all the Christmas stock coming into the shopping centre I was kept very much up to my eyes.

On the morning of 5th December, I got a phone call on my day off from Joe to come into work for a meeting at 2pm. I asked him what it was all about but he told me just to drop everything and come in. I left Aaron down in my sister's and drove to the shopping centre to meet with Joe. I met Joe and the head of security and was taken into a small store room.

I was first asked about a jacket I had picked up the day before while cleaning and left down in the basement, like we did with other things we ever found left lying around. I was accused of robbing the jacket. I was also accused of robbing the Christmas tree and table. They stated they had checked with Argos who confirmed both items were stolen from their store. I knew, as my mind started to panic, that I had lost the receipt. I felt a panic attack coming over me as they pushed me to write a letter to state I was resigning of my own free will. They said if I didn't, they would have me taken out of the shopping centre in handcuffs in front of everyone and they'd have me disgraced along with my family for the Christmas. I panicked and signed the letter and left the shopping centre in an awful state.

My world came falling down all around me, with Christmas just weeks away. The shock drove me right over the edge. When I got home, I had to face telling Karen. I spent the next few hours trying to make sense of all that had happened that day.

'But Patrick,' she said, 'when you bought the Christmas tree and table, you took the free Christmas lights home on the bike.'

I pulled them out of the press to find that the tag that's on all Argos items was still on the box. The next morning, I rang Argos and talked to one of the managers who took the details from the tag on the Christmas lights. He rang me back an hour later to confirm they could prove I did purchase the items and that they had it on CCTV. The manager asked me to drop into him the next day for a meeting to draw up a copy of the receipt.

The next day I went to Argos and made my way to a staff member to ask for the manager. But before I got to someone, I got a tap on the shoulder from a manager of the shopping centre and was asked to go outside. I walked out with him where he turned and told me I was barred from the centre. It turned into a heated exchange of words as I pulled the Christmas lights out of the bag with the tag on them and told him that I had the proof that the items I bought in Argos were not stolen, that I had been set up to get rid of me so May West could take over my job because I was in therapy. His face dropped when he saw the receipt and asked if we could talk. But I had had enough and left the shopping centre in another awful state.

I rang the manager back up and told him I had been taken out of his shop before I could see him. He told me he'd hold all the evidence for me, and said that I should go to a solicitor and get him to take a case and get them to contact him back. I took up a case for unfair dismissal and for defamation of character, and left the case in the hands of the same solicitor who was carrying out my abuse case against St Laurence's.

My Christmas of 2003 was in ruins. I gave up my therapy sessions and sank deeper into myself. I'd left myself wide open going for help with my past abuse, only for it to lead to losing my job in such a hurtful manner by people I worked so hard for and who I trusted with the sensitive information of my personal problems.

Over the Christmas and into the New Year of 2004 I was put on the sick by my doctor as my health started to drop to an all-time low. I became depressed as I watched my relationship with Karen fade away and die from my life forever. By the start of 2004, I wanted to leave the relationship and live alone. I couldn't take it living this way anymore. I wasn't like others who just stuck in a relationship for the kids' sake while the love between the two people was dead. It just wasn't me. I'd rather die than live like that for the rest of my life.

But my love for Aaron grew, keeping me strong. In the daytime I spent my time with him. He was the only one left in the world that sent a ray of love into my otherwise dead heart. At night I sat alone as the haunting feelings of what I once was came back racing across my mind and heart.

I was riddled with a dark sense of loss, and a sense of guilt and shame at what I'd become to Karen – half the man I once was. I felt a total failure as a human being that now lived his life on past memories. With court cases and abuse cases all ahead of me and the stress that such events bring, with no job, stuck on the sick, what could a man like me who had lost everything he ever loved expect? What could a man expect who found himself trapped in life and sinking fast to a place of total despair, a man who felt he was a total disgrace or was made to feel that way by his failures in life?

As the rockets lit up the sky and the noise of people counting down to the end of the year gone by and the start of the new one just beginning rang in my ears, I sat as my mind flashed back to that one close moment in Smugglers' Cave on that damp Saturday with Cathy. Eighteen years had passed since that amazing close encounter which seemed like a million light years away. With people wishing each other a happy new year all around the world, I saw nothing ahead of me for 2004 but a dark, painful existence that I tried to hide from as best I could. As the world held up their glasses to a new year ahead and drank best wishes to family and friends, I lay with my emotions bleeding, listening to these words from Aslan:

> *For you, for me, for the sake of sanity.*
> *For hell, for heaven, for the life I'm living*
> *Save me, save me.*
> *Games*
> *Aslan, 1994*

Little did I know 2004 was to unfold an old 16th century myth linking Smugglers' Cave back directly into my life in a way that would change my life forever. Out of my broken existence came what I often refer to as my last great war. An almost defeated man found the strength to pull up his own personal sword to rage one last war for freedom, for love, for his soulmate.

Chapter Fourteen

FROM THE CAVE TO THE CASTLE

Long ago your name
A shadow in my dreams
The wild brave still searching
Greying winds fall apart
I believe your heart.

Hope cries from the hill
The mist clears from your eyes
Your banner will promise
Let's remember the start
I believe your heart.

Tell Me Now What You Feel
Moya Brennan, Soundtrack, King Arthur, 2004

As I dragged myself into 2004, I was at my lowest that I could remember. Nothing was right within or outside my world. I was so unhappy in my marriage and was now face-to-face with that time in so many relationships when you have to ask yourself hard questions. Do I stay in this loveless relationship, or do I get out and risk losing what I already have – a home, a safe haven, food on the table, security surrounding me?

I knew my relationship with Karen was coming to an end. My feelings were gone and I realised I wasn't in love with her. But like most people, I couldn't face that and just pushed on, hoping this curse of not being free to love would lift and maybe I'd be OK again. But then there was the factor that I knew I could never settle for a relationship where the feelings were gone, because it went against everything I ever believed in about relationships all my life. I had always believed in finding my soulmate since I was a young teen in 1979 sitting alone in my old damp room listening to love songs on the radio. That dream, no matter how low I'd found myself in 2004, never left me. In fact it was more alive now than maybe the rest of me inside. At times, I felt this overpowering sense of pictures racing around inside my head and falling down into my heart. A sense of finding this person, holding her close and just knowing she's the one, the one I've been looking for to fit into this place in my heart forever. I could see that first kiss in slow motion.

People may think it's daydreaming, but it was the only dream keeping me from falling over the edge. I'd found such amazing loves in the likes of Cathy and what kept me going in the fight for her heart was the soulmate thing I stood for, and even after I split with her I never lost this part of me that kept saying, One day, one day, love will come back to you, just don't give up on love itself.

And I never did.

It was like I had a built-in compass that kept pointing me in this unseen direction to find this one person I was made to be with forever. To many people this may sound like pie in the sky, but I took it deadly seriously. It was something that went very deep into my life and history and I knew I was at risk of it dying if I stayed with Karen. I remember sitting, like I always did, in a room alone trying to remember back to when we were in love, when we were so close, and it did seem so amazing but now it all lay dead inside my heart. I knew it was a door that was closed forever. My mind would look back to standing face-to-face with Cathy, and it's there I saw how much I knew I could give to someone in a relationship. But the rows, the hurtful things said in those rows had burned my love for Karen away forever.

It came up a few times about moving out, but like most couples it's said and soon forgotten. For me it was Aaron, the thought of being away from him after building up such a great relationship with him, that stopped me – it seemed too hard to face.

But as time slipped by, I got more down and depressed as flash-backs to my past hurts growing up as a kid came back to haunt me. Even in my dreams I saw the faces of my abusers, then I'd wake up in a pool of sweat, gasping for air.

More visits to my solicitor over both the abuse case and now the unfair dismissal case didn't help my health, and he put it to me to try to go into therapy. Somehow I dug up the strength to ring up about doing just that, but it had to be near home and with someone new. I rang up Fesha who were set up for state-run school abuse victims and they got me in touch with a local therapist. I went along to meet with her with an open mind, not knowing what to expect.

I was met by one of the greatest people I have ever had the pleasure of meeting, Kate. From the moment I met this fifty-plus woman, we formed a bond and a great relationship. As I sat that first afternoon with my emotions bleeding all over her floor, I'd taken my first step into the unknown to start trying to rebuild my life from scratch again.

My self-esteem, my confidence was totally shattered and all my past hurts had taken their toll on my mental state as well, so I was a right mess inside by the time I got to Kate in 2004. But if you met me in the street, you'd think I was a happy-go-lucky guy, I hid the pain that well.

The sessions with Kate slowly gave me enough balance to think outside of all the fears that had held my mind and trapped my heart. I started to see some light at the end of what had become a dark tunnel of pain. I started to send CVs out to try get back working.

On the home front, things remained pretty much the same as the therapy just opened up my eyes in a big way that the love I once had for Karen was lost and had left my heart, and that it wasn't going to return, even with therapy. So the guilt of not being able to love Karen began to lift off my shoulders, and I felt a kind of release and even a hint at the truth that maybe I was at last coming back to life.

*

I called in for an interview with a security firm based in Swords who were hired by a goods packing company. The job was just checking people coming and going from the factory, checking in goods, CCTV camera checks and patrols of the grounds. Three days later I got a call to say I'd been given the job. So in June of 2004, I commenced employment again. It didn't take me long to get into the swing of the job, and I got on well with the guys I worked with as well as the staff who worked in the factory. I was very aware that I was just trying to find a stable place within myself and hold a hope that nothing painful or dramatic or crushing would enter into my life at such a time when I was slowly rebuilding it up almost from its very roots. It was a very nervous time filled yet again with concern, what ifs and wondering what was waiting around the next corner.

I was learning some things in therapy, but I knew I was a long way from understanding how to deal with the deep pain inside and how to overcome the fear that held my life still in its grip. If I looked inside for more than five minutes it became that dark reflective mirror of stories of loss, sorrow and deep regret that would creep up from its dark place, leaving me feeling I was drowning with self doubt and how I was being perceived even by those who I got on well with. It worried me now more than ever what people thought of me, and it made me feel sick to think people thought badly of me. It made me feel nervous to confront people in any shape or form.

Alone in my shell, one day on a long twelve-hour shift, my mother's face came flashing into my mind. I wasn't even thinking of her. There she was, her small face, her shy eyes looking into mine. It was a moment when I remembered her saying, One day, Patrick, you'll write a book. But I told her, I haven't got the right ending yet. But one day I will.

I got word from the Internet that week that Gary Numan was playing on September 11th in Shepherd's Bush, London, a five-minute walk from my sister's house. On top of that, Gary had an aftershow party going on where he would be after the gig. So I planned the trip, mainly to see Numan face-to-face for the first time in my life. It would be a dream come true to meet the man behind the music, and the time seemed perfect to ask his permission to write him and the influence of his music into the story of my life.

At this stage my idea was to get someone to write the book for me, as I had no educational background and my spelling was awful. In truth, I just had no confidence whatsoever in taking on such a task. With my job consisting of twelve-hour shifts from 8am to 8pm, it was a long day, and I had to run for a bus to get home by 9pm.

*

One evening I was offered a lift by a girl who was dropping another staff member home. I jumped at the offer. We dropped the other guy off and I sat in the front seat and just started chatting away. The girl's name was Sylvia Reilly, a really good-looking girl with a personality to match her amazing looks. She told me she was in a very unhappy relationship for thirteen years and wanted to get out of it, but knew the guy she was with would give her lots of hassle. We chatted away and got on so well. I told her I was in an unhappy marriage and going through a lot of personal issues in my life. We sat for ages laughing and joking about life in general. I asked her why she didn't just date another guy, and she said that most guys would be too afraid of the guy she was with. It all sounded like she was being held in a relationship of control and fear.

After that chat we saw each other in work and chatted away. Being in control of the security cameras, I often watched her on the cameras. One day I went out to pick up something for lunch and brought her back a teddy bear, and walked into the factory in front of all the staff and handed it to her. There was no way I was looking for any kind of relationship, as I was still very much living on the edge with my emotions and trying to find a way to try and just cope from day to day. But I must admit I got a very strange feeling when I talked to her, but couldn't for the life of me say what it was. She had this aura that seemed to surround her that I couldn't say I ever felt before from any human I'd ever met.

She told me she was going out one weekend with her mates to the After Dark Nightclub in Balbriggan. I told her I might meet her there. There was something drawing me to her, and every time I talked to her I got the same feeling sweeping up and down my heart. The last thing on God's earth I was looking for was a relationship of any kind, but it was nice to feel I had a friendship with Sylvia and we were both on the same wavelength.

I headed out on my own that weekend, following some strange instinct without being at all sure where it would lead. I bumped into her and her friends in the nightclub, and there was that feeling again shining down around us both as we talked and laughed. Whatever this bond was, it seemed to grow the more I talked with her, and it was something way outside my past experience. I was baffled by it but just went with the flow and enjoyed the wonder of being in her company.

As I walked her home and we chatted away, I felt like I had known her years. Now it felt like we were together a lifetime. When we got to her house I didn't keep her, as her boyfriend stayed in her mother's house and would be home from his own night out drinking. I asked her would she meet me midweek and I'd bring her somewhere. She agreed. So a date for that Tuesday night was set for 8pm. Sylvia had my phone number so we could keep in touch by text and through work. We both had to be careful as we were both still in relationships, and God knows what her boyfriend would do if he got wind of Sylvia talking to another man, never mind meeting up with one in secret.

When Tuesday came, Sylvia was to pick me up at the County Bridge in Balbriggan at 8pm. It was a mid July evening as I searched my mind to find the best place to bring such an amazing girl for our first real date. Sylvia thought I was going to take her to some lane and park the car for a few snogs. But I had something else in mind – a castle.

Two miles outside Skerries stood Baldangan Castle, and with its old stone walls it struck me as the perfect romantic place to bring a girl like Sylvia. As we drove the road to it, I gave her no hints as to where I was bringing her as I knew she had never seen the castle before. Just then it struck me as that for the second time in my life I was bringing a girl to a place to hide our relationship. It was eighteen years since I had taken Cathy to a secret hiding place, and here I was doing it all over again.

I knew danger surrounded what I was doing now as it had done all those years ago, except it was worse this time around. As we drove towards the castle grounds that night I had no idea what the outcome of all this was going to hold for us. I was being led by pure instinct. I took Sylvia's hand as we walked towards the castle gates and we entered the grounds side by side and just chatted away, unaware of the history on which we stood. The castle was steeped in stories of great battles dating back centuries. In 1642, two hundred men bled on the very grounds under our feet. There were stories of Cromwell, linking him to battles on these very grounds, but now in present time two people in their own personal battles opened up as the darkness fell over the castle and a mist came down, with only the moon now giving its light.

It felt so easy to just talk to her and laugh and joke about our lives. Just now and again she would drop her eyes down to one side, something I'd noticed her doing a lot since we first met. A shy look covered her face. She asked me to hold her, which I slowly did. You could sense her body wasn't used to being held like this. It felt so right holding her, and our bodies felt like they fitted together as if they were crafted to fit into such a moment as this.

The distinctive smell of Sylvia's hair and skin even seemed to be telling me something. I stood back on the castle grounds looking at the face of this amazing yet shy, beautiful woman who had a heart of pure love that had never been set free. A girl who had no interest in playing the games that so many people play in relationships and with people's hearts and lives. A girl trapped in a loveless relationship that had all but taken her very soul right away.

But under the moon that night her face and eyes filled the castle grounds with something so warm, so stunning and beautiful, yet I knew she wasn't seeing herself for what she was because of all that had been taken away from her, down through the years. My mind started to race back to all my ideas of love, the great ideas I had set up in my mind and heart of what an amazing relationship should be like.

Then, like a gentle breeze, there was that familiar voice, that feeling that followed me around telling me never to give up throughout my battle for Cathy all those years ago. There was that voice of promise that one day love would come back to me like some great reward that I now felt so unworthy of face-to-face with such beauty.

I could at last feel the great chain that had held me bound after losing Cathy break, the spell disappeared . . . and I was free once again. It felt like warrior horsemen had raced by my encounter with Sylvia and let swing with a sword, and cut something out of my heart that had held me captive for eighteen long years.

It all seemed so surreal, like a great plan unfolding, leading me forward to this moment – to this one person, Sylvia. I'd stood by the fact that soulmates weren't a myth. They were something very real, something deeply personal to me. Now here I stood with Sylvia on the war-torn grounds of a castle, of all places, with this soft voice telling me, Here she is, here's the soulmate you gave up so much for to battle and find.

A love came alive in my heart for this shy, beautiful woman under a full moon trying to break through the mist.

How could a man put words into any order when in a split second his heart is set free from what seemed like a cold prison cell to now love freely again? I was so conscious within that in front of me was the girl I'd searched my whole life for. I bent forward and drew Sylvia's face close to mine, her eyes drawing me deeper into her heart. Our lips touched softly, giving of a taste of feelings that seemed like they were dipped in the very core of love itself. And in that moment, within that kiss watched only by the light of the moon looking down upon the castle grounds, our love was sealed forever.

> *I'm wishing for something*
> *I don't know what I'm wishing for*
> *I'm dreaming of something*
> *I've never had before.*
>
> *Dreaming of Dreams*
> *Aslan 2000*

Into the graves below our feet, died all the empty lies of people who branded me cold-hearted, who said I'd never show love again, that I had nothing left to give in this life. All my self-doubt and dreaded fear of being unable to love again died and was gone forever from my heart. In its place, two souls were taken from two torn relationships that caused them both so much pain and were placed into an unbreakable love for the rest of time.

Flashes of the dream I had dreamt so many times of what often seemed as a kind of kiss of life that would one day wake me up from my coma state had now come to pass in fairytale surroundings. But this was no fairytale or fantasy. I knew all too well that beyond these castle grounds lay the real world of people who would try everything to tear down and break this love we had found together. Outside these walls lay a painful war that must be faced if we were going to stay together forever. I suppose it's true to say I pulled my own sword from the castle grounds that night to fight for the second time in my life for the heart of a girl.

Little did I know that, dating back to the 16th century, an old myth read that if you go into Smugglers' Cave two miles away and keep going, you'll come out at this castle's grounds. According to folklore it was only a myth and held no truth whatsoever. There was no connection, in spite of the old myth, through which you could tunnel your way from Smugglers' Cave to the castle.

But now, in 2004, there was a connection between the cave and the castle. My story. Two places I took the two girls I loved most in this life. Two forbidden loves separated by a gap of eighteen years. Two hideouts that were no longer connected by a mere myth but by two love stories.

I often wonder after that day, long after my first night taking Sylvia to the castle when I was told of the 16th century myth, was this the first time ever that an old myth became a myth no longer? It still sends a chill down my spine when I think how the two places were connected all those years ago. I'd wonder, in years to come, will people be telling their grandchildren this story as a kind of folklore love story.

It was time to head home and back out of the warmth of such a moment. The feeling hit me – This will draw you back into the spotlight. Even so, I'd talked to Karen about moving out, and the subject was very much on my mind before I met Sylvia. What about Aaron? What way would he take all this on board, and also, could my emotions take all this with my own deep problems that I was only beginning to try to sort out? Would my health be able to withstand another spotlight experience of this nature? I was back in the real world.

Some people have a very false view of meeting the love of their lives. That all your problems will disappear forever and ever and you'll sail into your lover's arms and that they'll fill your heart and soul with all you need to make you happy for eternity. But that's not the real world. I had found the woman of my dreams, but that didn't make all the mounting problems in my life disappear. If anything, it started a fresh painful new war in my life that was to be almost the death of me.

The next day, a friend in work who knew I took Sylvia out for a date asked me where I took her. I told him.

'Who do you think you are, Sid, King Arthur?' he said, laughing.

Another nickname that fitted the picture so well, I suppose.

We kept up our meetings at the castle, spending our time chatting, laughing, holding and getting to know each other better. We laughed, joked, kissed and loved each other under what we now called the castle moon. We kept everything hushed. I had talks with Karen about moving out, but I had to find a place to move to and somewhere I could afford. Sylvia lived at home with her ma and dad and boyfriend. So everything was pretty much up in the air. She was trying to tell her boyfriend it was over, but he wasn't listening to any of it. She hinted that she was in love with someone else, but he laughed it off and pushed it all to one side.

*

It was getting close to going to London to meet Gary Numan for the first time and see him play live again. My drug habit was creeping back slowly into my life as even with the therapy and meeting the love of my life I was still experiencing a lot of deep emotional pain and the tension at home was still ongoing. I started to take coke again. It numbed the pain and gave me the old back door feeling of getting away from what I was feeling. I'd sit with the old routine of listening to Numan on the headphones and have lines of coke on a CD cover hidden under the sofa on the floor, chopped and ready to snort. I'd slide it out, snort and push it back under carefully, and spend hours listening to the Pure album again. I heard Gary Numan was working on this new album, a kind of Pure Part II. But I knew that Gary had written Pure under the awful pain of the fact that he and his wife, Gemma had lost a couple of kids. Since then, Gemma had given birth to a girl, and I had a strong feeling that Gary's new album would be different. For some reason, I felt it was going to have a very big impact on my life like no other Numan album. The album was to be called Jagged Halo, but news was that it wouldn't be out until late 2005 or early 2006.

So it was London next, and the prospect of meeting Gary Numan . . . it was very surreal just thinking about it. I stayed with Breda, and as always had a great time chatting about my life, and about Sylvia and Aaron.

The gig was super as always. Numan sang with that stage presence that just can't be matched by any other singer in my book. And so to the aftershow party, and bang – there I was standing five feet away from my idol. My mind raced back to when I was alone listening to him in my damp room back in 1979. All that I drew in such a personal way from his words that had kept me sane for years came flashing into my mind.

I walked up and just said into his ear that I was going to write a book, and would it be OK to quote some of his songs. I didn't even let him answer, I asked him for a photo and that was it. Looking back, I was star-struck but didn't know it. I just stood there, one foot away, looking at him. He was very nice, and as he was leaving I asked him not to forget to come back to Ireland.

'I'll be back next year,' he said.

That was it. An amazing feeling, and with that experience I was back in Ireland facing the wars.

*

On the 13th October I found a place in Balbriggan to move into – an estate called Tara Court. With everything going on, I kept telling myself that Aaron would be OK about all this and understand it was for the best.

I couldn't have been more wrong. When Karen and I split the first time, Aaron was two years old and didn't understand, but he was now six years old and we had formed a very strong bond. Now he felt his dad was leaving him for good. The stress of watching him crying tore me up so badly, but I hid it well. It was the worst moment of my life to watch my own kid crying for me to come back home, to see his hurt, to see his face, knowing I was the cause of it. It did something to me, but it had come at just the wrong time for me.

I knew I couldn't go back. Even if Sylvia walked away from me, I still wouldn't have gone back to the relationship with Karen – it was over for good, but I was the only one who seemed to know it. Then the 'Eastenders fans' jumped into the frame – the kind of people who leap in when there's a problem to fuel the fire and to hand out bad advice when they'd be better off keeping their noses out. People said I didn't care about Aaron, that I was just interested in what I wanted in life. Nothing could have been further from the truth. There's always people who will want to hurt you more with their words for walking away from any relationship and to be honest, it opened my eyes to who were my true friends.

I was experiencing enough pain in my life and people just showed me how cold they really were by making me out to be some kind of monster for walking away from a loveless, failed marriage. Not one person asked me how this was affecting me. No-one cared. If you were to ask me today do I regret walking away, the answer would be no and will always be no.

The only thing I deeply regret is that my son got hurt by it all.

I still remember him ringing me in work just after I left, crying and screaming for me to come home. I still remember the first night he stayed over with me. I was making his breakfast when I heard him talking, and went into the front room to see him on his knees, with tears running down his small face, praying to God for his dad to come home. It just broke my heart. What do you say, what do you do in such a moment? It was an unspeakable, heartbreaking situation that no amount of words could ever explain. What do you say to the child you love with all your heart and soul that you can't go back home?

I knew people would say that if I didn't have Sylvia in my life, the break-up wouldn't have happened. They forget she wasn't there in 2000 when it fell apart. My leaving was on the cards well before she ever came into my life.

Two weeks after moving out I still hadn't let anyone know about myself and Sylvia, as she was still trying to find a way to get it out and make it stick that her relationship was over with her boyfriend, and that she was in love with me. I'd told her she was under no pressure from me when to do it, to take her time. But he was starting to cop on. Her boyfriend took Sylvia out to a restaurant, and over the meal she told him it was over, but wouldn't give the name of the person she was seeing. She came down to me after the meal and I told her not to do it for me, but for herself.

'Go up, Sylvia,' I said, 'and take your life back from him.'

She found the courage, went up to her house and told him and gave him my name. She got a kick and a box. Her dad pushed him out the door and told him never to return. But this was now the start of the war.

I talked to Karen and told her there was someone else. The timing wasn't great, but what time is right to break this kind of news? Sylvia's phone was ringing that night every two minutes, with threats being made on my life.

With a marriage at its very early stages of ending, with my dear son Aaron left crying and devastated at my leaving, with my therapy for my childhood problems still at its early stages, I was truly putting everything on the line and risking a serious breakdown in my health if I was going to make it to freedom with the love of my life. I had been pulled back into the spotlight once again for a woman's heart, and into another fearful unknown future.

Chapter Fifteen

BEYOND THE VISIBLE

Here is my small black box
Filled by hurt sent by you
Here is my small black book
Filled with lies told by you
Here is my small black house
Filled with fear, thanks to you
Here is my small black heart
Filled with shame left by you
Here is my small black doubt
Filled with tears cried for you
Here is my small black wish
Filled by dreams lost by you.

Pressure
Gary Numan, 2006

One of the greatest tragedies in life is the assumption that we can scope a person's character. If we spend enough time with another person we really think we have the right to give a true account of that person to another on the grounds of their actions and what they tell us. I once heard a man say that it wasn't until something happened in his life at the age of fifty-two that he truly knew who he was. He was amazed to find he never fully understood or knew himself till then.

If something very dramatic happens in your life at an early age, you will spend the rest of your life trying to live out of that painful experience rather than your true and real identity. It's like the child never grows to be who they are actually meant to be. Instead they grow up with a false identity, or as I'd put it, a false passport in life, going around from place to place under a fake persona, trying to fit in around people. The tragedy of this truth is that the person has no idea that this is true about them. They have no memory that can reach back to anything else but a painful existence as a child. They live their whole life from a place of pain, like a bone being pulled out of place that's never detected and left to continue to cause pain for the rest of their lives.

What's worse is the person is always trying to protect themselves from people getting in and causing deeper pain. They spend years working on their false passport to be seen as normal and themselves as someone that's accepted in the world by people they come into contact with. It becomes their life's goal. Always hoping the world will love them and take great notice of them. And if people don't, then the hurt they feel plays havoc with what already causes them hurt from their past.

Some people make sure everyone sees the good in them and are very skilled at dealing with others. They end up in some cases loving a person a great deal, but only to make themselves feel good about themselves and to feel safe and secure in their relationship. Always smiling, always the centre of the party. All of what I'm trying to explain can possibly be explained in a better way by an expert in the field of therapy, but what's important for me in this book to explain as we near the end of the story is this – I was running since I was a two-year-old child under a false identity. I'd spent forty years in this life carefully covering up pain after pain. It was something I was a master at doing. I'd started young and knew all too well how to hide away in my dark room of pain with my own heart and life – a room that I had carefully built.

But the tragedy of doing this is that you grow up with no idea of who you truly are and what your true identity is. And if it's unknown to you, then it's the same for everyone that comes into contact with you.

This is why I pointed out that it's nearly impossible to know a person's identity, and all you're left with is what you see them do or say. From that you can draw up a portrait of that person – but it's just a picture from what you see and what they say, nothing more than that. Your end result is always going to be the same, a fake portrait. You don't know that person as much as they don't know themselves. It's so tragic, yet so true. The horrific consequences of such an existence show themselves in so many ways. The most apparent is a discomfort in your own body. You just don't feel good in your own skin. There's this fear that doesn't just come and go, but that controls your life. Do what you may, you can't break free.

For me, I spent my whole life like this, and not for a split second was I aware of it. I never saw my true state and condition. All my life, up to this point and beyond, was made up of storing pain inside and putting out to the world around me that everything was OK. I always knew how to brave-face everything bad that happened to me, while underneath I was drowning in the pain of everything that had occurred down through the years. I'd always been this person I was. So how was I ever going to understand within myself that down under the floorboards of this dark room of anger, hurt and pain lay buried the priceless unknown true identity of one Patrick Bentley?

Unless I found it, I could never be the real me. I'd never be comfortable in my own body, in my own skin. If I could find it, my fears would be broken, and my worries about what the world thought or said about me would be banished from my life forever.

But all this was something I was totally blind to. I was in a dark place and still trying to pass through life with a false identity card. All I was used to in this world was fear and hurt that seemed in itself hard to cope with at the best of times. But conflict with people has been the curse of my life. My life from a kid onwards has been spotlighted because of an early life of crime, prison terms in abusive state-run schools like St Laurence's, terms in St. Pat's, Mountjoy and this all kept my long running clash with people in authority ongoing.

I've been wrongly imprisoned. I've experienced long-running battles with people for falling in love with a girl. I've had my life turned around by God only to see it slip away time and time again. I've had a broken marriage and a long-time battle with a Class A drug. I've watched as my six-year-old boy was hurt badly by my marriage break-up. Everything that's happened only served to enhance my fear of the world outside me. The very thought that I may be labelled as self-destructive and a reckless individual by people hurt me maybe more than anything else.

I had no identity to fall back upon, so all I felt was rage and anger and hurt towards people holding any bad view of me. People up to this point in my life could only come to one conclusion in their minds regarding me. I was heading for a completely destructive end. I don't blame people coming to such a conclusion, but anyone who held that view was sadly not dealing with all the facts of my life. They were falling into the trap of painting a portrait of someone who was unknown to them and to himself. I knew so little about myself, yet so many felt they had me all figured out in this life. How wrong we all were in the end.

My best friend down through the years, as I've said, was John Fold. He was the person who got closer to my world than anyone else. We both thought alike to the point where I wasn't sure if he was me and I was him at times. He would know what I was thinking before I said it. He was the only person who could sit down with me in a pub and we'd talk in code between ourselves and know what we were talking about but no one else had a clue. Any mess I got into in my life, he was always there to help me out. We laughed, drank and did everything mates do. I let him into my world, yet I let him into a counterfeit world. So, not even my closest friend knew the real me.

The true me lay trapped and alone in what now seems like another world. I've always been my own worst enemy as I stumbled to understand my problems. My falls in life have always been public, and it was always me that gave people the stones to throw at me. I gave people, in a sense, the guns. I even gave them the bullets to shoot me down with all my life. I then stood a wide open target, as always, as one by one the bullets came my way. Shots fired by people who even claimed to love me. Even now, people who knew I was in therapy for abuse showed no mercy. I had to stand time and time again and brave-face it and pretend it didn't hurt me at all. I couldn't show a weakness of any kind or I'd be playing into people's hands. I had to be strong and stand my ground for the one I loved, Sylvia, and take what came my way. But inside, the true story of what was happening beyond the visible was unfolding. A staggering story was waiting to unfold that would give me the perfect ending to my story, an ending I could never had foreseen.

One of the most important sides to this whole story is how and why the child in my past created this dark room within his heart that was unknown to the world outside. We all know the stories of a kid being hurt who over the years puts up walls to protect himself from people. It's the same idea, but I just saw it as this old dark room where for years growing up I saw this picture of a kid sitting alone looking out a small window. Hurt, trapped and always cold and looking like he's just trying to live, to survive. He couldn't speak or even try to explain how he felt inside. In order to remain alive emotionally, he maybe even created a mirror, and through this mirror he found the only way he knew to talk of how he felt, who he was, his anger and pain.

It became the mirror to reflect emotions and stories, but needed sound. And that sound, in my case, was the voice and music and words of Gary Numan. Numan's music was so perfect as it gave the air of feelings to do with isolation, hurt and anger at being unjustly treated by people. It's a running theme throughout all his work since 1979.

I was using the music for the same reason as the next person – because I loved the voice, the sound – but I had this other added dimension that ran very deep that I had no idea about over the years. Once Numan's voice hit my ears, it would travel to this dark room and express perfectly just how it felt living inside my heart.

I often said to Karen that if anyone took the time, they'd find me in Numan's music. It sounded like a joke at the time, but became a very true statement. For anyone who loves music, I'm sure there's always something very personal that's drawn you to a certain type of band or sound. Something that moves you, that you find hard to explain to someone else and at times to even yourself.

I'd spent twenty-six years studying Numan's music, album after album, because it spoke into my world year in year out. It never failed to reflect my life at its deepest level, from Replicas in 1979 to Pure in 2000. But what was to come in Numan's Jagged album was to far outreach them all. There was a closing of a ring waiting to be revealed in this album. Gary dropped the Halo from the name and just stuck with the name Jagged purely in an attempt to drop the idea of it being about God, plus his record label was called Jagged Halo. It was to be Gary's first album in five years so, understandably, all Numan fans were waiting for this eagerly. The expectation was mounting, but before I got to that part of the story, I had to stay afloat and avoid sinking and being lost in the seas of battle.

*

I wouldn't let a soul say a word against Sylvia. She and I stood side-by-side and let people throw whatever they wanted at us. A part of me tried to hide the fact that Aaron was, understandably, hurt by my break-up with his mother, but it was slowly tearing away inside me. It is something I wouldn't wish on anyone, but I had to get through it, like everything else.

However, only two days after we broke the news, windows were put in a couple of doors up from me, but the target was actually my house. That was just the start. A few days later, Sylvia's car was scraped with something rough down the sides. The cops were now in the picture. We knew who it was, but we had no proof and couldn't do anything about it. The next time 'Dog' was scraped on the bonnet. Threats were ongoing, and soon it was the talk of the whole town. The cops took statements, but even after seeing the guy running away one night after scraping the car, they still did nothing. Even with threats left on Sylvia's phone, no arrests were made. €3,000 worth of damage was done in an attempt to instil fear into our relationship and split us up.

When that didn't work, we were attacked in broad daylight coming home from work. We pulled into the driveway and Sylvia's ex jumped off a bike with a hammer in his hand. I hadn't time to get into the house where I had a baton just inside the door. Maybe it's just as well I didn't get my hands on it as he'd be dead and I'd be locked up. He got Sylvia in the stomach with the hammer, winding her, and he broke the windows in the front door. Again, no charges were made and the threats kept coming, so Sylvia changed her number.

I remember a guy I worked with saying to me that it would all cool down one day soon.

'No, it won't,' I said.

'Why do you think that?'

'If a person like Sylvia's ex controls another person's life for years,' I replied, 'and then that hold is broken, they are the ones who never get over it.'

It's a drawback, a life sentence, once someone loses control over the soul of another. It's nothing to do with love or losing someone they love, it's losing the control over them that kills them in the end. I saw this sort of thing all my life so I knew the war would rage on for a long time yet.

With our relationship out in the open we could go out from hiding in castles, but we always took trips up to the old hideout. The bond to the place has never left our hearts. We went out drinking where we had people coming up to me to say how different Sylvia looked, like she was a new woman, that I had saved her life. I'd just smile and made sure to say that all the credit should go to Sylvia for where she is today. I knew why they were saying Sylvia looked a million bucks, but for me she was the same woman I fell in love with the first time we dated. But now she was a free woman, and our love was getting stronger even with the pressure surrounding both our lives.

When Christmas 2004 came, I wanted to do what I could to make it less painful, so I stayed up with Aaron in Karen's on Christmas Eve and made the best of the time in such circumstances. The pressure was telling on me as I had to cope with attacks upon myself and Sylvia and her car, and abuse thrown at us in the street. I had the fallout of the marriage and Aaron's pain to try to cope with. How do you explain to a six-year-old child why he has just seen his dad leave home? It was like a cut that was bleeding inside of him. I tried to look like it was all OK with me. But my mounting problems were too much for me to handle so I started back into dabbling with coke to numb out the pain.

If I was going out clubbing I'd take ecstasy – the coke was for more personal use, sitting alone, snorting, listening to Numan. An escape from my growing pain into myself and down to the dark room inside. It never got in the way of my relationship with Sylvia, which is amazing when I look back at how bad things started to get with the coke. But I had to start taking these trips through the old familiar door into my self-made world to hide from what I felt, or to release what I felt through the music. I just felt so safe and so secure from the cold world outside. I could see the faces of people who now wanted my downfall to happen, who wanted me to fail and bleed. The intense anger was rolling along in the music and the words. I could see so clearly in those moments.

For hours I'd sit alone wondering as pictures and feelings raced through my mind, trying to make sense of my own feelings and caged world within, but couldn't. It was left always to Gary's songs to explain my feelings.

> *Who hasn't made a big mistake?*
> *Betrayed a love or turned to hate?*
> *You think it's you?*
>
> *Who hasn't told a small white lie?*
> *Or felt revenge was justified?*
> *I think that's you.*
>
> *Who hasn't had a secret need?*
> *A truth to hide, desires to feed?*
> *You think it's you?*
>
> *I look inside, a big mistake*
> *I'd make it stop, but it's too late*
> *I think it's you*
> *I know it's you.*
>
> *Halo*
> *Gary Numan, 2006*

*

With a drug problem now part of my life again, we drifted into 2005. After more damage to Sylvia's car we moved up to Baron's Hall, Balbriggan into a nice apartment where nobody could find us. Baron's Hall is such a big place that it would take an army to find out where you lived. We both worked away, and I went about trying to be there for Aaron and build a life together. Building up a relationship with him again was slow and the guilt was cutting me up badly. There were always times God came rushing across my mind and a deep sense of shame with it. I talked to Sylvia about it and she felt it was amazing to listen to. But I'd tell her,

'Don't look at me as an example of the Christian life – I'm its biggest failure. There's so many Christians who do live the life and don't have these setbacks like me. They'd be better to talk to than me.'

I knew the news of my marriage break-up was out in Christian circles, which just added shame upon shame. I could just imagine some folk saying, 'There goes his life again, another disaster.' I'm sure the story they got was I just upped and left, but whatever was said or not said, I knew it wasn't anything good. Sylvia took a big interest in what I told her about the Bible, but it just took me to a place of fear that I let God down one too many times. It haunted me from time to time like a ghost. In the night there came that lingering feeling that I was going to snap one day soon and be lost forever.

Looking back at my therapy session with Kate, she was like a lost mother to me and therapy surely saved my life from the point of total collapse. But I had barely touched on the big issues in my life and was still very much lost to the huge problems that held my life in such a dark grip. I was merely talking through stuff to get me through another week. But it was a learning experience, a stepping stone into the world of therapy for which I am forever grateful to Kate. I never told her I was having problems with drugs; I kept it hidden and wasn't facing up to it. I felt I was moving forward so I was improving somewhat. But really, I was starting to live a double life. One was loving Sylvia and having a ball being around her warm heart; the other was the desire to switch into my dark room and block even Sylvia out. Numb and coked up to the eyes, it was time to visit the dark room and hide from the uncaring abuse by people and my past junk.

Aaron slowly started to come and stay with us, which was great. He gradually opened up to Sylvia and they became best friends, which was super to see happen. Kids do bounce back from stuff like this, but it didn't help my sense of guilt for what he was still going through. It's never left me even up until today as I write this book. But breaking the ice with Sylvia started us down the road to rebuild our relationship, which I'm so thankful for.

The abuse in the streets with Sylvia's ex came to a head when he got too close and I gave him a few boxes. He picked up a rock and followed me up the street and tried to get close enough to throw it. We ended up in the middle of the street stopping cars getting by as he tried to get a shot back at me with the rock. The cops came and he was arrested, but I was charged with a public order offence as well. We were both fined, and the judge told us to shake hands outside after the court hearing.

*

I was looking for some inspiration and direction after the court hearing ended, and it came in an unexpected form – the 2005 film Cinderella Man starring Russell Crowe. Films have always played a big part in my life down the years. It's the same for us all, we all have our favourite through the course of our lives that somehow touches something deep inside us, and we never forget the moment we saw it and how it felt. To name just a couple of films, one that truly touched something in me down the years is This Is My Father, with James Cann and Aidan Quinn, a true story of forbidden love. The Shawshank Redemption, and Instinct with Anthony Hopkins, both touched something deep within that's never left me. But no film ever touched me as deeply as Cinderella Man.

The film is the true story of a boxer named James J. Braddock who went to the top as a boxer in the late 1920s, early 1930s. He had it all – money, fame, the world at his feet. But with the Great Depression of the 30s looming, Braddock, nursing a broken right hand, lost everything and ended up in poverty. With his wife Mae and his kids to support, he ended up working the docks. The film is about Braddock's climb out of a dark hole and certain ruin, and against all the odds getting back into the ring and fighting like a different boxer than the one who had lost everything. Braddock was now fighting to survive, and within twelve months he was given a shot at the Heavyweight Championship of the World. In 1935, from labouring in the docks with a broken hand, Braddock carried the hopes and dreams of the working class on his shoulders and faced the overwhelming favourite, Max Baer. James. J. Braddock, the 10/1 outsider, took the title off Baer to become the sport's most popular World Champion in history and was famously dubbed the Cinderella Man.

I'm sure at a time in my own fight and struggle I saw something of myself in Braddock. My whole life seemed to reflect a long-running battle that seemed always against the odds. I always seemed to be so close to victory in life that I could almost taste it, but each time it would be lost or taken away from me. The game went on but victory always eluded me, leaving me full of self-doubt and anxiety attacks and frequent nights of poor sleep. I was uptight and stressed in my body due to frequent flashbacks to my childhood abuse and loss, particularly of my mother's tragic death. But certain things such as the Cinderella Man story gave me a hope that one day I'd win this conflict. Sylvia bought me the book The Cinderella Man which inspired me further. If she was texting me she'd call me the Cinderella Man, a name she still calls me face-to-face as well from time to time.

*

With Aaron slowly on the return to himself, things seemed to be turning around slowly for me. I hoped my luck was at last changing as some flashes of light seemed to be opening up a road ahead of me that I hoped would bring my world within to some place of settlement.

A date was set in March 2006 for the release of Gary Numan's Jagged album, with a launch gig in the Forum in London. Sylvia liked his music too, so we planned a trip over to the gig as a breakaway from the pressures of the past year. I was still working in the security job and was doing nightshifts. I wasn't sure of the venue for Numan's gig so one night while working I went on a break and sent an email to a Numan fan on a computer just to give him my number to ring me. I told him not to email me back. I went home and slept and woke up to a message left on my phone not to go into work but to go to a meeting the following day at head office. Word got to me before the meeting that it was over the email.

When I got to the meeting I wasn't given any pre-warnings or asked to have a witness present to hear what was said. I was just taken in and sacked over the one email I'd sent. I didn't think anyone would mind me sending one email. No written warnings, just sacked. I appealed it, but the sacking stood, so I took another unfair dismissal case. It was now November 2005 and it left me with no job for Christmas. Another fight to try to overcome. But the cleaning case came up to the employment courts and I won my case easily. It felt like a great revenge over what they had done to me. But such feelings are never healthy and only ever pushed me further out emotionally to a darker part of the sea that was already drowning me in its anger.

*

I started to have a string of strange nightmares about my mother. She was always smiling and telling me to move on with my life. I'd wake up not knowing what to make of them and always in a pool of sweat and deeply upset. I still couldn't hold a clear picture of my ma in my mind and unclear feelings about her tragic death began to haunt me. But like everything else I pushed the feelings to the back of my mind and switched everything to just moving on with my uncertain future. All I looked forward to in life was Sylvia, Aaron and what was now becoming a kind of holy grail album, Jagged.

I'd say I'd worn out all of Numan's albums and had come to a very sad and painful time in my life that matched nothing that had gone before. The album Pure covered another time that maybe by now I'd passed through, and something inside craved a whole new and fresh Numan album that just maybe would again reflect what had now become the breaking point years. I suppose the wear and tear of years of trying to cope with failure, hurt and pain and abuse covered with the haunting sounds of letting God down so badly had now pushed me to a new place within, and I craved to reflect how it felt to be now breathing and alive within my own body and soul. Something so deep inside wanted to tell a story of how it felt that I couldn't explain humanly. It shows me, now looking back, the measure of pain, hurt and anger I was trying to hold back and conceal.

All of this was very much going on in my subconscious. I'd no idea Gary's music was being used to this degree in my life since I was fifteen years of age. I had no idea it was coming to a climactic ending. All I saw were the warnings from time to time. Sometimes I felt what I could only describe as a flash in my mind of me screaming louder than any sound I'd ever heard, like a bomb going off inside.

With just two days to go to the Numan gig in London, and just days after the release of Jagged, we were shopping to pick up a few last bits before heading off. I planned to pick up the album in London as I never imagined it would reach here in such a short time. But to my surprise, Sylvia just popped into HMV and came out holding the one single copy they had. Well, you can just imagine me tearing off the plastic to open it. I couldn't wait to get back to the car to put it on. I still recall those first seconds of the song at the start of this chapter, Pressure. A haunting, slow build up of Eastern Arabian sounds, then came the voice:

Here is my small black box.
Filled by hurt sent by you.

Before the first song had ended I knew Jagged had moved, touched and captivated me like no past Numan album had (or had even come close to). All my pre-instinctive feelings about Jagged being something so different and so deeply personal were met with a sense of being totally lost as each song, in word and sound and feeling, held up before me the perfect dark un-told picture of everything I'd been through and felt but could never say since my mother was killed in 1995. I don't think it will ever be possible for anyone but myself to ever understand just how much that bit of music, word and sound meant to me. It held up a statement of a man devastated by something outside of him and things he did as a result of that, an album of hidden pain and desires. For me, it told a story of hurt, pain, fear and failure. It was the album that looked back at all that had taken place and now spoke of all I'd been through. There was in the words of a song like Pressure a statement to certain people who hurt me but got away with it, because all people saw was my failure rather than the truth. It was really a statement to those who cut me down over the ending of my marriage. Even the music bore a feeling that matched the words to the song.

The song Fold, which was second on the CD and which I put in the chapter Hope Bleeds, told for me the story of when I was falling down to my lowest in 2000. It's a song of justified anger at people who fed on seeing me in pain and how I wanted to fold them out of my life forever. Halo was for the self-righteous people who tried to make sure they looked innocent and sinless to the world around them. In so many ways Jagged is about my own fear of being where I now found myself in life. It's about a man who feels a very intense fear that he's shamed God to the point that there's no hope of being forgiven by him. There's a song called Blind that musically and lyrically may go down as the one perfect song that captures my fall from God and how it felt inside for years.

> *I look at what I've become*
> *I'm a pure and perfect lie*
> *Like a blind man falling*
> *Scared and helpless*
> *And I'm still falling from grace.*
> *I stumble*
> *In the depths of my sin*
> *On my knees*
> *I'm a sick man drowning*
> *Don't leave me blind*
> *I'm so cold.*

Now armed with what I could only describe as the last in a great long-running story of albums, Jagged is the last great symphony of sound of a man lost, angry, in a lot of pain and now at the threshold of delivering a final statement of his deepest feelings of what he felt and who hurt him, and the lies that people told to cover up their own shame.

I sat at home that evening after getting my hands on Jagged. I played it over and over, soaking it into and down to the darkest recesses of my nightmare existence. What would this amazing album sound like live in London in a couple of days' time? What need would it feed? I was in love with Sylvia, yet holding my world together by my fingertips, but feeling like my world lay safe and happy under the sounds of Jagged. But deep down inside this self-made dark room of pain and hurt, unknown to me, a crack was appearing that was going to lead to a leak, and from that leak I was led face-to-face with certain death and beyond to the Born Identity.

Chapter Sixteen

BORN IDENTITY

Fear can hold you prisoner. Hope can set you free.

The Shawshank Redemption

> *I pray every night*
> *And I'm losing my faith*
> *Sometimes I call out for you*
> *And sometimes I'm afraid.*
> *So I beg God*
> *For salvation of an angel*
> *And I ask God*
> *Can he forgive me?*
> *I think it showed me heaven*
> *And now I know why I'm scared to die.*
> *Am I a fool in the dark?*
> *Am I the ghost in my dreams?*
> *Am I afraid of the truth?*
> *I don't know.*

> *In a Dark Place*
> *Gary Numan, 2006*

The lights dimmed as the haunting intro music from banks of synthesisers sounded out and up through the floorboards under our feet, causing the hairs on my neck to stand. After a couple of bags of cocaine, my senses were hyper sensitive and experiencing a deeper pleasure as the sounds raced up my body. The music died down and out walked Numan as cool as ever, voices chanting his name filling the air over the dying sound, and then it was an hour and half of the whole Jagged album which, of course, sounded far better than the CD. I held Sylvia from be-hind and drank in the words and music in the deepest and most personal way as Numan gave what a lot of fans felt to be his best gig to date. For me, Gary was sensational and the new album sounded and felt like nothing he had ever done before; it sang deep down inside yet again and fed a hunger and need inside my heart like a great antidote to all I now felt and was experiencing in 2006.

With my arms wrapped around Sylvia, the sweat running down my face, I hung on every word from Gary's mouth as if my life depended on it. Feeling so close to her and hearing Numan play to us both felt like a perfect moment in my life. But in the wider scope of things, I was a man in a lot of pain and was merely now using a perfect album of music to help me air that out. Deep inside, I was troubled and very much on a spiral plunge.

When we got back home to Balbriggan, I moved back to Skerries, my own home town, with the intention of getting away from some of the hassles of Balbriggan. On the outside it worked fine and I was far happier to be living back in Skerries, but there was a steady increase of the inner pain deep inside. Kate, my thera-pist, moved back to Wexford and I didn't pick up with anyone else. I gave her a lovely framed picture of Sylvia and me at the gig in London just before Numan came on. It was very hard say-ing goodbye to her; she was such a great person and such a help to me over the past two-and-a-half years, and in many ways her work with me saved my life from breakdown in 2004.

*

My relationship with Sylvia grew closer and closer, which was no small miracle, considering my inner turmoil. She gave me so much love and support that it is still hard to believe a girl can love as much as she can. But my back door to escape, to mix co-caine with joints and cover my mind and heart with the sounds of Jagged, was becoming a big problem. When Sylvia would be away working, I'd take weekly trips to my dark room existence where I'd feed the craving hunger to visit all that was truly me on the inside, away from the all-seeing eyes of the world and all that I felt wanted harm to come to me. I'm sure to many it was just a dangerous game of drugs and dark music. But to me, it was nothing short of a case of survival from some total collapse within the frame of my body.

Once Sylvia and I were in love and getting closer I'd be OK, I thought. What harm was I doing sitting alone in a room listening to music and taking coke? When we went out it was more of the same, cocaine and a few Es to be washed down with drink, and then I was untouchable. For me, there was nothing that matched a night out in the Milestone Disco in Balbriggan where the friendly DJ there always played a song from the Jagged album for me. Standing with outstretched arms on a dance floor as songs from Numan screamed into my drug-filled mind. Those five minutes were so well disguised in a dance, yet in reality terms I was downloading forty plus years of hate, anger and injustice which was truly ripping my world apart. The dance always looked something so out of the ordinary; at the end of the day it was Gary Numan. But I loved it. I could always nearly taste the feelings that raced up my body and into the air around me. It was that intense. It became a kind of therapy to me again, like it was back in 2000. Only now, it was just all slowly running out of control before my very eyes.

In June, I made another trip over to see Gary in Hammersmith Palais, where again I was very much out of my head on coke and Es. The gig was super and after it ended I met his lovely wife, Gemma, who is such a down-to-earth woman. After talking to her, I met Gary for the second time in my life. The first thing I said to him was would he give Sylvia a kiss, which he did. Then there I was standing face-to-face with Gary Numan again. So much happened in those moments; I wanted to say, Gary, I think Jagged is your best album and I just wanted to explain how much it meant to me. But I was lost in the moment, and then someone else asked him something and that was that.

I stood up at his car next to him as he chatted to his fans and just took in the moment. Someone took a photo of me talking to him, but I've never liked it – it is so clear I'm on drugs. But a lovely moment all the same.

Back home, the cracks deepened inside and my emotions caused me deeper upset as concealing the pain of what I truly felt got harder to hide from the world outside mine. The next big event was my youngest brother Simon's wedding to his beautiful girlfriend Corrina. He asked me to be best man, which I was only too proud to be. Simon, like me, had a very hard upbringing, so it was a fairytale ending for them both to make it to where they now found themselves, having worked so hard. Looking back to that proud day, it amazes me how well I hid the true nature of what was happening inside me. The turmoil underneath stayed under control until late that evening when I found myself alone in the car park in Sylvia's car listening to Jagged, coked out of my head.

The frustration was so unpleasant as the echoes of past hurt crept up, forcing me to merge myself with the sounds as I chain-smoked out the window. Inside, I slowly retreated back into the shadows, out of sight, out of sound. It's another small miracle that my relationship with Aaron still seemed to be improving all the time. When I was with him, my love for him always just took over the moment and I entered a different zone in which I just felt as one with him. I always loved taking him to the Skerries 100 Road Races and bringing him around to see the top riders and get photos taken with them. He loved the buzz and just hanging out together.

By 2006, the main interest on the bike scene came from a local rider, Martin Finnegan, from just down the road in Lusk. Martin was winning the likes of the Skerries 100 and most of the top races around Ireland. For the fans in the South of Ireland to have a rider with such talent was unheard of in the history of biking in the Fingal area. The following he had was surreal. He was simply loved by thousands of fans everywhere he went.

By this stage I was drawn to a rider by the name of Darren Lindsay who, in my opinion, was one of the nicest guys the sport ever produced, along with Martin. You never felt it was a wrong moment to come and chat to him. He always wore a childlike smile that would light up any paddock on a rainy day. I took Aaron over to him with a birthday present that day and he couldn't thank us enough. As good a rider as anyone in his day but outside of riding bikes he was one of the most down-to-earth and warm human beings I've ever had the honour to meet.

After a win at the Ulster Grand Prix, Darren was back at Skerries for the September Killalane Road Races. I had Aaron staying that Saturday and didn't go up to the practice as I was taking him up for the racing next day. The phone rang. It was John Fold to tell me there had been a serious crash at the practice. It wasn't long before it emerged that Darren Lindsay had been killed off his 600 Honda. The sense of disbelief at the news just left me numb all over. It's probably true to say Darren was the most fun-loving character the sport of road-racing had ever known. His death shook me far more than I expected, mostly because I had never let myself admit how much he had impressed me as a person. It just struck me after he passed from this life. I still find it hard to look at a picture of him, as I do often with riders I loved who lost their lives doing what they loved best.

*

On a brighter note, I was still doing my own research into how I was going to write my book, and one of the things I was hoping to get as part of the project was the famous Smugglers' Cave painting I gave to Cathy back in the late 1980s. To do that, I had to try to get in touch with her. I gave my phone number to one of her friends, and a couple of weeks later she texted me. I'd only talked to Cathy a handful of times since we split up back in 1990, and we had both moved on in life and matured a lot. The painting had been misplaced over time and couldn't be found. But Cathy and I stayed in touch and talked through the relationship break-up. We cleared the air, and became great friends. It was great for once to have a girl I dated as a friend. I was so used to break-ups that ended with no-one ever talking to each other again, or some bitter root left behind that spelt out the truth that some people never loved each other at all; they merely needed the other person to block something out in the circles of their insecurities. When they lost the relationship, all that was left was pure hate which, in my opinion, exposes the truth that they never loved the person to begin with.

The next stop was the Electric Picnic festival where Numan was playing in the three-day event. I went alone as the tickets were €175 and I was only going to see Gary – I had no interest in anyone else. I stood up at the front with what was only a handful of Numan fans surrounded by a multitude of people who would never have heard Numan play before. So I put in the extra shouts, to make sure Gary knew there were fans in the crowd. He walked out on to the side just before the gig and gave us a wave and away we went into what was, for me, his best performance ever. Not bad, I thought, for a man struggling with Asperger's Syndrome.

*

By Christmas 2006, I was really struggling with my emotions and fears. I wasn't making it any better for myself, as my co-caine habit was getting way out of hand. I spent all Christmas Day coked out of it. I had to tell people I had a cold so they wouldn't get suspicious as to why I was snuffling all the time. I was suffering serious flashbacks to just about everything bad that happened to me growing up and in later years. I was feeling so uneasy around just about everyone now, bar Sylvia and Aaron. I'd ring John Fold and ramble on about a load of rubbish, trying to drag out of a fag as my body raced from the coke. I lived and slept trying to coke out pain all the time. My body was growing weak and I looked awful. I felt like a tormented soul from the time I got up to the time I slept. I suffered from nightmare after nightmare, and slowly felt beyond the point of help. Sylvia knew I was using, but not to the extent that I was. Once our relationship was close it didn't matter after that.

But things took a sudden and major change on the night of my birthday that February. Unknown to me, Sylvia was listening to a CD from a Christian group I had picked up on the streets of Dublin in the summer of 2005. On her way to work that night, she asked God to save her and to come into her life. When she told me, and I saw the change in her life, it had a big impact on me for the good. I gave up all the drugs and started to sort out taking Sylvia to a Christian church in Dublin. For the first time in many years, I saw hope at last in getting my relationship with God back, the loss of which I considered to be at the root of all my unhappiness. We moved into a smaller church near our home in Swords, Co. Dublin where we really started to get our lives sorted out. Knowing how much I loved Sylvia and having my relationship with God back felt like a light at the end of what was a very long, dark tunnel of drugs and inner conflict and pain. There was just one problem if we were going to make it together, and it was a problem I wasn't ready for.

To remain in a relationship with Sylvia, I had to get a divorce as I was still legally married to Karen. It was even said to us by a pastor that we should split up until I got the decree of divorce. From what seemed like light at the end of a tunnel, the vision within my own tunnel seemed to get dark again. Sylvia and everyone else took it OK but all of a sudden I felt trapped, as all my inner fears and pain arose to start haunting me once again. I was a guy very much in love who saw at last a hope to make my life work, only now I had to face a divorce.

I asked Karen about it and she had no problem with the fact there was no possibility of reconciliation, plus Aaron was being well taken care of. The only problem was that by law you have to be separated for four years, and Karen and I were separated for only two-and-a half. My case was that we lived apart long before the marriage ended and that's the date I put on the document. I just hoped Karen wouldn't contest the document, and I'd be free to get on with my life and not have this holding me back. I became more and more stressed out as this awful feeling of being trapped in my life came over me to haunt me along with my other problems.

A date was set for the hearing in June 2006. Four weeks before the case came up, the tension spilled over with Karen over our conflicting statements as to when the marriage ended. My case stood that my state of health emotionally made it impossible for me to hold a relationship down with Karen of any kind. But she had her rights, and from her point of view we were still married until the day I left in October 2004. So by now we were not on speaking terms. One of the last times I took documents to Smithfield's Family Law Courts (as I was representing the divorce myself), I got this amazing sense of God's peace that spoke these words in my heart: I am going to set you free. It was so strong that it left me feeling everything was going to be OK at last in my latest attempt to salvage my life.

On the morning of the hearing, I felt sick all over. I had my case, but I was hoping Karen would stay at home and I could get my divorce and move on with my life. I kept watching the clock on the wall as it hit 9:55am. Sylvia was cool and kept saying,

'It doesn't matter if you don't get it, you'll get it next year.'

But in my mind, if I didn't get it I couldn't move on with my relationship with God and Sylvia without giving people something to hold against that relationship. So it was again the fear of what people think and say that was fuelling my fears in the end.

10:00am came and in walked Karen. I kept telling myself, Don't worry, God said he's going to set you free, so stop worrying. But as we both got called to face the judge, all my fears of courtrooms as a kid and people in a state place of authority swept over my heart and mind, and panic set in. I started dropping papers and stumbling over my words. Everything I seemed to be saying was mixed up and I could feel a panic attack gripping my body. Karen just stated about the four years of being apart being the law. The judge asked if I had anything to ask Karen. I had stuff to ask in order to bring my case forward but I was finding it hard to breathe, so I just said no. The judge gave the verdict that if it wasn't four years, he couldn't grant the divorce and that was that. Where was the promise from God that I'd be set free? Why did I make such a mess of the case?

I walked out of the court and my vision went blurred. I put my hand in my pocket and took my phone to find an abusive text from someone who lived beside Karen. I rang the number to make sure it was the right person who answered the phone. I just hung up and left it. My body felt like it was drowning as Sylvia said,

'It's grand, Patrick, you'll get it next year.'

But what nobody knew was I hadn't got another year. This experience was to prove too much, even for me.

Something cracked that day in court, and now after forty-three years of hiding, running, blocking out pain after pain, finally the vital blow struck a leak within the well-structured walls of my self-made dark room of pain. As I tried to get air into my lungs that day and gather my thoughts, the vision in my sight remained blurred and shot with an overwhelming sense of inner pain. The next day when we picked Aaron up from Karen's, we were met with sneers and laughs from certain people who live up that way. It just brought home to me how people would rather see you dead than happy. Christians in the small church near Swords said,

'Sure there's always next year – don't worry about it.'

But no-one saw my state inside, no-one knew the history of pain I was concealing all my life.

*

My life from the day of the divorce hearing onwards was like one long battle to hold on to my sanity. I felt myself unable to cope as the leak of pain from within began to poison every part of my day with a deep discomfort, as if my body was trying to cope with the toxic waste of years of anger, pain and hurt. But now a crack had struck the wall of a great dam, and it was only a matter of time before I'd reach for the painkillers – cocaine and my Gary Numan music. And if I slipped out of God's hands this time, I felt like my last chance would be gone forever. What awaited me seemed like the last fall into the depths of total despair where everyone would wash their hands of me and stand back as I sealed my own fate in my own blood, forever.

I sat alone snorting coke as Sylvia headed off to work, surrounded by guilt, shame, and overwhelmed by the dreaded sense of failure yet again. I held my mobile phone in my hand as I sank down into my dark room to visit my pain and anger through the loud sounds of Jagged to try to dull out my senses to pain. I felt like texting Karen and telling her, Karen, I don't have another year, let me go.

But fear of people reading into my unprotected heart drew me back. For the first time since I sat down to draw from Gary Numan's music back in 1979, it wasn't working for me. I pressed from one song to the next screaming inside for some kind of relief, but something was wrong. All I could see were the faces of people who hurt me for forty-three years. The anger was choking me inside. I wrapped my arms round my body, took some sleeping pills to knock myself out.

Come Saturday, I asked Sylvia to come out with me. I thank God she did. I took coke and popped an E tablet. Everything seemed

OK. We went to the Bruins Pub in Balbriggan and I came up on the E tablet, which was very strong. We were out in the smoking room when someone who had been giving me and Sylvia dagger looks for a couple of years came in. One smart, cold look from her became the final push. I never got my composure back after that. Years and years of people's rejection of me made me snap in that moment, sending me into a nightmare.

Everyone I tried to talk to afterwards, I couldn't click with. Like a painful noise in my head, everything seemed cold and disjointed all around me. Even talking to Sylvia seemed out of place. I tried to click back into a warm, nice buzz but I couldn't. We went up to the Milestone Disco up the road. I walked in and up to the DJ and she said,

'Which song from Jagged do you want me to play?'

'I think the one I've never danced to, the song itself, Jagged,' I said.

A song that told my feelings of pain and anger, a song I felt was a true reflection of what I thought was nearing the end of my story of how I thought people saw me, and in part what I thought of them.

As I walked out on to the dance floor, sweat dripping down my face, my heart pumping with anger and pain, it truly was a fitting song for a fitting end. The lights of the dance floor shone down over my head as the crowning of the Jagged Halo song sang out its final statement, its final painful cry of forty-three years of injustice and of self-hurt, the final destruction of my life was now complete and on show for everyone to witness.

They say I'm forgiven and I have to pay
They say that I turn innocence to panic
But I don't care.
I sink to my knees
Head in my hands
So now I'm just a shadow
On their bleeding hearts.
What have we become?
What does a confession ever do
But take my guilt away?

Jagged
Gary Numan, 2006

I gave it everything I had left inside. I slowly walked off the dance floor clutching the most intense anger I'd ever experienced. Then in a split second, the death of my mother engulfed me, flashes of the lorry hitting her small body, plunging her to death and out of my life forever became real. The place started to spin as I tried to fight the feelings off, but in the end I told Sylvia to get me home.

When I got home the pictures returned, but this time the painful feeling ripped up my insides. I lay on the bed holding Sylvia and let out a scream or what may have sounded like an intense screeching cry and slowly came out of it. I sat up and for the first time since that awful morning when I had heard the news of my mother's death twelve years ago, I felt I was back to the person I had been before the shock of that morning. It began to dawn on me that the loss of my mother had sent me into some kind of emotional coma, and now I'd just woken up from it and felt the pain of her loss for the first time ever.

Everything seemed to make sense of the way my life went after her death. The day back walking up the town in Rush when I felt a sudden pain that dimmed even the light around me that day. I talked to Sylvia for hours, and made up my mind to go up to Karen's and tell her I didn't blame her for everything that had happened with the marriage breakdown, that the awful change in me was due to my ma's death.

I went up and put flowers on my ma's grave and started to deal with it slowly. But within my own body things didn't change as far as the pain, the anger, the dark room were concerned; the curse remained hanging over my life. If anything, the pain increased from that experience. The fear of everything that had happened and what people thought of me deepened. I feared like never before in my life.

*

I woke up on the morning of August 31st 2007 with one thing on my mind: I've got to get some cocaine and some grass and numb out these feelings before they swamp me with pain. I picked up three bags of coke and grass around 6pm, and headed back to the house to get lost in a night of blocking out everything that was clutching at my heart and soul. It was the day I gave up on ever sorting out my inner pain, it was a day like no other I've ever known. I was a completely broken man inside. The coke was chopped up and put into lines, and the night of blocking out started around 8pm. Line after line went up my nose as I dragged on a joint of grass. The clock on the wall ticked by as Gary Numan's DVD of the Jagged gig in London played on the TV. The clock hit 12:30am.

Time stood still as I took those couple of potentially fatal last lines of coke and walked down towards the loo. Then bang, the awful whispering voice and the dreaded words, You are dying from an overdose. You have stepped over the line.

The panic, the fear rising, the feeling that my very soul was being taken from my body.

'It's over, it's all over. I'm dying, Sylvia.'

240

Then the next minute I was on the sofa, gasping for air as I slipped in and out of time, out from the world we can all see around us to the unseen world. Everything was about to unfold, as if a grand plan was coming to a close with me at the centre. At a time when I'd given up all hope and in truth, everyone had given up hope in me, now sitting after taking a load of coke, the one person me and everyone else never imagined would turn up did – God himself. But it wasn't all nice. The first thing I saw that I'll never forget as long as I live was God standing back, maybe to let me see what's really behind the world of cocaine, maybe just to wake me up to tell others.

Sylvia was standing over me trying to get me back from where I had slipped to, when over her left shoulder came this black, faceless thing that opened like a black wall to the point where I couldn't see Sylvia anymore, just this black being that went for me and pinned my hands to the wall of my apartment. I screamed because I felt like it wanted to take my life and kill me.

But God just pushed it back and it left. I kept seeing it in the room trying to attack me, but each time God pushed it back. If anybody really wants to know what's behind cocaine, what sort of power you're dealing with, well, I've seen it up close and personal. I put a name on it, the Spirit of Illusion.

*

I thank God for his mercy that night, for showing me this, yet keeping me safe from it. After this black faceless wall was taken out of the frame, God, in a sense, put his hand inside me and BANG! – there was a sudden rush of the strongest emotional pain I'd ever felt. What happened was that God blew away for-ever this dark room of pain that stayed inside me since I was a child. The root cause of all my pain and suffering went up in smoke. All the fear that had controlled my life since I was a child was broken forever. All the fears of what people thought of me, how all my life was just one long painful story of trying

241

to fit in, trying to get people to like me and fearing all the time they didn't, suffering pain all the time as a result. All that was removed from my life that night forever.

The carefully built room inside that was constructed by a child was gone. All that remained from the blast was splinters; the main work was done by a miracle of God. The splinters could now be removed, one by one, in time. What mattered was that it seemed that God in his mercy set a time and place to meet up with me and heal my life once and for all, and set me free from the need to hide, to take cocaine and stay behind the door of a dark room of pain and hurt and fear.

I had no idea that night that all this was happening. It took time to unfold and to become clear to me. I remember crying that night as all the hurt, pain and fear that I'd spent my life concealing within the walls of this room finally burst its banks and poured out. But before this encounter came to its close with God, he did one last thing for me, and then the experience was complete and ended.

After God removed all this stuff from within that dark room inside me, he, in a sense, resurrected my original, lost identity from under the rubble and smoke of the remains and put into place the one thing I've never had, the Real Me, like a bone that was out of place since birth suddenly being set back into place, removing forever the pain I had been blocking out all my life. In truth, I'd spent forty-three years never comfortable in my own body and skin. A bit like Jason Bourne in the film The Bourne Identity, always trying to find out who he was. Now I knew who I was for the first time in my history and my long, painful search was finally over.

I'd never have to spend my days trying to fit into this world or to try to get people to like me or accept me. I was me, the real me. I became the person I would have been if all the hurt, pain and abuse hadn't happened. I was set free in the end by the one and only person who truly knew me, who knew my pain, my hurt, my hidden tears and fears.

The timing was so perfect when I look back now. I'd been written off by just about everybody. My whole life was one of almost making it, for it to cave in every time. People got tired of me, and my yo-yo life made no sense to anyone in the end. At the point of what seemed like my last great fall in life, God, in his great mercy and love, stepped in to do what the whole world could never do for me, heal me and give me my identity and place me back in time to enjoy the rest of my life as the Real Me.

*

I awoke the next morning still unaware of any of this, still coming to terms with what had happened the night before. I walked out to the sitting room and the first thing I did was turn on the TV and found that Gary Numan's DVD Jagged was still in the DVD player. I put it on, and after less than a minute, I noticed something very odd about it but couldn't make it out. The songs were the same as last night, but something was missing that took a while to figure out. There was no pain, no anger, no hurt or injustice. Just a clean feeling inside my heart. I still loved the music, but the unhealthy crutch I had used Gary's music for was gone from within my heart.

My mind raced back to the young fifteen-year-old sitting in his damp room listening to his first Gary Numan album Replicas and how he'd used the music ever since as a dark reflection of a dark room within which all his pain had been stored.

But now God had removed all that, and there I sat looking at the face of Gary knowing just how much the man's music had kept this one man sane for twenty-nine years.

From where I was sitting, I peered out through the glass door next to me, out and up to the blue sky above. How could I ever describe what it felt like after all I'd been through in this life to have all that pain removed from my body for the first time in my life? What did it all mean to me? If there was ever a time in this book when I felt completely lost to explain something, it's here.

God had moved into my life even though I had let him down over and over again. He turned up and broke out of his timeless world to touch me and set me free. The whole thing is so unworthy of human words; it's so priceless and means so much to me.

I'd received a real second chance to make it with God in this life, and I knew nothing would be able to remove this miracle from my heart. I was put to the test very soon when I told people who I thought would find this amazing, only for them to say,

'God doesn't turn up when you're on drugs.'

If someone had said that to me before September 1st I'd have been so hurt, but now it didn't matter what people said or thought about me. I knew who I was, and I was learning for the first time in my life to like who I was outside of what people said or thought of me. I felt the freedom of being me without being pulled down by what people thought of or tried to say about me. That was so priceless, and the sense of freedom of the experience was truly overwhelming.

The first thing I did was to ring up and get back into therapy and work on picking out the splinters inside after the bomb. I was put in touch with a therapist called Carolyn from Rush.

After Kate, I wondered if we could get on as well as that. But Carolyn was perfect for the job ahead, a true person who has had such an impact on my life. I was ready to work on anything now and learned so much working with her. I'm forever thankful to God for, yet again, putting the right person in place to work with me after Kate. My life was like that of a child being born, full of smiles, and full of new life.

*

With no educational background whatsoever, I sat down one evening with a dictionary on one side and a pen and paper on the other and told Sylvia that now I was going to write my book. I knew I had to go back and open every hidden door to all the hurt and write it down without any writing skills whatsoever, word for word. I wrote Smuggling Love first with the hope that someone would rewrite it for me into a chapter, but the local editor I got encouraged me, saying I could write this whole book myself, that my writing was great. It took me a long time to believe her, but I kept writing and I do thank her for the push she gave me.

There's a book you could write about writing The Jagged Halo. It's just been the most painful, hurtful, yet life-changing and amazing experience. Now off drugs and even the fags, I jogged to stay fit for the task of writing that lay ahead.

By Christmas, the Northside People newspaper did a bit of a story and an ad to track down the lost Smugglers' Cave painting by Steve Hope. They said I was writing about it, and again the word was out and down came the spotlight on my life. But thankfully, it was a very different spotlight than the dark light I'd been used to all my life. From taxi drivers to local people just stopping to encourage me in the writing of this book, I couldn't thank them enough, it all meant so much to me.

As each chapter got handwritten, each one felt like a great splinter of pain being removed. And with each splinter that I took out, it gave way for my identity to blossom and spring more and more to life. Most of the writing of The Jagged Halo was written listening to Gary Numan on my headphones to create and relive all those authentic emotions I had lived in his music and relive all those links again. Is it any surprise that Gary's new album due out in 2010 is called Splinter?

I had some people who put me down for trying to write this book on my life, but I expected that. I remember watching The Shawshank Redemption late one evening and it was like a picture of my life in one of the closing scenes when Andy Dufresne crawled through the sewage pipe the size of five football fields and came out clean on the other side, with arms spread out in the night rain. My whole life seemed like a dark tunnel going on forever and ever until I finally made it out the other side to freedom.

One day myself and a mate, Dermot, went to Smugglers' Cave and then on to the castle to take photos for the book – the land-owner was the guy who told us about the 16th century myth linking both the cave and the castle. That story always makes the hairs on my neck stand up. I got more into my relationship with Aaron and Sylvia, probably because I had so much free-dom inside to give more love. I went to more bike racing and just enjoyed being me. But yet again there was more hurt in los-ing riders we all loved.

In May 2008, Martin Finnegan lost his life at a race meeting, sending the world of bike racing once again into deep mourning. A sense of shock and numbness was felt, as Martin lived just up the road in Lusk. Before we all had a moment to let it sink in, the Northwest 200 came up two weeks later. On the Thursday night, Robert Dunlop, Joey's brother, was killed off his 250 machine. Both Robert's sons, William and Michael, were in the same prac-tice session and came across the crash. Come the Saturday, race day, everyone thought the two boys wouldn't race, but what un-folded was something that, for me, pushed the meaning of fairy-tales to a new level. The first race of the day was the 250 race, and both Michael and William were on the grid. Hanging over them both was the deep emotional pain of losing their dad who had not yet been laid to rest. William broke down on the warm-up lap, so it was left to a nineteen-year-old carrying all this on his young shoulders to make his dad proud. In my mind, I thought he'd just ride around midfield. But this young man had Dunlop blood running through his veins and went for the win.

I've watched great races since the 1970s and I've seen everything from close racing to great riders win great races and then lose their lives. The sport of bike racing has seen it all down its long running history, but this was different. Nobody foresaw what happened that day as young Michael raced into the lead in the race. I'm sure Joey, Robert, Martin, Owen and all those riders who gave their lives for their beloved sport pulled back the clouds to watch what was the most amazing achievement, not only in Irish road racing but in sport full stop, in my opinion. Michael crossed the line in first place to a flood of emotion, and I'm sure his win meant more to his dad Robert than all his wins around the Northwest put together. I felt blessed to be there and told myself that day that I'd write it into this book.

*

I can still remember writing the end of From the Cave to the Castle chapter, which was the hardest chapter to write, and I sort of hit writer's block. I didn't understand it at the time. I think it was that I'd pushed myself for a year writing this book and my body, mind and soul was tired out. Then as I started Beyond the Invisible, the last splinter came out and I felt so complete inside. A warm feeling raced up my body that just left me in tears. My mind flashed back to the awful low times when I felt so lost as a human being, drugged up to the eyes on cocaine in the flat in Bath Road, no hope, sinking fast to the point of no return, struggling with so much pain and hurt. Yet here I was, completely healed and restored to my original self.

On 6th September 2008, I stood with Breda in London at a Gary Numan gig. I was a new man watching Gary perform a lot of the Jagged and Pure songs that used to reflect my pain, only this time it all seemed to reflect someone I knew, but who was no longer with us. I enjoyed the gig like no other gig of Gary Numan's because I was clean inside emotionally and could now enjoy the music from a whole different place inside.

I met Gary on his 50th birthday touring the Replicas album in Manchester in March 2008. Standing with Sylvia alone face-to-face with him on his tour bus was very surreal, yet it was amazing to meet him without all the anger, pain and hurt that were reflected through his music for all of twenty-nine years. I just thanked him for the show that night and told him he didn't look anywhere near fifty. He thanked me with that almost shy look that's always been part of the real Gary Numan. As we left I put my hand on his shoulder and told him to take good care of himself. I think he sensed we really did care about him. Gary Numan will always mean so much to me. Without ever knowing it, his own struggles that were reflected right across his long music career found a place in one fan's broken up world and held that world together, stopped it from going over the edge into an emotional breakdown that I'm certain I'd never have recovered from.

*

Now here I am, at the end of writing The Jagged Halo, my whole life story. Healed, restored and free to be who I was always meant to be. Me.

My walk in this life was set in motion at the very beginning by a terrifying experience of fear at the tender age of two, when having been left alone I reached for my mother to come back, feeling and sensing I'd been abandoned forever. In that moment inside I closed down and sealed the child in me away forever to protect him from hurt, pain and fear. From there, I began to walk down the road of this life in what seemed like a long, dark, narrow lane with tall creeping wall-to-wall trees that hung their long branches over me from one side of the lane to the other, blocking out all light from the skies above. The only sound that awoke my senses and that of the child's was the distinctive voice and music of Gary Numan, and like the theme music to a film, it followed me every step of the way. His voice whispering through the cold air at night when all the light to my life seemed almost gone.

*

As I walk this dark laneway, flashes of my life appear like a highlights tape playing my life out before me.

I see myself running late into school with no books and no hopes, into another beating like so many other kids of that time.

I see a child stealing to feed the hunger inside.

I see my dad smiling and the sweat running down his face as my brother and I are taken away to St Laurence's.

I see a child collecting stories of pain and fear and storing them in a small, dark room within.

As I move forward, my body grows, but the child remains the same.

I see prisons, fear and rejection at every turn.

Haunting shadows sweep down from behind tree branches sending me deeper into the world of fear.

I see Kate smiling into my eyes and throwing me a kiss for good luck for the years ahead.

At last there's a break in the trees and a light shines through, sending a note of hope. It's Cathy. I reach out and touch her face, her eyes reach into my world. It feels like freedom is reaching down into my dark existence.

The hand of love tries so hard to push the trees apart to help me but the shadows pull together and the light fades, and I fall down for the first time on my knees, alone and lost again. I try to get up but I can't.

Then I hear a rushing sound, the sound of thunder.

I look up helplessly.

I hear a voice so beautiful, beyond that of any man's.

I stand up, and above me between the thick branches above, a light is shining down and into my troubled heart.

You belong to me, Patrick.

A rush of love not of this world overwhelms my lost, empty heart.

I sense I've been found, and all my dark pain and hurt is over and my life is at last about to start.

But the shadows of fear come again, closing out the light that once shone so brightly in my heart and soul. It's darker now than ever before and my fears have grown, but the child remains the same, locked away in his dark room of pain.

I stumble forward and reach out, and a hand catches mine. It's Karen. A voice whispers, You'll be OK now.

But a sharp branch falls from one of the trees above, cutting me deeply on my left side. Before I can get up to stop the bleeding, another one breaks, cutting me on the right side. I can't stop the bleeding. I cry out in the dark night as the fading pictures of my ma and dad slip away from my sight and life forever. I try to block out the pain as best I can, but I still can't seem to stop the bleeding.

It's now darker and the shadows have taken everything from me again. The light from above sweeps down and offers to help me with real hope, but each time, like before, my blood-stained hands slip away and it all seems to go dark around me.

I stumble on, still trapped and bleeding. All the lights are gone now but I live in hope. I stagger on, holding only a picture in my heart of a child.

The laneway seems wet. Is it my tears?

Another light breaks through the dark trees. And the most beautiful woman I've ever seen walks towards me holding a sword in her right hand. It's Sylvia. She places the sword in my right hand and places her head against the side of my face and whispers, We'll love each other forever.

The shadows sweep down to block out the light of love again. But I turn fast with the sword and I cut them down.

She walks with me along this dark laneway trying to help me, trying to stop the bleeding, but I'm getting weaker inside. The pain and fear haunt me like a ghost in the shadows of the night.

But I know how to hide, I've always known. As I stumble on, I see the trail behind me of used bags of cocaine. A magic powder used to numb the pain and slow down the bleeding from the open wounds.

It's September 1st, the pain has been too bad. I feel like I'm dying inside.

I can't breathe.

Help me.

Someone help me.

*

I close my eyes to die.

I open them again so slowly.

It's hard to see now, as all I see is a blinding warm light that my eyes have never beheld before.

After a long struggle, I get my eyes to open. I'm trying to catch my breath in disbelief.

The dark trees are gone, as are the hanging branches and dark shadows. Open before me are bright blue skies and rays of golden sunshine, the sound of beauty is everywhere. I'd never imagined all this existed on the other side of the dark world I'd lived in all my life.

I slowly get up and gather my thoughts to try to make sense of what's happening. My eyes are trying to take in the beauty surrounding me.

In the distance, just out of sight, I see the outline of two people standing next to a door. As I slowly walk towards them, I notice my bleeding has stopped and the scars have even healed. Something sinks into place inside my heart, and for the first time in my life I know who I am.

A joy floods my heart at the knowledge that the dark room of pain within has been removed forever, and in its place now rests my true identity from above.

As I get closer, my heart almost stops in a moment of disbelief and astonishment.

There, standing by the doorway, are my mother and father, holding hands. My ma dressed in a bright blue dress, my dad wearing a dark brown suit.

I look into my mother's face and a warm smile breaks out across it, her eyes shining with joy.

'Patrick,' she says, 'you made it. We're so proud of you.'

She bends over and kisses me on the cheek. A tear trickles down her face.

'I love you so much, my son.'

'God, I love you too Ma,' I say through my tears. 'I always have, you know.'

I look into my dad's face. His voice breaking, he says,

'Well done, Patrick.'

I bend over and hold him in my arms, not knowing what to say. Silently, I think the words:

I love you dad, you know that, don't you? I'm so sorry I was too late to say goodbye.

'It's OK son,' he says, 'I understand. I love you too.'

With both their hands joined together again, they stand back and my ma, looking at me now and pointing towards the door, says in her soft voice,

'You know what you have to do now Patrick, don't you?'

She smiles.

'We'll see you again one day soon.'

As I stand at the door, my ma and dad fade from my eyes, and now it's just me and this door. Slowly, I put my hand over the handle and press down and give a small push. The door opens, and it seems dark and damp and musty as I step forward.

My eyes look right, and there in the corner stands an old damp cot with a child with tearful eyes looking at me. His small arm stretches through the bars, his hand reaching towards me.

With tears streaming down my face, my heart unable to take in the moment, I bend over and pick the child up. I hold his small, trembling body as close to mine as possible. He whispers softly in my ear,

'Thanks for coming back for me.'

I walk back out the door holding him, his tiny head resting on my left shoulder. His tears turn to smiles, his eyes fill with joy. The moment I leave the room the doorway fades and I see Sylvia waiting for me with her warm, caring smile.

With one arm holding the child, I place my free arm around her.

A laneway opens before us, paved with new hopes and new dreams.

With blue open skies above and the sound of birds singing in brightly coloured trees, I look up.

A ray of sunshine breaks from heaven above onto my face, and upon its light I rest my smile forever.

> *I in them and you in me; may they be brought to complete unity to let the world know that you sent me and have loved them even as you have loved me.*
>
> *John 17:23*